AN ESSAY CONCERNING SOCIOCULTURAL EVOLUTION

THEORY AND DECISION LIBRARY

General Editors: W. Leinfellner (*Vienna*) and G. Eberlein (*Munich*)

Series A: Philosophy and Methodology of the Social Sciences

Series B: Mathematical and Statistical Methods

Series C: Game Theory, Mathematical Programming and Operations Research

SERIES A: PHILOSOPHY AND METHODOLOGY OF THE SOCIAL SCIENCES

VOLUME 34

Scope: This series deals with the foundations, the general methodology and the criteria, goals and purpose of the social sciences. The emphasis in the Series A will be on well-argued, thoroughly analytical rather than advanced mathematical treatments. In this context, particular attention will be paid to game and decision theory and general philosophical topics from mathematics, psychology and economics, such as game theory, voting and welfare theory, with applications to political science, sociology, law and ethics.

The titles published in this series are listed at the end of this volume.

AN ESSAY CONCERNING SOCIOCULTURAL EVOLUTION

Theoretical Principles and Mathematical Models

by

JÜRGEN KLÜVER

University of Essen, Germany

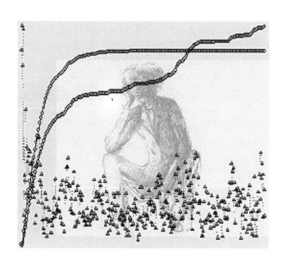

KLUWER ACADEMIC PUBLISHERS
DORDRECHT / BOSTON / LONDON

A C.I.P. Catalogue record for this book is available from the Library of Congress.

ISBN 1-4020-0750-7

Published by Kluwer Academic Publishers,
P.O. Box 17, 3300 AA Dordrecht, The Netherlands.

Sold and distributed in North, Central and South America
by Kluwer Academic Publishers,
101 Philip Drive, Norwell, MA 02061, U.S.A.

In all other countries, sold and distributed
by Kluwer Academic Publishers,
P.O. Box 322, 3300 AH Dordrecht, The Netherlands.

Printed on acid-free paper

Printed in the Netherlands.

TABLE OF CONTENTS

PREFACE

Writing about sociocultural evolution is always a complicated enterprise, because the subject is not only difficult in a scientific way but also in a political one. In particular since the events of September 11, 2001 the debates about the differences between cultures and their evolutionary developments have left the fields of pure scientific research once and for all. However, there have probably never been scientific discourses that did not touch the realms of political discussions - Darwin, Marx, the atomic physicists and the recent debates about genetic engineering are just a few examples.

The aim of this book is not to take part in these debates but it is written as a contribution to the foundations of evolutionary theories in the social sciences. The readers will have to judge if I have succeeded with it. Perhaps essays like this one will help to clarify the problems we all have to face just now in regard to intercultural discourses. Theoretically and mathematically grounded insights into cultural development as the source of many political problems will not solve them immediately but may serve as signposts to how to deal with them in the long run.

No book could have been finished without the help of others. It is my pleasure to thank Udo Butschinek and Jörn Schmidt for reading a first version of this book and giving me a lot of critical advice in particular with respect to my English. The same thanks go to two native speakers from Kluwer Academic Publishers. All mistakes in the final version are of course my responsibility alone. Magdalena and Christina Stoica did a very nice job with the picture at the beginning of the book; Christina Stoica had a lot of difficulties with the layout, which she managed in an admirable way. In particular I am very grateful to Bernd Röske for his work on the pictures in Chapter 3. My thanks go also to Helga Andresen who inspired me to play with Bateson's concepts of competence and meta competence in a geometrical fashion. Prof. Leinfellner gave me some valuable advice for the final version. Finally, I wish to thank Charles Erkelens and Jolanda Voogd from Kluwer Academic Publishers: it was a pleasure to co-operate with them and to renew the pleasant experiences I had with respect to my last book.

1. SOCIOCULTURAL EVOLUTION: A CONCEPT AND ITS DIFFICULTIES

There are probably few concepts in the social sciences which bear so many difficulties as the concept of sociocultural evolution. The reasons for it are at least twofold: on the one hand theories about evolution of societies were often mixed with ideologies about race, nation or sociocultural classes; on the other hand since Darwin the concept of evolution has more and more been identified nearly totally with biological evolution. Therefore social theorists who tried to develop a theory of sociocultural evolution had not only to defend themselves against the reproaches of ideology, but had also the task to classify their approaches in regard to the overwhelming paradigm of Darwinian biological evolution. It is no wonder that often social theorists declared the concept of evolution to be useless for the social sciences.

To make matters worse, it was (and is) not even very clear what may be meant when speaking of sociocultural evolution. For example, is sociocultural evolution the same as (human) history (cf. Habermas 1976)? A lot of scholars would deny an equivalence between the two terms, in particular historians. And more: if there is such a thing as socio-cultural evolution, what exactly does evolve? Human beings for example and if yes, in what sense of the term? Or do ideas, beliefs, norms or social structures evolve? For all potential candidates there are supporters in the long history of social evolutionary thought.

Darwin, as is well known, defined rather precisely (according to his time) not only the concept of biological evolution but also the *mechanisms* by which evolution occurs, namely variation and selection. By adding the genes as evolutionary units after Mendel's discoveries it became possible to define these mechanisms even more exactly: mutation and heterosexual recombination (crossover) vary the genome, natural selection chooses between phenotypes and affects the genomes via the different reproductive success of the phenotypes. That is the classical Darwinian scheme which, as far as I know, is still the basis for most of the recent biological evolutionary theories (cf. Dawkins 1986). Of course, things are probably not quite so simple as this scheme

1

suggests; for example, some biologists think that the DNA is not the only hereditary system but that, e.g. epigenetic hereditary systems must also be taken into account (Falk and Jablonka 1997). Biological evolution may, after all, have some "Lamarckian" aspects. From quite another point of view Kauffman (1993 and 1995) argues that selection, in contrast to the traditional Neodarwinian approach, is not the only important factor and that systemic self organisation also plays a decisive role. I shall come back to these problems in Chapter 1.3. The main factor I wish to emphasise here is that in biology not only the units but also the mechanisms of evolution are rather well defined and, at the latest since the great works of R.A. Fisher (1930), can also be treated mathematically.

Neither is the case when social scientists define sociocultural evolution. There is not only, as I mentioned, no consensus in regard to the units of sociocultural evolution among social scientists but also no precise mechanisms of evolution have been developed. Of course, there are exceptions: Cavalli-Sforza and Feldman (1981) for example constructed a mathematical theory of cultural transmission, using the mathematics of population genetics, and identified learning and acceptance of ideas as the mechanisms of cultural evolution; in a similar spirit Boyd and Richerson (1985) saw "social learning" as the main mechanism of the evolution of culture and used the same mathematics. Yet these approaches had no great impact on social evolutionary thought for reasons I shall deal with later. The main stream of evolutionary sociology and/or cultural anthropology does not contain precise definition(s) of evolutionary mechanisms.

This being the case, one should perhaps abandon the task of developing evolutionary social theories and in particular mathematical ones. A lot of social theorists believe anyhow neither in the possibility of evolutionary theories outside of biology nor in mathematical social sciences. But in my opinion, and fortunately not only in mine, this would be a voluntary capitulation before one of the greatest tasks with which social science has to deal: the theoretical and systematical reconstruction of our history. I am quite sure for reasons that have to be shown later that even a *logically* complete theory of sociocultural evolution will not explain thoroughly all the difficult courses and events of human history; but I am equally sure that without such theories we never get a real understanding of our past (and no idea how to shape our future either). Science, after all, always has to look for theoretical, i.e., general explanations. If there are at present no theoretically sufficient explanations of human history, i.e. theories of sociocultural evolution, then this just signifies that it is a very difficult task. However, this well known fact certainly is no reason to refrain from it.

This study offers no complete theory but, as the title says, theoretical *principles* for developing complete theories and some mathematical models by which the principles are tested. However, we shall see that even with such a relatively modest claim it is possible to gain some insights into the evolutionary logic of human history. The evolution of the social *sciences* will hopefully demonstrate whether the ideas presented in this book can be enlarged to real theoretical understanding of our common history.

As there is no consensus in the social sciences about the concept of sociocultural evolution , which is unfortunately rather often the case with fundamental social concepts, it is my first purpose to give a brief description and evaluation of the numerous and different attempts to capture sociocultural evolutionary processes. It is neither my task nor my interest of research to give a comprehensive overview of this subject. Several authors, to whom I can fortunately refer, have, in recent years, already done this (e.g. Sanderson 1990; Trigger 1998; Turner et al. 1997). I just try to explain rather briefly why the social sciences had and have so many difficulties in dealing with evolutionary theorising. But I also wish to demonstrate how much has already been achieved, despite my rather pessimistic remarks above, which gives foundation to build upon. The fact that I try to develop an own model of sociocultural evolutionary processes and to transform it into mathematical schemes does not devalue in the least the great attempts of scholars from whom I have learned very much.

It is also not my subject, by the way, to give a theoretical reconstruction of human history in terms of the concepts and mathematical models with which I shall deal. Such reconstructions have been done rather often and in particular recently by such outstanding authors as Sanderson (1995) and Turner (1997) from different points of view. I presuppose in this text that readers are, if only in a general sense, familiar with the courses that human history has taken and that they know about the great transitions from hunter-gatherer societies to agrarian state societies and finally to societies characterised by industrial capitalism, functional differentiation and so on. The intention of this book is to establish a theoretical model for sociocultural evolution and to demonstrate the transformation of this model into a certain mathematical algorithm. which serves in turn as the mathematical realm of performing experiments with the theoretical model. I am well aware of the fact that such a theoretical and methodical approach is still comparatively unusual for dealing with sociocultural evolution. That is why I explain this approach rather thoroughly. However, as I explained elsewhere at some length (Klüver 2000), this may be a way to make the social sciences more precise without losing its content and to gain in this way new insights that cannot be achieved in the traditional manner.

As evolutionary biology was and is the leading science in dealing with evolution, I also sketch some of the main ideas of current evolutionary biology. Of course, as a social scientist I am neither competent nor interested in valuing the different opinions that can be found there. Yet if one tries to speak about evolution in a scientific sense, one has to be aware of the achievements of theoretical biology in this respect. Evolutionary social sciences have to solve their own problems by themselves and no natural science can do the task for them. However, it is often very useful to look to other, and in this regard more advanced, scientific disciplines, either to learn from them in order not to reinvent a scientific wheel, or to learn from their mistakes.

1.1 A SHORT REFLECTION ON THE HISTORY OF SOCIAL EVOLUTIONARY THINKING

Nowadays it is quite common to identify "evolution" with biological evolution and each evolutionary theory has to define its own relations to *the* theory of evolution, that is the Darwinian model of biological evolutionary processes. Yet it is well known that the concept of evolution is far older than the Darwinian and Neodarwinian theories in biology and that the idea of the development of systems through time was first thought of in relation to human history. Darwin himself, as he said in a famous remark, got the main idea of the evolution of biological species by learning about the evolution of languages, a concept developed in the first half of the 19th century by the emerging comparative and diachronic linguistics. Gould (1982) emphasises in addition the influence of the concept of the "invisible hand" of Adam Smith. Therefore it is no exaggeration to claim that the idea of evolution is a heritage of the emerging social sciences and humanities.

In a detailed reconstruction of social evolutionary thinking, Trigger (1998) identifies two main positions in regard to sociocultural evolution. The first one originated in the Enlightenment: human history was looked upon as *progress* of the whole race; all human beings were considered to be principally equal and capable of the same achievements; therefore the different cultures and societies mankind had developed so far had to be judged as variations of the same theme; in particular different cultures had to be evaluated as earlier or later stages of a universal scheme of succession; the driving force of history or sociocultural evolution is the capability of humans to invent new ideas and to act according to them. As doubtless the European societies in the time of the Enlightenment were the most progressive ones in terms of new ways of thinking, they defined the criteria for progress, that is, they defined the goal of development, which sooner or later all societies would reach.

It is important to note that originally, during the Enlightenment, this "Eurocentric" view of human history had nearly nothing to do with racism or beliefs in the "natural" supremacy of European nations over the rest of the world. As Trigger emphasises, the political connotations of these evolutionary ideas were mainly directed against the old feudal regimes, in particular at France, the main centre of the Enlightenment. The idea of the equality of rights of all human beings forbade all speculations about a superiority of the European races. The concept of the "noble savage" illustrates this quite clearly: men are good by their (biological) nature and only bad social norms and values, including those of the European societies, can corrupt people and lead them to deeds contrary to their nature.

Of course, the ideas of the Enlightenment about the nature of mankind and the inevitable progress of the human race were quite idealistic and two centuries of social research have demonstrated that things are a lot more difficult, including the concept of the noble savage. Yet it is interesting to note that the founder of Historical *Materialism,* Karl Marx, has exactly the same premise at the bottom of his own theory of human history: the driving force is the development of the *Produktivkräfte* (forces of production), which are the incorporation of human creativity; in the beginning there is a natural state of *Urkommunismus* (primordial communism, in which people lived peacefully together and only the social development of the *Produktionsverhältnisse* (relations of production) finished this ideal state; finally the logic of history is defined as a succession of always the same states of development and the European societies of industrial capitalism define the criteria for progress, though not the end of history. In this sense, and not only in this, Marx obviously was a true child of the Enlightenment. I shall come back to the model of Marx in the next chapter.

The Enlightenment founded *one* line of thinking about mankind and in particular about sociocultural evolution. Therefore modern theories about cognitive or social "universals" must also be looked upon as carrying the heritage of the Enlightenment. That becomes very clear for example in studies about social universals (Brown 1991) and linguistic universals. Pinker (1994), a pupil of Chomsky, claims explicitly the tradition of the Enlightenment when analysing verbal competence as a universal trait of mankind

In contrast to the Enlightenment stands the position of Romanticism, which was founded at least partially as a counterpoint to the ideas of Enlightenment. Especially by the influence of the German philosopher of history J.G. Herder, history was understood not as a universal succession of the always same stages, but as the unfolding of *different* cultures; these are not to be valued as earlier or later stages of one universal schema of evolution but can only be understood as unique, singular manifestations of the human mind. In particular, cultures can only be understood, according to the romantic point of view, "from within", that is from their very own norms, belief systems and so on. Therefore it is not possible to value different cultures against each other; each culture represents an equivalent contribution to human history, though different from every other culture.

The romanticists, whose intellectual center was Germany, did not believe in progress as an inevitable course of history. They appraised the past, in particular the Middle Ages, and criticised the present as having lost the spirit of former times. Therefore they simply denied the idea of sociocultural evolution. The Enlightenment postulated a universal schema of human history; Romanticism emphasised a relativistic point of view with the principal equivalence of all cultures.

It was certainly no accident that the centre of Enlightenment had been France which was the leading nation in Europe during the 18th century, and that the centre of Romanticism was Germany, which could not compete with France, at least culturally at this time. Especially in Germany Romanticism was deeply combined with the postulate to strengthen the traditions of German culture against the overwhelming influence of the French. [1] A leading culture has good reasons to define itself as *the* or one goal of history; an inferior culture on the other hand must in contrast be interested to emphasise the principal equivalence of all different cultures and to deny a universal stage of succession. The contemporary discussions about Multiculturalism versus Eurocentrism mirror these different interests: partisans of so called underdeveloped or primitive cultures tend to deny sociocultural evolution and criticise the concept of it as a form of cultural imperialism; social scientists who believe in sociocultural evolution must, if they belong to the leading Western cultures, defend themselves against the reproach of cultural oppression and of denying the values of extraeuropean cultures.

I will not give a solution just now in regard to these fundamental differences but only want to demonstrate that at the beginning of thinking about sociocultural evolution in a systematic way stood a combination of philosophical ideas about human history and political and cultural interests. Yet it is important to note that neither the philosophers of Enlightenment nor of Romanticism had originally in mind the intention of declaring groups of people or other cultures as inferior. That was the questionable achievement of the late 19th century when, under the influence of Darwinian evolution theory, biological evolution became the key concept for explaining differences between cultures and societies: they were thought to mirror differences between human *races.*

The rather melancholy history of the legitimising of European imperialism by using biological metaphors has often been described; Trigger (loc. cit.) gives a profound depiction of the impact of Darwinian

---

[1] Even progressive reforms in Germany after the lost Napoleonic wars as for example the famous foundation of the Berlin university 1810 by Humboldt and Schleiermacher had the goal to restore German culture and to reduce the French influence (cf. Schelsky 1962).

theory on social evolutionary thinking. The infamous quotation of the "survival of the fittest" was of course never meant by Darwin in the way the "Socialdarwinists" used it (see also Turner et al. 1997). Yet the consequences of Darwinian theory for thinking about sociocultural evolution were rather ambiguous: on the one hand the social sciences got a fascinating scientific paradigm for their own problems with evolutionary theories; on the other hand social evolutionary theories had to carry the heritage of using biological concepts for ideologically legitimising colonialism and imperialism. In this sense the central idea of the Enlightenment was twisted round: the European societies were regarded as the goal of history but only because the Europeans represented a superior race. The concept of equality of all human beings, which was stated explicitly during the Enlightenment, was simply denied.[2]

To make matters even worse, the very independence of the social sciences was threatened because the boundaries between the social and the biological sciences became fluid (cf. Weingart et al. 1997). It is no wonder that many social scientists, especially theoretical sociologists, refused such a questionable heritage and abandoned the concept of evolution for the social sciences (cf. Blute 1979).[3]

The impact of Marx, the other great evolutionary theorist of the 19th century, on the social sciences made things still more complicated, though for different reasons. Marx, as is well known, represented the concept of sociocultural evolution as a universal succession of different stages. Therefore every social scientist who defended a universal theory of sociocultural evolution easily got mixed up in the fights against or for Marxist positions. As even the suspicion of being a Marxist could have severe consequences for academic careers in many countries and not only academic ones, the option for particular theories of sociocultural evolution was always not only scientific but also political.

Yet despite the numerous errors of the sociological followers of Darwin and/or Marx and the frequent intermixture of scientific and

---

[2] The famous quotation of Kipling of colonialism as "the White Man's Burden" illustrates that twisting round quite aptly.

[3] The title of Blute's article is clear enough in regard to the resistance of many sociologists to evolutionary theories: "Sociocultural Evolutionism. An Untried Theory".

ideological positions in the debates about sociocultural evolution, some important aspects must be clarified: in a very general sense it is rather inevitable that reflections about human history and in particular about the differences and similarities among the many societies humankind has generated so far are always in danger of losing scientific neutrality. The old and famous remark *tua res agitur* (your problems are dealt with) illustrates this quite well: even as social scientists we are always involved, namely as members of a particular society, when speaking about sociocultural evolution. The position of the Enlightenment implies the problem of Eurocentrism, that is the valuation of all cultures just from the aspect of how far other cultures are still away from the European standard (and way). As most social scientists are members of Western societies, it is obvious that their own traditions and belief systems are strongly involved in such a position.

The romanticist position on the other hand implies a multiculturalistic view and is relatively free from the danger of Eurocentrism. Yet "modern romanticism" (Trigger loc.cit.) must face the reproach that it simply abandons scientific research, that is the search for possible universal features of human history, in order to become free of the imperialistic heritage of Western nations. Perhaps this inevitable involvement is the reason why there are a lot more cultural anthropologists dealing with the subject of sociocultural evolution than there are for example sociologists (Stichweh et al. 1999; see also footnote 3), because anthropologists, if they belong to a Western society, usually do not have to deal with their own societies.

I said above that it is neither my interest of research nor the subject of this book to give a detailed overview of the history of evolutionary theories in the social sciences. However, even this short digest should be sufficient to indicate some of the problems, with which each theory of sociocultural evolution has to cope. Yet there is no way to refrain from this problem: as in all sciences, the social sciences have to deal not only with the *structure* of their subjects, whatever that may be, but in particular also with the *dynamics* of social systems (Klüver 2000). Social dynamics means, in more sociological terms, social change and the development of social systems in historical time. Therefore the search for a theory of sociocultural evolution is nothing else than the outlook for dynamical regularities in the unfolding of social reality. Each science has to fulfil this task with its particular subjects; if social sciences want to belong to the scientific universe then the construction of theories of sociocultural evolution is one of their most important, and unfortunately a bit neglected, problems.

1.2 THE BIOLOGICAL PARADIGM

When dealing with sociocultural evolution, social theorists have so far taken one of three positions in regard to Darwinian evolutionary theory:[4]: (i) they took it literally, which means the attempts to transfer the main concepts from biology to the social sciences; (ii) they ignored evolutionary biology and tried to develop theories of sociocultural evolution independently from biological ideas; (iii) they took over some of the biological concepts but only in a metaphorical way and used them as their own conceptual tools.

As with each classification this one also consists of "ideal types" in the Weberian sense. Though even a cursory view upon the history of social evolutionary theories shows that this classification is far from unjust. To give only some examples: the mentioned theory of Cavalli-Sforza and Feldman (loc.cit.) as well as that of Boyd and Richerson (loc. cit.) are clearly of the first kind, as they try to apply the concepts (and mathematics) of population genetics to cultural evolution; the Marxist approaches are definitely of the second kind because they have developed their own conceptual and theoretical traditions and an author like Luhmann (1996) belongs in the third category: Luhmann rather often uses concepts like "variation" or "selection" or "recombination" but he never defines them in an exact manner and he never claims that he uses these concepts in the same sense as they are used in evolutionary biology.

A reductionistic variant of the first position are attempts to reduce the social sciences to biology or to look for biological foundations of human social behaviour, respectively. Rather famous in this aspect were and are

---

[4] I am quite aware of the fact that since Darwin there have been other approaches to biological evolution, for example the so called saltationists (cf. Dawkins 1986; Depew and Weber 1995). But for the purposes of this book it is quite sufficient to identify biological evolutionary theory with (Neo)Darwinism and the attempts to enlarge it.

sociobiology (Wilson 1975) and evolutionary psychology (Cosmides and Tooby 1987; Thornhill, Tooby and Cosmides 1997). I deal with these positions in Subchapter 1.4.

Neither of these positions or mixtures of them are able to make evolutionary biology fruitful for the tasks with which they have to deal. The first position usually has to presuppose that sociocultural processes can be described in literally the same manner as biological ones, which may be true for some cases but has certainly not been proven for most of the important sociocultural developments (see below 1.4.). The peculiarity of social processes in comparison to biological ones simply gets lost. Moreover, this position depends on new insights and results of evolutionary biology: there is for example much doubt whether the classical mathematics of population genetics is sufficient for the understanding of biological evolution (see below). Accordingly, adherents of the first position have to change their theories if and when evolutionary biology yields new results.

Partisans of the second approach of course neither wish to nor can learn anything from biology. Sociocultural evolution has, according to these traditions, its own logic and must be exclusively analysed in terms thereof. The independence of the social sciences in particular from the natural sciences is a premise held without doubt; each discipline has to solve its problems within its own framework of concepts and research traditions because the peculiarities of the different subjects only allow different and separate approaches.

The third position finally only borrows of the some semantical and conceptual grand tradition of evolutionary biology; their adherents usually tend to overlook the fact that the concepts of evolutionary biology make sense only in a rather strict methodical framework. In biology it is quite meaningless to speak of "variation" or "selection" if these concepts are not combined with specific methods for measuring them empirically and/or mathematically. As the use of biological concepts in theories of the third kind is mainly metaphorical the concepts may have some heuristic value in these theoretical social sciences but no more.

I agree with the second position insofar as social processes have their own logic, which is not the same as that of biological ones. Yet I firmly believe that it is possible to learn from the tradition of evolutionary biology in a rather general sense: just like the social scientists biologists have to deal with very complex (adaptive) systems whose features are rather similar to those of social systems. That is not to say that both kinds of processes are the same, which would be a kind of reductive fallacy. It means that the *type of problems* evolutionary biology had and has to cope with are in a *formal* sense much the same as those that social theorists have to analyse. As biology has much more experiences in dealing with such problems it is always fruitful to see how another and more advanced discipline struggles with the same *type* of problems as one's own. In addition, I believe that some very general principles underlie all processes of evolution, biological, physical, cognitive and sociocultural ones, despite the differences of the particular mechanisms (see below chapters 4 and 5). So let us have a look at some recent discussions in evolutionary biology.

In 1.1. I referred to the fact that theories about sociocultural evolution always get mingled with social ideologies and interests. The theory of Darwin, of course, had the same fate. Hundred years after his death Gould wrote that "his name still causes fundamentalists to shudder and scientists to draw battle lines amidst their accolades" (Gould 1982, 380). Accordingly Dawkin's famous "The Blind Watchmaker" (1986) has the main intention to show that and how Darwinism is the only rational explanation of life, against creationists and other disbelievers (cf. also Dennett 1995). Apparently it is very difficult to speak about evolution without hurting *someones* feelings.

Yet in the middle of the twentieth century it seemed that Darwinism was not only well grounded but also the one paradigm in biology that unified the whole discipline. The key concept for this belief among biologists was the "Modern Synthesis" (Huxley 1942), which Gould (1982, 382) describes as follows:

"Synthesis occurred at two levels: (i) The Mendelian research program merged with Darwinian traditions of natural history, as Mendelians recognized the importance of micromutations and their correspondence with Darwinian variation, and as population genetics supplied a quantitative mechanics for evolutionary change. (ii) The traditional disciplines of natural history, systematics, paleontology, morphology and classical botany, for example, were integrated within the Darwinian core, or at least rendered consistent with it."

The second level of the modern synthesis is of no great importance here; it is up to biologists of course whether this claim of the synthesis is still valid. (It may well be, by the way, that a complete theory of sociocultural evolution could also present a unifying paradigm for the social sciences in the long run.) The first level, by comparison, is more relevant for our considerations: it expresses the now classical mechanism of biological evolution, namely the famous distinction between genotype as the level of variation (mutation and recombination) and phenotype, the level of selection. In particular the synthesis emphasised the central role of selection: there are other evolutionary mechanisms like drift, but selection is the main force of evolution, which drives organisms to more and more complex forms. Indeed, as both mechanisms of variation are "blind" (Dawkins), that is random and *not* goal orientated processes, selection has to do the "creative" (Gould) task of generating better and better adapted organisms.

The modern synthesis has been attacked during the second half of the last century from different directions which cannot be discussed here (see for a thorough overview Depew and Weber loc. cit.). The two most interesting attempts, at least for social scientists, to revise the synthesis may be refered to as (i) abandoning the monopoly of the single organism and its genotype and (ii) introducing self organisation as a second evolutionary force besides selection. I shall briefly discuss these approaches because they represent problems that will also be important for the analysis of sociocultural evolution.

(i) The first attempt to enlarge the synthesis is twofold: on the one hand scientists like Gould and Lewontin (e.g. Lewontin 1970; Gould 1977) argue that selection does not operate on single organisms alone but also on "groups", that is species or even clades. Therefore the adaptive fitness of an organism as product of variation and selection may be due in particular to selective processes operating on the whole species, to which the organism belongs. Therefore the selective force of evolution must be understood as something operating between different though interdependent "levels" (Gould). As a logical consequence it follows that the concept of adaptive fitness may not be measured on the individual level alone, an individual organism is not only in regard to its *natural* environment more or less well adapted, but also in respect to its *social* environment, that is, its species whose fitness in turn determines the fitness value of the organism.

On the other hand recent researches have apparently demonstrated that there is something in biological evolution that is suspiciously "Lamarckian" (Falk and Jablonka 1997; Jablonka et al. 1992). Of course, nobody seriously believes in direct transmissions of acquired characteristics; not only since the infamous Soviet genetics of Lysenko this concept has been buried for good. Yet for example during the ontogenetic development of the immune system several genes might be rearranged, which will be transmitted to offspring; another example is "specific changes in the DNA of flax plants in response to growth conditions" (Falk and Jablonka 1997, 398). In general these and other results seem to indicate that epigenesis can play an important role in evolution also which, as far as I know, was first postulated by Waddington (1956); the variations of the DNA, the generation of a phenotype and the selection of it are not the only mechanisms of evolution. As epigenesis is often influenced by the environment in which the organism develops, we may safely conclude that the interaction of the developing organism with its environment may play a role in evolution that is not to be neglected.

Social scientists will be on familiar ground when reading such considerations. I shall come back to these biological thoughts when I present a theoretical and mathematical model for sociocultural evolution. However, before leaving biology there is still another attempt of enlarging the synthesis to be considered, namely the introduction of self organisation into evolutionary theory.

(ii) This approach is mostly connected with Kauffman, a biologist who has worked continuously with the Santa Fé Institute for research into complex systems (Kauffman 1993 and 1995; Depew and Weber loc. cit.; Waldrop 1992; Lewin 1992). The main idea of Kauffman is that selection is not enough to generate "creatively" more and more complex forms; there must be another evolutionary force, that is self organisation, which determines the path of evolution independently of but in interaction with selection. As Kauffman operates with methods with which biologists and social scientists are still not familiar, I give a rough sketch of his approach; similar methods (and results) will be demonstrated in more details in Chapter 3.

Kauffman experimented with Boolean networks (BN), that is, artificial systems. BNs are mathematical models, similar to cellular automata (CA), whose units represent the elements of a network and whose "rules of transition" are the expanded rules of propositional calculus. The units may take one of two values, 0 or 1, and each unit is connected with several other units. The rules determine how the values of the units are changed by the effects of the other units with which they are connected; the dynamics of the whole network is generated recurrently via the changes of the individual units.

BNs and CAs are discrete (artificial) systems; therefore their rules may be expressed as particular combinatorial rules. Despite their simplicity they have an important characteristic: they are (potential) universal Turing machines which means that each computable system can be modelled by a suitable BN or CA. I shall come back to this aspect below.

The general results of Kauffman's studies in these artificial systems are this: BNs which he sometimes calls "genetic networks" express features and behaviours that are strikingly similar to those known from biology about genomes and adaptive behaviours of organisms. For example, Kauffman found out that the number of (simple) attractors in a BN with N units is roughly the same as the number of different cell types in an organism with N genes.[5] Therefore he concluded that in a mathematical way the differentiation of cell types during epigenesis is nothing other than the attaining of different attractors of the genome, that is ,the genetic network. However, this is only due to the self organising capacity of the genetic system; no selective forces play any role in the process. Of course Kauffman does not deny that selection plays an important part in evolution. Yet the power of self organisation constrains selection: when a genome, a genetic network, has been varied by mutation and/or recombination, then the self organising processes step in and determine the further development of the particular system. Selection then has to judge whether the result, the phenotype, fits adequately to its environment but the creative force (Gould) relies exclusively upon self organisation. For other results of Kauffman see his books and e.g. the

---

[5] A simple attractor is something like a steady state of a system, that is, a state that the system does not leave anymore or to which it returns after a short period though the transition rules are still operating on the system. For a more detailed explanation see Chapter 3.

instructive overviews in Depew and Weber (loc. cit.), Lewin (loc. cit.) and Waldrop (loc. cit.).

The most important aspect, at least for me, of Kauffman's *methodological* approach is this: Kauffman did not model any particular biological systems but he analysed BNs for themselves and tried to find general laws that determine their behaviour (see below chapter 3). Therefore his results are valid not only for biological systems but for complex self organising systems in general. That is why this approach can also be taken for the analysis of social systems as well. Yet this methodological procedure is, as I remarked, quite unusual not only in biology and it is no wonder that Kauffman has often been criticised as being "reductionistic" and/or "mechanistic" (cf. Depew and Weber loc. cit., 453-457),which meant the reproof of reducing biology to physics and neglecting the unique complexity of living systems (e.g. Rosen 1991; Ulanowicz 1994).

As this point is also important for my own researches I wish to deal with these reproaches a bit more thoroughly because it does not concern only research in biology. Analysing formal systems like BNs or CAs has *per se* nothing to do with physics proper or biology or sociology. It is a kind of "experimental mathematics" (Hofstadter 1986) whose subject is the analysis of "programmable matter", as Rasmussen et al. (1992, 214) describe it in a beautiful metaphor. The very logical simplicity of these systems of programmable matter makes it possible to discover regularities that could not be seen in any other way in natural systems. Of course, as Depew and Weber correctly remark in regard to Kauffman (loc. cit. 432), calling such artificial systems for example "genetic networks" does not make them valid models for biological systems. Yet their fundamental property of being universal Turing machines makes it possible to draw conclusions from the behaviour of these artificial systems to the behaviour of natural systems in general: if BNs as such exhibit certain regularities, then in principle all those natural systems must exhibit the same regularities which can be mapped on suited BNs. The universal characteristic of BNs guarantees that there must be always such a BN or CA. So if the models of Kauffman are reductionistic, then it is only in the sense that they attribute *general* characteristics of biological systems to those of mathematical models. If this is "mechanistic", then each mathematical science must live with this reproach, but I think it can do so.

After this little excursion into the realms of experimental mathematics, which we will get to know a bit more thoroughly later it is time to come back to evolutionary biology. The modern synthesis is challenged, as we saw, from different directions. On the one hand there are arguments against the exclusive role of the single genome and accordingly the single organism as the sole site of evolutionary processes. As a sociologist I am a bit minded to characterise these arguments as a postulate of "dialectics": biological evolution must, according to these aspects, be seen as an interdependent process between the single organism and its "social" environment on the one hand and between the ontogenetic development and its natural environment on the other hand. I am of course not competent to judge whether these arguments are biologically valid. However, it seems clear to me that at least sociocultural evolution must be thought of in just such dialectical ways. Social scientists may learn this from biological evolutionary research that probably even the processes of biological evolution have to be conceived in terms that are very familiar to the theoretical tradition of social theory.

On the other hand there is the problematic relation between selection and self organisation. We shall see that this is also a good old acquaintance of social scientists, though not in these terms. In the social sciences one speaks of the difference between, e.g., internal and external factors of system's development or of the dichotomy of functionalistic versus causal explanations. As these differences will play an important role in the later chapters I shall give the problem of selection versus self organisation some further considerations.

Depew and Weber (loc. cit. 480) give a list of the logical cases how self organisation and selection may be related; according to their analysis a "middle position" seems rather probable, that is, both play a significant part in biological evolution. From a more mathematical point of view this rather vague statement may be clarified a little.

Some years ago the computer scientist John Holland constructed a mathematical model of the evolutionary process of variation and selection, the so called "genetic algorithm" (GA) (Holland 1975; Holland et al. 1986). A GA consists simply of strings of symbols, for example binary numbers, and an evaluation function which attaches to each string a numerical value, the "fitness". The strings are recombined, that is, parts of them will be exchanged (crossover) and several units of the strings are changed at random (mutation). The evaluation or fitness function decides which of the new strings are the best; these are preserved, selected, and changed again by mutation and crossover. This procedure is repeated until the strings have reached sufficient fitness values (see Klüver 2000 for sociological applications of the GA).

The interesting aspect in regard to selection and/versus self organisation is the fact that the GA practically always reaches an attractor, that is it generates strings that have better fitness values than at the beginning, the values get better until a certain threshold is reached and then the *strings will change no more* if the rate of mutation is not drastically increased. This, on first sight rather peculiar, behaviour of the GA, can be demonstrated as a mathematical necessity: it follows from a famous theorem in metrical topology, the so called Banach fixed point theorem (Michalewicz 1994), and it means here that the GA can be seen as a "contractive function", that is, the distances between the fitness values of the strings get smaller the longer the GA operates. Therefore either the GA reaches a certain fixed point in finite time, which it does not leave anymore, or the GA gets nearer and nearer to the fixed point without reaching it, the fixed point is mathematically speaking an asymptote. In terms of mathematical systems theory this means that biological species may be seen as attractors in an evolutionary space; this might explain, by the way, why species do not change over long periods of time although the evolutionary processes of variation and selection are still operating on them. So it seems that not only systems dynamics in the sense of Kauffman but also the *adaptive* processes themselves bear characteristics of self organisation, here contractive properties, which together with selection determine evolution; in Klüver 2000 I have therefore called this phenomenon "self organisation through adaptation". (The GA and its dependency on the fixed point theorem will be analysed a bit more thoroughly in Chapters 2 and 3.)

It seems to me that this kind of (mathematical and systems theoretical) reasoning can also be fruitfully applied to the problems of sociocultural evolution (see below Chapter 3). At any rate, the lessons that the new developments in evolutionary biology may give to the social sciences are at least the following: on the one hand biological evolutionary processes obviously have to be understood in ways that are rather familiar to social scientists; therefore a theory of sociocultural evolution has to conceive its subjects at least as complex as those of biology. However, that is something that the history of social theory has always postulated. On the other hand the social sciences must consider how to achieve a methodological standard comparable to those of evolutionary biology without losing the peculiarity of their subject. The modern synthesis in biology, which was often taken too literally in the social sciences, is obviously enlarging and new paths of development are open. That seems like a good time to undertake once again the task of thinking about sociocultural evolution.[6]

1.3 A GENERAL DEFINITION OF EVOLUTION

Unfortunately it is not always very clear what is meant by "evolution" outside of biology, in particular in the social sciences. Sometimes evolution is identified with "development" or also with "dynamics" (e.g. Doreian and Stokman 1997). As among other goals it is the intention of this book to develop a *mathematical* model of sociocultural evolution, the concept of evolution must be defined in a precise manner.

The Oxford Dictionary (9th edition) gives eight different definitions for evolution; for our problems definitions 1 and 3 are the most important ones, which I shall consider in detail[7]: (1) "gradual development, esp. from a simple to a more complex form; ... (3) the appearance or presentation of events etc. in due succession". The first definition corresponds roughly to the idea that is behind biological evolution, in particular the concept of evolution as a process that leads to rising complexity; the second definition is in contrast more or less equivalent to the physical concept of dynamics, which is not the same as biological evolution. Let us examine these two definitions in more detail.

---

[6] As a sociologist I am not much concerned with the question whether these new paths of research in evolutionary biology are just an enlargement of the classical Darwinian frame or quite another theoretical approach (for discussions of this question cf. Depew and Weber loc.cit.; Dennett 1995). In my opinion it boils down to the question "what Darwin really meant" which I gladly leave to historians of biology.

[7] Definition 2 is the standard biological definition as the development of species, definition 8, for example, is a mathematical concept like, e.g., the extraction of a root.

In the most general sense the dynamics of a system may be defined as the *rule generated succession of the system's states*. Each system is characterised by its elements and the rules of interaction between the elements; these rules operate on the elements and thus perform the transition of the system from one state to another. In a mathematical sense the rules of interaction may be understood as a mapping or function, which maps one system's state onto another. The system's trajectory, that is the succession of its states in a state space, is determined by these rules and its initial state, namely a state at the beginning of the observation of the system. It is important to note that nothing more is needed to understand the dynamics of any system; of course, the difficulty in science is mainly the discovery of the interaction rules.[8]

This physical definition of dynamics is necessary but not sufficient for a concept of evolution, which does not simply reduce biological or sociological concepts to those of physics. Of course, each evolutionary process is a succession of states, generated by particular rules of interaction, and therefore the definition of dynamics also fits evolutionary processes.. Yet evolutionary processes must also be defined by another important characteristic, which purely physical processes lack: the property of *changing and/or enlarging the structure of evolutionary systems*. This is the logical core of evolutionary systems and that is why simple reductions of biology or sociology to physics will never succeed in grasping the logic of evolutionary processes.[9]

Before I examine this property of evolutionary systems in detail, it may be useful to refer to the kinds of evolutionary systems so far known. Without claim of completeness there are at least

   – biological systems;
   – sociocultural systems;
   – cognitive systems, that is, minds and/or brains;

---

[8] Quantum theory and chaos theory both stress the fact that it is not possible to characterise any initial state as precisely as it would be necessary to predict the future trajectory of quantum systems or complex chaotic systems with total precision. These additional problems, however, need not concern us here.

[9] To be sure, there are also variations of structure in physical processes like, e.g., phase transitions or structure transformations in crystals. However, because the meaning of structure in these physical processes is different from that, which I use in regard to adaptive and evolutionary systems, I shall not deal with these problems in this book.

– computer programs with the ability to learn and to evolve
– and finally the physical universe itself.

I leave the case of the physical universe gladly to the astrophysicists as it is in every sense of the word a case by itself (see below Chapter 5). When considering the remaining four, a very general definition of evolution is obviously applicable to all of them, namely that they are able to generate not only different states, i.e., generating a particular kind of dynamics, but also different *structures, that is rules of interaction.* However, these systems do not change their structures *ad libitum* though random processes may also play a role in this. They all operate within a particular environment, which is the criterion for acceptance or negation of the structural changes.

The importance of the selective force of the environment for biological evolution has been known since Darwin (see above) and need not be stressed further. Sociocultural systems are the subject of the next two chapters; therefore the discussion of the meaning of environment for these systems can be postponed. The evolution of cognitive systems is of course dependent on their material environment on the one hand and, most important for human systems, on their social environment, that is in particular on parents, teachers and social peers on the other. These and other persons decide on the success or failure of the particular ontogenetic processes and thus give the next stages of individual ontogeny new directions. Yet it has been known since Piaget that these processes must be organised by the learning individuals themselves, and that there is no simple reaction to the social environment. The same goes, in a formal sense, for learning computer programs: they get fixed criteria about the goals of their learning processes and develop their specific structures, that is their rules of interactions between their artificial units according to the feedback from their goals set by the programmers.

In neither case the systems "adapt" in a colloquial sense of the word, which would mean that environment determines the changing of the structures unambiguously, and also the resulting structure. The evolving systems just get feedback, that is information on whether the structural changes have been successful or not. If not, the system has to do the tedious task of structure changings again as long as it is necessary, if it has time enough to do so. Therefore any evolving system is of course self organising in the sense that it organises its processes by its own rules;

environment can only tell whether the system is on the right track. As evolving systems are also adaptive, they react to the demands of the environment by changing their rules of interaction by their own logic; again we may speak of adaptation by self organisation. To mark this important difference between pure self organising systems and systems that are capable of adaptive self organisation the physicist Farmer (1990) distinguishes between "dynamics" and "metadynamics" which means the difference between systems, which change only their states and those, which also change their "architecture" (Farmer), that is their rules of interaction.

In order to illustrate these concepts I would like to introduce a computer program that belongs to the kinds of evolving systems mentioned above. Jörn Schmidt and I constructed a so called "hybrid cellular automaton", that is a (stochastic) cellular automaton (CA) combined with a genetic algorithm (GA); the aim of this construction was the simulation of social differentiation, in particular the evolution of stratified class societies from simple tribal societies (Klüver and Schmidt 1999 a). The formal system is self organising in the respect that it operates only according to the rules of the CA; the CA models the society in its different stages of evolution. The CA's development is measured by an "evaluation function", which values the achievements of this artificial society in regard to an (also artificial) environment. The GA operates on the rules of the CA, that is the operations of the GA change the CA rules if and when the "values" of the CA are not sufficient according to the environmental demands. In a logical sense the operation rules of the GA are "meta rules" of the whole hybrid system, as they only act upon the CA rules. The hybrid system of course has no "goal" or "intention" in the usual sense but only self organising dynamics and the capability to change its structures according to the environmental criteria. Obviously such artificial systems both *are and model* evolutionary systems. As they contain not only rules of interaction but also meta rules for changing the rules, I think the term "meta dynamics" suits them rather well (see below 3.1.).

In my opinion the fact that there are no goals in the artificial system above is a precise demonstration that evolution generally may not be conceived as goal oriented processes. It is well known that there was (and perhaps still is) a lot of confusion about this point. Evolving systems do not follow any goal, neither in biology nor in sociocultural evolution. They just evolve which means that they have the capability of structure changing and *reacting in this way* on their environment, that is on the problems that the environment presents at a certain time. The only "goal" that can be found is the need to get along with a particular environment, which is the only goal we put into our formal system. Of course, some adaptive systems are able to anticipate, which means that they can think and plan about potential futures. In a formal sense the artificial system just described does exactly this. Yet they do this to cope with the *present* problems, not to follow any goal to which they are predestined by some Creator or Hegelian *Weltgeist*. Therefore, if by "goals of evolution" there is meant something other than the need to maintain ones existence in the face of complex environments, I can see no use of this concept.[10]

The same goes, by the way, for the identification of evolution and the rise of complexity. Apart from the fact that it is very difficult to define "complexity" in a precise manner (cf. Klüver 2000) there are a lot of examples in biological and sociocultural evolution where no perceivable rise of complexity occurred; to be sure, there are also a lot of examples where enlargements of complexity happened. In other words, there is no general law that combines evolution with some inevitable rise of complexity. Whether adaptive systems increase their complexity or not, whatever this means in particular cases, is a question of the trajectories of these systems in their past and that means a question of their history (I shall come back to this question later in the last chapter) For the case of sociocultural evolution we shall analyse these problems in more detail and in a specific manner; in particular we shall see that the rise of complexity is sometimes not traceable to particular environments.

So what after all is evolution, distinguished from simple dynamics? It is a dynamical process of systems that are both able to change their states by rules of interaction and their structure via meta rules; often the

---

[10] Of course our artificial system does not prove in a mathematical sense that evolutionary processes have no goals. However, the fact that it is possible to model evolutionary processes in a mathematical way without using such questionable concepts like goals or direction of evolution is strong evidence that it is not necessary to use these concepts in scientific explanations of evolution. Occam's razor tells us that a theory that does not need such concepts is to be preferred to those theories that need the concepts.

changes are due to certain environmental demands, but always the changes are just part of the adaptive self organising capacity of the system. These meta rules may be those of a (natural or artificial) genetic algorithm, they may be the learning rules of cognitive systems and/or artificial neural nets and they may be the combination of social and cognitive changing rules, which will be described in the next chapters.[11] The *fundamental* logic of adaptive systems, and evolving systems are always adaptive too, is always the same, at least on this level of abstraction. Yet even cursory glances at the different kinds of adaptive systems show that it is not to be expected to find the same kind of rules and meta rules everywhere, that is, the same type of evolution. Whether there are biological, cognitive or sociocultural systems, each type has to be examined for its own sake, combining in this task the differences between different types of systems and their similarities.

One additional remark has to be made in advance. It seems that at least sociocultural and cognitive systems exhibit not only the two kinds of dynamics just discussed, but also a type of "third order" dynamics which might make these systems unique in an evolutionary sense. In Chapters four and five I shall deal with this subject in detail.

1.4 EVOLUTIONARY SOCIAL THEORIES AND THEIR DIFFICULTIES

Despite the fact that especially in theoretical sociology the theme of sociocultural evolution is often only of secondary importance, there are nowadays already a lot of rather different evolutionary theories (cf. Turner et al. loc. cit.; Sanderson 1990; Trigger loc.cit.; Stichweh et al. 1999). It is quite impossible to deal with all of them and I can only try to summarise them with the help of a very crude classification. In order to do this I refer to the traditional sociological distinction between micro- and macrotheories (Alexander et al. 1987), though I vary this a bit.

When considering the term "socio-cultural" evolution it is clear that there are two dimensions of the problem: on the one hand there is some

---

[11] I leave it to theoretical physicists and writers of science fiction whether the physical universe also has meta rules, i.e. whether the physical laws of the universe change over time. Some authors seem to think so but of course only in a very speculative way (cf. Hawking 1988; see below Chapter 5).

"social", which evolves, on the other hand some "cultural", which does the same. In some ways these two sides of one problem are interdependent but whether both are equally important or whether one side is the more relevant, and if so, which one, is one of the main differences between the various theorists. In general it may be said that with few exceptions most theorists deal only with one side of the matter: They either (1) concentrate on cultural evolution and thus mirror the traditional microtheoretical approaches in sociology or (2), they think in terms of social development and/or social evolution and analyse the evolution of society in a macro fashion. Of course, there are always exceptions, that is (3) theorists that deal with the evolution of social structures and norms in a microtheoretical way. This is in particular true for rational choice theorists and other authors who follow the tradition of action theories influenced by economics. In this research line evolutionary game theory often plays an important role; the famous study of Axelrod (1984) may be called paradigmatic for many researches in this field (see also Schmid 1998). Finally, it is certainly possible to do research with another combination of the four dimensions mentioned above, namely analysing culture in a macro theoretical fashion. Classical philosophy of history did it this way, in particular Spengler (1926/28), Sorokin and Toynbee (1934-61). Yet, as far as I see, contemporary studies mostly follow one of the first three orientations; I shall deal with them in this order of succession.

(1) Theories of cultural evolution are rather seldom in mainstream sociology; the main representatives of this approach are to be found in cultural anthropology and psychology. Although the numerous authors differ in important aspects, they may be united in the common belief that cultural evolution can and must be treated in generally the same fashion as biological evolution. "Biological evolution" means mostly the "modern synthesis" (see above 1.2.); therefore the task is to first identify units of cultural evolution in analogy or parallel to genes in biological evolution and second to define the mechanisms of "cultural transmission" (Cavalli-Sforza and Feldman 1981). The concept of "memes" (Dawkins 1976 and 1986) has become rather famous in this context for the first task; the mathematical mechanism of population genetics is accordingly often used for the second one, though sometimes only metaphorically.

There can be no doubt that these approaches give important insights into the matter of cultural evolution. However, they have two fundamental difficulties, which show that they are not wrong but insufficient for the task of explaining sociocultural evolution. These insufficiencies may be called (a) the problem of cultural units and (b) the integration of culture and society.

(a) The success of the modern synthesis was based mainly on the fact that genes are discrete units that could be identified experimentally. Therefore the mathematics of population genetics could be applied very satisfactorily and without fundamental difficulties (cf. Hofbauer and Sigmund 1984). Treating cultural evolution in the same (Darwinian) manner means that there have to be cultural units, which are discrete and are transmitted in a way at least similar to the biological transmissions of genes. Paradigmatic in this context are Boyd and Richerson (1985), who take over the concept of memes and treat their transmission processes in a mathematical way according to population genetics. They simply postulate that this way is a sound one because the mathematics is already at disposal. One need not go so far to take biological evolution literally. Sperber (1996) is much more cautious when he stresses the point that ideas, concepts and thoughts are usually changed when taken over from one individual by another. In contrast to biological evolution the recipient of an information nearly always plays an active role in the transmission process. But even Sperber speaks of "epidemic" processes and the "epidemiology of representations and beliefs", though only informally. Therefore he also seems to believe that processes of cultural transmission underlie regularities that are similar to biological ones.

Durham and Weingart (1997) give a critical overview of the different attempts to identify cultural units and come to the conclusion that often the analogy of cultural units, especially memes, "is suggested terminologically, rather than by careful definition and empirical demonstration." (1997, 310). In particular, results from cognitive sciences like Lakoff's theory of linguistic category (Lakoff 1987) seem to indicate that cognitive units, if there are any, are rather unlike genes (Durham and Weingart loc. cit. 303); cognitive units are clustered around prototypes (cf. Rosch 1973:) and integrated in semantic fields that are different in distinct individuals, depend on the respective culture and so forth. Therefore there are serious doubts as to whether the analogy of genes makes more than metaphorical sense in cultural evolution, and even those metaphors might be quite misleading. Dawkins, by the way, the inventor of "memes" has become much more cautious when speaking about the analogy between biological and cultural evolution (cf. Dawkins 1986).[12]

As the units of cultural transmission are a questionable concept, so are the mechanisms. Neither the processes of population genetics nor those of epidemiology can be easily transferred into the domains of culture. Of course, it may well be that *some* cultural processes follow the rules of genetic or epidemic transmissions, but that must be demonstrated empirically in each case and is not to be taken for granted; that would mean a too simple *petitio principii*. A general proof (in an empirical sense) of the efficacy of some of the biological mechanisms just mentioned in cultural transmissions needs to have a convincing candidate for cultural units. However, as far as I see, the sceptical observations of Durham and Weingart are still valid and I see no way to overcome the difficulties mentioned above.

(b) Even more serious is the second insufficiency, that is the problem of linking culture with social structure. In no way is it to be seen how purely cultural approaches, even if they solve problem (a), can give insights into the evolution of social structures, that is, social rules and norms. The simple transmission of concepts, ideas or "memes", whatever these may be, is never enough to explain the rise and changes of social structures. Of course, the evolution of ideas has a lot to do with the evolution of social structure, as we shall see in Chapters 2, 3 and 4, and the mechanism of "social learning", which is discussed in detail by Boyd and Richerson (loc. cit.) is very important in this context. However, an exclusive concentration on the transmissions of ideas from one person to another will never reach the *social* level of sociocultural evolution. To be sure, social rules must be expressed in verbal concepts in order to make them understandable for those persons who should obey them. But the

---

[12] Some defenders of the meme concept like Dennett (1995) even think that only this concept allows one to analyse cultural evolution in the exact way of the natural sciences; memes belong in these theories to the realm of Platon's ideas or the Third World of Sir Karl Popper. However, the eloquent manner in which e.g. Dennett argues for his position does not alter the fact that the concept of memes is psychologically questionable and sociologically rather useless (see below).

evolutionary development of such rules. from the rules of hunter-gatherer societies to the institutions of the functionally differentiated societies of the modern kind, cannot of course be explained by reference to rather simple and questionable mechanisms of transmission of concepts or ideas.

I mentioned above the fact that the importance of epigenesis for biological evolution seems to be underestimated by the modern synthesis; therefore it is not by chance that a defender of the modern synthesis like Dawkins propagates a concept of cultural genes, which neglects totally the role of social structures, the formal parallel to the organism. As contemporary evolutionary biology acknowledges the importance of epigenesis, evolutionary social science must do no less.

Some of the difficulties of the cultural approaches to sociocultural evolution may also lie in the fact that they deal mainly with transmission and/or learning processes, i.e., taking over processes of ideas. They take only seldom regard of the rather plain fact that ideas must first be invented, or discovered, before they are transmitted. Evolution is after all also the emergence of something new; therefore the course of sociocultural evolution may not least be dependent on the manner *how* new ideas are generated, accepted and *then* transmitted by teaching and learning. Tomasello (1999) is one of the few exceptions I know of who stresses the importance of dealing with the emergence of new ideas, though he also does it only informally.

Sociology of knowledge has, since Marx, emphasised the point that our ideas are at least partially dependent upon our societal context, that is upon our cultural *and* social environment. As much as we are the producers of society, we are the products of the social and cultural contexts, in which we were raised and live (Berger and Luckmann 1966). Therefore, both the invention of new ideas and the acceptance and passing on of them are certainly dependent on this "dialectical" (Berger and Luckmann) process. Any approach to sociocultural evolution that does not take this insight into account must be regarded as unduly reductionistic.

Though concepts like "coevolution (of culture and genomes)" (Durham 1991), "sociobiology" (Wilson 1975) and "evolutionary psychology" (Cosmides and Tooby 1987) do not belong strictly in the field of research of cultural evolution I would like to deal with them briefly here. Sociobiology as well as evolutionary psychology have the aim to decode our biological heritage and to explain human behaviour and thinking by demonstrating its biological, that is mostly genetic foundations. Both lines of research have become rather famous, and infamous; in particular they attacked the autonomy of the social sciences by reducing them to biology and/or biological anthropology. It is not the subject of this book to analyse these modes of thinking in detail (for sociobiology see Turner et al. 1997). Here it is sufficient to note that the reference to biological foundations of our mind and behaviour is certainly quite useful in many aspects, but that there is not much to be gained by it for the problem of sociocultural evolution. There is no question that the ability of humans to develop new ideas and to change their social rules is biologically founded and that it is an important task to uncover these foundations. That is a truism. However, especially in regard to the obvious flexibility of the human mind, the resulting fact that human beings are not determined to an unequivocal course of history, in contrast to animals, leads to the actual interesting question, *why* sociocultural evolution took the paths it did and whether there are regularities or even general laws to be discovered. Here approaches that argue from biology cannot contribute much because these are questions that have to be answered from the logic of social and cultural processes. The grand manner, by the way, in which sociobiologists and evolutionary psychologists sometimes criticise the established social sciences is not based upon an abundance of convincing results and confirmed theories.[13]

The hypothesis of the coevolution of genes and culture (Durham 1991) produced without doubt some interesting results, especially with regard to the dependency of modes of food production on some genetically caused diseases. Yet I do not think that Durham seriously believes in the important role of special genes for sociocultural evolution in general. Apart from hopeless racists, nobody, for example, would believe in particular philosophical or mathematical genes of the ancient Greeks during the Golden Age of Perikles or in the sudden emergence of musical genes in the German population during the time from Bach to

---

[13] The modularity of mind/brain, for example, which is postulated by evolutionary psychology (Thornhill, Tooby and Cosmides 1997) is neither confirmed by contemporary neurobiology (cf. Edelman 1992) nor by mathematical models with, e.g., artificial neural nets (cf. Mainzer 1997). Both prefer connectionistic approaches.

Beethoven and Brahms.. In the same manner I suppose that Durham
would be the first to scorn the idea that the English acquired special
genes which enabled them to invent modern capitalism. Therefore the
hypothesis of coevolution might be a way to explain some particular
paths of development, especially in societies with only few alternative
options for food production and other kinds of answers to environmental
problems but no more. In general, as far as I know, sociocultural
evolution is much too fast, especially during the last four millennia and
even more so in the last four centuries, that it could have significant
effects on the human genome; therefore coevolution of culture and genes
could not have been an important factor for sociocultural evolution.

(2) Macrotheories of sociocultural evolution belong mostly to
sociology in a strict sense and they are using the established concepts of
theoretical sociology. In contrast to the theories of cultural evolution they
deal explicitly with the emergence of social structures and their changes
during the course of human history; because they are macrotheories they
need not look for discrete units of evolution. Yet as they do not have the
problems of the culturalistic theories, they have their own problems,
which may be considered as complementary to those of the first kind of
theories.

(a) Macrotheories in general are always only able to reconstruct the
dynamics and/or evolution of systems as a whole. They can demonstrate
the trajectories of the system during the time of the observations and, in
the case of the natural sciences, they can give mathematical equations for
the description of the trajectories; in many cases it is even possible to
make rather accurate predictions in regard to the future behaviour of the
system. Classical examples of these approaches are Kepler's laws of the
planetary motions or the equations of Lotka and Volterra for the
dynamics of predator-prey systems. Yet macrotheories are not able to
define the concrete mechanisms that *generate* the observed dynamics and
evolution. This is possible only from a microtheoretical point of view,
which concentrates on the interactions between the elements of the
systems, which are to be observed and explained. In the natural sciences
a system is understood only if the concrete rules of interaction, which
explain the observed dynamics of the system, are known. Therefore, the
planetary system was only understood in a strictly physical way when
Newton added his law of gravity to Kepler's laws because Newton's law

defined just the rules of interaction between physical bodies. As physicists do not speak of macro- and microtheories, one may instead speak of top down in contrast to bottom up models.

When we apply these general considerations to macrotheories of sociocultural evolution, we find just this deficiency. Take for example the theory of "Evolutionary Materialism" of Sanderson (1995). In the tradition of Historical Materialism, Sanderson postulates a causal theory of social evolution and defines the following factors:

"The principal causal factors in social evolution are the material conditions of human existence, i.e., the demographic, ecological, technological and economic forces at work in social life." (loc. cit. 8) He continues in regard to the relevance of adaptation: "Adaptation is a process pertaining to individuals and never to any social unit larger than the individual. Social groups and societies ... are only abstractions" (loc. cit. 10/11). These "individuals are egoistic beings who are highly motivated to satisfy their own needs and wants." (loc. cit. 12)

On first sight this sounds like a theory based on the needs of individuals and their actions; in particular individuals produce part of the causal factors of social evolution themselves, i.e., the "technological and economic forces", which in turn drive social evolution like the other factors; this reminds one of the "dialectical" processes in Marxian theory. I agree with most of Sanderson's premises with the exception perhaps of the seemingly inevitable selfishness of human beings. Yet by reading the comprehensive reconstruction of human history in terms of evolutionary materialism one finds only the development of whole societies and groups, the "abstractions". Particular combinations of especially demographic and ecological factors cause the evolution of particular societies which, as Sanderson notes (loc. cit. 9), "embody different evolutionary logic". It seems that Sanderson favours a form of causal theory borrowed from physics: given one certain cause or a special combination of causes, then equally special developments will occur. As these causes operate on whole societies or groups via the mediating factor of individuals, only the effects of the causes on the societies must be taken into account. In the end evolutionary materialism is a macrotheory, with strong orientations to world systems theory (e.g. Wallerstein 1974), which lacks any definition of the mechanisms how the processes that react to the effecting causes must be understood.

As I said, I sympathize with many of Sanderson's assumptions and his work is to be valued highly. Nevertheless his theory shares the deficit of all macrotheories: they reconstruct the past on the basis of a general theory but they are not able to define the concrete mechanisms that generate the trajectories of the systems observed. Strictly speaking those theories explain only half of the problem.

Contemporary evolutionary theories of social differentiation like that of Turner (1997) make this deficit even more evident. Turner himself acknowledges that "in some ultimate sense, institutional systems are composed of individual interactions" (loc. cit. 280). He is quite right when he continues that these interactions can only be understood in the frame of general social structures and that therefore the investigations of the development of these structures, social subsystems like economy or polity, must be a special level of analysis. However, this valid methodical claim again leads to a theory where only the evolutions and interpenetrations of macro units like social subsystems are discussed and where nothing is said about the generating logic of interactions, which cause the development of the macro units. By using the example of Kepler and Newton again, these macrotheories of social evolution remain on the Keplerian level and still wait for their Newton.[14] The same can be said even more explicitly about world systems theory (Wallerstein loc. cit.; Chase-Dunn 1989); for other macrotheoretical attempts see Trigger (loc. cit.).

I do not wish to be misunderstood: social macrotheories are extremely fruitful and yield important results in reconstructing the past as well as understanding the present. This is in particular the case with the theories I just mentioned. Pure microtheories are in a special manner "blind" to the large scale consequences of individual actions and interactions, i.e. the whole of society, and,. as Adorno once said, *das Ganze ist das Wahre* (the whole is the truth). Yet no theory of sociocultural evolution can claim completeness if it is not able to define the generating logic of society and sociocultural evolution. Of course, all the theories I just mentioned are written in a rather informal manner, that is they do not use mathematical tools, in contrast to some of the culturalistic theories

---

[14] Who is not me, to be sure, because I just give some general *principles* and several mathematical models in this book, not a theory with the claim of completeness.

mentioned above. It is quite impossible to give a thorough account of human history on the basis of "individual interactions" (Turner) by using only an elaborated natural language. Therefore the mentioned deficiency is mainly due to methodological reasons. The contemporary possibility of constructing mathematical models and testing them via computer simulations, however, has changed this situation drastically. We shall see in the next chapters, whether a complete theory of sociocultural evolution based on elaborate computer simulations is at least a "concrete Utopia", to quote Ernst Bloch.

(b) All these macrotheories aim at the reconstruction of *social* evolution and mention only barely the term *sociocultural.* To be sure, both Sanderson and Turner, for example, analyse domains like religion, education and science and describe their relevance for social evolution within the conceptual frame of their theories. Yet obviously they see no reason to distinguish between social structures and cultural ones. This makes sense in large comprehensive theories of society, which take culture for granted and which deal mainly with the evolution of *social* structures. Again, as in the case of the theories mentioned in (1), there may be some doubts as to whether things are so simple.

If we define culture according to many authors (e.g. Habermas 1981) as the set of all knowledge that is valid in a particular society, then clearly culture cannot be reduced to social structures. The knowledge that individuals possess and acquire is of course not the same as the social rules they have to follow. Therefore, as mentioned above, the question of the relation between culture and social structure is not a trivial one. The problem is even deeper: Sanderson of course is right when he maintains that only individuals act and change society, in particular the social structures that usually regulate their behaviour. But they undertake these changes only on the basis of some knowledge and/or beliefs, whether they are valid or not. One has to know, like Bruno or Galilei, that the geocentric theory of the planetary system is false, and one has to know also that the Catholic church is wrong. Then one is able to act and change by these actions parts of the social structure, in this case the rules of obeisance and obedience to the church. The social consequences of this new knowledge, that is changing of the society, are well known. Theories that concentrate only on social structures miss these important aspects of social and cultural evolution and they too are incomplete in this regard.

It is perhaps no accident that, as far as I see, contemporary macrotheories of social evolution are more or less systems theories, whether in the Parsonian tradition like Turner or in the combination of Materialism and systems theory like Sanderson and Wallerstein. Systems theories tend to define their subjects rather uniformly, which means that they regard social systems only in one particular manner: they consist of one and only one type of elements, e.g. social interactions, communications (Luhmann) or egoistic individuals who only seek the fulfilment of their needs. This one-sidedness may be the cause for neglecting the important difference between culture and social structure; not by chance the sociology of culture is a subject for only few specialists and the concept of culture is often restricted there to the arts or perhaps religion.

It is certainly not a very new insight that complete theories of society or sociocultural evolution have to combine different approaches to capture the complexity of their subject. When I repeat this rather old postulate by demonstrating the inevitable deficiencies of one sided theories I certainly do not wish to criticise authors, who obtained important results for the sake of criticism alone. I just try to demonstrate which criteria must be fulfilled if one tries to speak about sociocultural evolution in a scientific manner.

(3) Theories of individual rational actors finally look neither for cultural units as the basis of cultural evolution nor for the development of whole social systems and subsystems. Their main question may be formulated like this: how is social order possible in a world of egoistic actors (the classical question of Hobbes of course) and how can we conceive the emergence, i.e. evolution of the structures of social order that we observe in history. In a strict sense they also deal only with social evolution and do not pay culture special regard; in contrast to most social macrotheories, mathematical tools are used here fairly often, especially game theoretical ones.

The famous study of Axelrod "The Evolution of Cooperation" (1984) is in several aspects paradigmatic. Axelrod analysed one of the most famous dilemmas in social decision theory, i.e., the Prisoner's Dilemma (PD) which was already investigated by Parsons (Parsons 1968), by using different game theoretical models and exploring them by computer simulations. One of the well known results is that a "mixed" strategy, that is the strategy "tit-for-tat" (TFT) came out best in different computer tournaments. Independently of Axelrod's experiments Maynard Smith confirmed these results in his evolutionary game theory (Maynard Smith 1982) by demonstrating that TFT belongs to the so called "evolutionary stable strategies" (ESS), which are a mixture of co-operative and aggressive substrategies and which are likely to be evolutionary successful in a population of competing strategies. There are several of coordination dilemmas like PD (cf. Schmid 1998) and the aim of rational decision theory is to analyse possible solutions and then to look for evolutionary conditions which favour one or several of these solutions (Schmid loc. cit.).

These are in particular *Wertegemeinschaften* (communities of value) and institutions for maintaining social order, which emerge from successful negotiating of different actors, who solve the dilemmas of their different interests by compromise or exerting power (Hobbe's Leviathan). Social evolution therefore is considered in this theoretical tradition as the emergence of social order, that is rules, upon which different actors agree *nolens volens* to co-ordinate their actions. Selection mechanisms support these emergent processes in order to reward adequate behaviour and to sanction deviant behaviour; the most important of these mechanisms are power, morality and markets (Schmid loc. cit.).

Evolutionary theories of rational actors obviously have the advantage that they are able to identify an evolutionary mechanism, which generates the evolution of social order: it is nothing more than the rational and interest driven interactions of social actors who are forced, in order to solve their co-ordinating dilemmas, to look for possible solutions and to introduce rules of social order to maintain these solutions. In this sense the criticism with regard to the lack of an evolutionary mechanism is not valid here. These theories also define their evolutionary units: these are the social rules actors agree upon, who are in a manner of speaking the bearers of the social evolutionary process. From a logical point of view therefore the theories of rational actors come out the best and it is certainly not by chance that even system theorists like Parsons were much attracted by them. The fact that a lot of researchers in this field are using mathematical, i.e., game theoretical models makes them even more attractive for mathematically minded scientists like me.

As is the case with the theories mentioned above, there can be no doubt that theories of rational action are very fruitful for the task of investigating sociocultural evolution. Yet, as nothing is perfect, to generalise Billy Wilder, these theories also have their severe shortcomings . The main crux is the concept of rational egoistic actor of course, as has been noted very often; this problem will be investigated a bit more thoroughly.

The distinction between *homo oeconomicus,* the rational egoistic actor who makes free decisions in each situation, and *homo sociologicus,* the rule following actor, is an old one and it goes deeply through the social sciences. It is not my interest to renew this old debate; rather I would like to argue, like many authors in recent times, that these alternative positions are far from incompatible. *Homo sociologicus,* to be sure, is certainly also a rational being who chooses between different options according to his needs; *homo oeconomicus,* on the other hand, is also a social being who lives in a social context by following the rules that define it. Therefore pure theories, in this case of *homo oeconomicus,* that deal only with one aspect of human nature, will surely miss important points about social reality. Vanberg (1994, 17-19), an economist, names three reasons why it is evolutionarily favourable that man evolved as a rule following being: (a) the variable nature of man provides us with only few instincts; therefore institutions, i.e., sets of social rules, had to be created in order to remove us from the burden of having to make decisions in each situation; common rules also make the behaviour of other people more predictable. (b) following rules that have proved to be effective in the past may often be a better strategy than risking mistakes by trying new strategies in every new situation; (c) if an actor is known for the fact that he will follow a particular rule in a specific situation, he may obtain benefits by just following the rule, Vanberg illustrates this by a man of whom is known that he will not give in to blackmailers; as a consequence he will less likely be a target for blackmail. A fourth reason is to be mentioned here as a variant on reason three: if an actor is known to follow rules of co-operative behaviour, then other actors will more likely behave co-operatively against him.

In general, apart from these cost-benefit reasons for rule following, it is simply an empirical fact that social actors usually act according to the rules that define their social context. *Homo oeconomicus,* to be sure, is certainly no myth, but it is an unempiricial construction that simply neglects the fact that all social actors have a biography and are no rational *tabula rasa*. This means that social actors are products of processes of socialisation and with it they have "internalised" (Berger and Luckmann loc. cit.) the habit of following rules. The arguments Vanberg mentioned demonstrate why this is evolutionarily favourable for a *Mängelwesen* (deficit being, Gehlen); if this is true then it is impossible to build a theory of sociocultural evolution on the concept of *homo oeconomicus* alone.

Two other aspects must be considered. The assumption about the inevitable selfishness of human beings who share the theories of rational actors with, e.g., evolutionary materialism, is equally problematic. Of course people are egoistic, i.e., they act according to their needs. However, if this is all that is meant by it then the proposition becomes rather empty. The needs may be material needs like hunger or thirst, they may also be the need for religious solace in times of peril, they may be the need to help other people, they may be the need for doing ones duty and they may be the need for new knowledge, a spiritual hunger, so to speak. Therefore the egoistic actor simply boils down to an actor with particular goals who tries to reach them. Nothing is said about *how* he does it; empirical sociology tells us again and again that in most cases people do that by following those rules that they have learned and internalised.

The second aspect is that of culture, that is the accepting, learning and inventing (of) new knowledge. Theories of rational and egoistic actors apparently have no place for the importance of culture and the way in which the behaviour of people is influenced by it. It is an historical truism, for example, that people followed the rules of the church and the feudal lords in the European Middle Ages because they *believed* in the truth of the church's sayings; obviously their "needs" were such that they obeyed the religious norms quite willingly. I do not know whether this is rational but it is certainly human.[15] When during the Renaissance, the Reformation and the Enlightenment religious knowledge as a universal

---

[15] In "Das Leben des Galilei" (The Life of Galilei) by Bert Brecht this point is beautifully illustrated: a "little monk" who defended the prohibition of Galilei's theories by the church pointed out that the poor and ignorant people needed the religious norms and pronouncements in order to accept their miserable life.

truth was shattered people changed their rule following behaviour; accordingly they looked for new rules.

In nuce, to understand an actor in a given situation one must certainly take into account the goals that the actor achieves, but also the rules which the social situation requires and finally the cultural knowledge as the basis of the actions. Culture often even determines the goals, as can be seen in the example of religious belief. Therefore no theory of rational actors can capture the factual behaviour of people in real situations without considering at least these three components.

Let me summarise: at best theories of rational actors can cope with the emergence and evolution of social ordering structures, but they are blind to the importance of culture. That is not to say that these theories are worthless, on the contrary. They give important insights into the problem, what people can do when in doubtful situations, where no established rules fit. In particular, as we shall see in Chapter 2, social rules often leave open a space of freedom, i.e., the rules do not unambiguously determine the adequate behaviour for each situation of decision. It may well be that in modern societies there are a lot more of such situations than in older ones, which gives these theories their topicality. However, it is not possible to reconstruct sociocultural evolution without taking into account the fact that human beings are rule following actors and without considering the great importance of culture for the evolution of social structures.

My critical way through the three main approaches to the problem of sociocultural evolution and the analysis of their shortcomings has a constructive goal: each of these research fields has its merits and no theory of sociocultural evolution will be complete without taking into regard the results obtained by them. The theoretical principles I present in the next chapter must be valued whether they take into regard at least the respective principles of the mentioned theories. Often sociologists and other social scientists deplore the heterogeneity of their disciplines and wish for unifying theories. Perhaps they will come someday. In the meantime we may console ourselves with the Evangelist John "in my father's house there are many rooms" (14, 2). Let us take the special treasures from each room.

2. A THEORETICAL MODEL OF SOCIOCULTURAL EVOLUTION

If there are at present no complete theories of sociocultural evolution, i.e., theories that capture at least principally all important features of these complex processes, then one has to proceed in a way that has often been criticised as "eclectic". This means, to be sure, that one picks from different theories the concepts, and if necessary the results, one needs for one's own task. I have to admit that I never fully understood why some social theorists scorn an eclectic procedure; apparently they believe that each theoretical social scientist has to develop a theory of his own or must avow to some particular theoretical school. But science does not make progress by valuing theoretical paradigms for their own sake. When the great behavioural scientist Bateson once noted that all new ideas are *de facto* recombinations of ideas already known, then scientific progress is also possible only if everything is taken into account that may be learned from different theories already developed. The fact mentioned in the last subchapter that the main theories of sociocultural evolution are all incomplete in some way or other must not make one blind to the insights they all give in their different ways. When I sketch the theoretical foundations of my own model of sociocultural evolution in the following subchapter I try therefore to keep in mind this eclectic way of proceeding.

2.1 SOCIAL ACTORS, ROLES AND SOCIAL SYSTEMS

What is to be learned from the theories discussed above? Obviously at least the following aspects: (a) cultural evolution as one of the two dimensions of sociocultural evolution depends on the mechanisms of social learning, that is the taking over of new ideas from other people. Boyd and Richerson (1985) stress this fact in particular and characterise the ability of social learning, referring to Bandura (e.g. Bandura 1986), as an ability characteristic for the human race and perhaps in this degree only for humans. There are some doubts as to whether this ability is in fact mainly restricted to the human race (c.f. Maynard Smith 1996), but the overwhelming importance of social learning for cultural evolution cannot be denied (cf. also Tomasello loc. cit.) I shall deal with the concept of social learning more thoroughly in the next chapters. (b) Evolutionary materialism and rational actors theories both tell us that the focus of research must be the social actor and the interactions among different actors. Therefore there is no need to look for some more or less ill defined units of culture like "memes", which operate seemingly independently from concrete actors; it is enough to study the rule governed behaviour of actors who are in a particular way determined by their beliefs, their ideas about the world and about what is right or wrong. (c) Theories of social differentiation tell us, though some theorists think them to be outdated (cf. Schmid 1998), that the relations between subsets of social rules change over time and produce an important part of the whole sociocultural process. Therefore it is not enough to study rules of social interaction and their changes by adaptation; one must also take into account rules between sets of rules, i.e. rules that define relations between different institutions or subsystems.

Let us start with the concept of social systems, the "abstraction" of Sanderson. As usual with social concepts there are many ways to define a social system; perhaps the most famous definitions are those of Parsons and Luhmann, which are, as is well known, not the same. I do not intend to enumerate and discuss all the different proposals that have been given in the history of social theory. In regard to the lessons one may learn from the evolutionary theories sketched above, I favour a rather pragmatic definition, which is consistent with the remarks about general systems theory made above in 1.2. and 1.3.: a social system consists of social actors whose interactions are determined by specific rules; the (intended or unintended) consequences of their interactions produce other interactions with particular effects and the successions of these interactions generate the dynamics of the system; the changing of the rules of interactions and/or the enlarging of the rule sets of the system generate the metadynamics or evolution of the system. So far, so simple, but of course a lot has to be clarified.

When speaking of *social* actors it must be understood that I do not simply mean human beings. From Marx to Luhmann social theorists have rightly stressed the point that the social sciences do not deal with human beings but, as Marx put it, with the *relations* between humans. Human beings, as Luhmann frequently emphasises (e.g. Luhmann 1984) are not a unity but are composed of several facets, each of which is subject to a particular scientific discipline like biology, psychology and of course, the social sciences. Therefore sociology deals only with the *social* dimension of humans, i.e. their behaviour, beliefs and thoughts insofar as these are determined by society and conversely are producing social reality. The concept of social actor refers to humans in the degree that they act according to social rules on the basis of belief systems and/or knowledge, which are part of the culture of a society. The key concept for this very traditional definition of social actors is that of social *roles.*

The classical concept of *homo sociologicus* as a rule following actor is intuitively rather clear. Yet theorists of rational actors, in particular those of rational choice, have rightly pointed out that it is by no means self evident that people obey rules, i.e. laws, norms and so on. Among other intentions people are obviously also looking for their own advantages and as humans are no simple automata they are free to choose between different options in each situation; in particular they are free not to obey rules if it is more profitable for them. Because people indeed sometimes tend to disobey rules, "governments are instituted among men", as the Declaration of Independence put it, that is institutions that guarantee social order. Why then is it an undeniable fact that most people do follow rules and that the concept of *homo sociologicus* is confirmed by empirical evidence?

The answer to this question was of course given by sociology long ago. In perhaps first the political essay of Western culture, the *Politeia*, Platon already emphasised the importance of (social) education for creating and maintaining social order and for keeping people on the right track, in his case of course the social order of an aristocracy of philosophers and guardians. In more modern terms G.H. Mead (1934) described the process of socialisation as the growing capability of role taking, i.e., understanding "objective" social rules and internalising them, that is believing in their rightness and acting according to them. It is well known how Parsons dedicated a great part of his work to investigating these processes and to analysing the importance of social roles for the integration of society (e.g. Parsons and Platt 1973).

The answer therefore to the question of the theorists of rational actors is rather simple: people follow rules because they learned to do so as part of their socialisation, i.e., their role taking processes. During the processes of socialisation and of intentional education, humans are integrated into the social network of rules, i.e. laws, norms, customs and so forth by taking particular roles appropriate to their stage of development, and sometimes abandoning these roles when, during their social ontogenesis other roles seem to be more adequate. If one follows the classical distinction between primary and secondary stages of socialisation (e.g. Berger and Luckmann loc. cit.) then it seems that some roles are more fundamental than others, for example roles founded on gender, and these fundamental roles contain a lot of people's "social identity".

Of course, people sometimes refuse to take specific roles and so "deviate", that is they declare other rules to be obligatory for them than the ones society postulates as valid. In most of these cases deviant people are treated as criminal or mentally retarded and/or not responsible for their actions, as the concept of social maturity implies in all societies the capability *and willingness* to act according to the rules the different social roles consist of. In a few cases, however, the deviating people are able to maintain their new rules against society and thus create new roles, these innovators become something like founding fathers (or mothers) of new social structures and traditions.

Actually, this is common knowledge to social scientists. I remind here of these truisms for the simple reason that in theories of sociocultural evolution these thoughts are seldom considered to be important; one of the few exceptions I know of is the theory of Habermas (1976) and Eder (1976 and 1991) but this theory is only a very rough draft and has never been carried out in more detail.

Before analysing the concept of role a bit more thoroughly, I have to go back once more to the theories of rational and egoistic actors and the question of Hobbes, because they still have an argument left: it may be true that people are basically *homines sociologici* by socialisation and education, and it may also be true that in the sense of the arguments of Vanberg (see above 1.4.), rational reasons can be found why this *social* behaviour is more profitable than permanent free and arbitrary decisions in each situation. Yet the question remains as to how this behaviour emerged during the evolution of mankind. Concepts like socialisation and even more education always have to presuppose an already existing society. If the question of Hobbes is to be understood how such a society is possible at all so that people can get accustomed to social rules and roles, it seems a logical circle to answer Hobbesian questions by pointing to society and processes of socialisation and education.

Strictly speaking this is not a question of (evolutionary) sociology but of evolutionary biology and not by chance many evolutionary biologists have dealt with this question (e.g. Maynard Smith 1982 and his concept of evolutionary stable strategies). Biological ethology has found overwhelming evidence for the fact that practically all higher species of animals live in some kind of social order, some of them comparable to particular human societies. Especially famous are the social groups of subhuman primates (e.g. Goodall 1986). Therefore we may safely assume that the capability to organise social groups, that is social order, and thus to avoid the Hobbesian *bellum omnium contra omnes,* is part of our biological heritage. To put it even more plainly: if, as Hobbes said with one of his famous metaphors, *homo homini lupus,* man is to other men like a wolf, then we know from numerous ethological researches that wolves are fundamentally social beings that often behave very nicely to other wolves and in particular follow the rules of their specific pack. Therefore, there is a very high probability that the Hobbesian premise that man is by nature an anti-social being is wrong. The sociological interesting question is therefore not how social order is possible at all, but how and why mankind developed different types of social order and whether there is a general logic behind it.

Evolutionary biology has of course dealt with the Hobbesian question and asked what evolutionary advantages are combined with the evolution of *social* behaviour; this is not necessarily the same as *co-operative* behaviour. Especially famous has become the theory of kinship selection (for a mathematical treatment see Parisi et al. 1995); I already mentioned the answers Maynard Smith gave from the point of view of the Theory of Games. It seems that individuals have more chance to survive and to reproduce, the fundamental criterion for biological fitness, if they acquire, via the genetic mechanisms, the capability to live in groups and act according to the specific rules of these groups. As a social scientist I think therefore that it is quite enough to assume that there are biological reasons for the emergence of social behaviour during the course of *biological* evolution and that the very premise of Hobbes and his modern followers is not valid. I shall give some mathematical reasons for special social structures and their emergence during biological *and* sociocultural evolution in the third chapter. Therefore it is not a logical circle to emphasise the importance of socialisation when explaining the fact why social actors follow rules: socialisation, i.e., the process of becoming a social being by understanding and obeying social rules is as old as mankind itself because men as social beings by their biological nature always had some kind of social order with them even in the dawn of their history.[16]

It is time to come back to the concept of role. The classical definition given by Mead and Parsons, as is well known, says that a role consists of "generalised expectancies of behaviour". The important term in this definition is of course "generalised" because by this it is possible to distinguish between a concrete individual and the particular role that he/she has taken over. It is not necessary to remind of the reasons why Mead, Parsons, Berger and Luckmann and many others defined a social role from the point of view of the partner in the interaction, that is from someone who has to interact with the occupant of the role. By turning this point of view to the role actor it is logically equivalent to define a role as a set of social rules that the occupant has to obey, and *which make his behaviour predictable, that is expectable in a general sense.* Therefore the taking of a role is the same as accepting particular social rules as obligatory. The famous oath of Hippocrates illustrates this quite clearly: taking the role of a medical doctor is accepting a rule like "helping ill people by all means and in each situation" as obligatory. As each patient and everybody else expects this rule following from a

---

[16] Metaphors like "the egoistic gene" (Dawkins) can be dangerous because they tend to mix two different things: it is one aspect of the whole problem to assume that the ultimate fitness criterion is the capability of reproducing and such being able to give one's genes to the next generation. That seems to be biologically valid. It is quite another thing to assume that beings orientate their life towards the chance to reproduce in a maximal fashion. The second does *not* follow from the first because it is quite enough to assume that living beings tend to live as well as possible and that they are "interested" only in their personal welfare but not in maximal reproduction. The capability to reproduce is a valid indicator for biological fitness but not necessarily the goal of the individual life. Obviously the organism which deals best with the problems of life has more chances to survive than those which are not as well suited and *therefore* the best suited organism has better chances to reproduce, not because this is the prime goal of its existence.

doctor, the equivalence of the two definitions is quite clear: the expectancy is generalised because the behaviour is expected from each doctor; the individual who occupies the role of a doctor may claim this role only if and because he/she follows the particular rules, i.e., accepts them as obligatory. Therefore the taking of a role is combined with the internalisation of the social rules that define the role during the process of role specific socialisation as obligatory.

To be sure, people who occupy specific roles may deviate from them. Doctors may not be interested primarily in the health of their patients but more in the money they can get from pharmacy firms if the patients get specific medicines, regardless whether the medicines are good at all for the health of the patients. In these cases the role specific socialisation was not wholly successful in the sense that the norms of the role had been fully internalised by the occupant. If such deviant cases are still an exception then the particular doctor is criticised and sometimes punished as a deviant case. If, on the other hand, more and more role occupants exhibit behaviour not consistent with the societal definition of the role then it is perhaps time to redefine such roles. I leave it to the everyday knowledge of the readers as patients whether the role of medical doctors nowadays has to be redefined.

When I defined a social role by its special social rules an important part of a role was left out: each role does not only contain rules of social behaviour but also a particular *knowledge* which is a necessary condition for filling a role. In the case of professional roles like our doctor above, this is quite clear, as the taking of a professional role may be done only after a shorter or longer time of professional education, that is acquiring a set of specific skills; in cases like parents, members of a political party or a club or guests at a dinner party it is usually assumed that the particular knowledge that is needed for all these roles has been acquired during the process of *general* socialisation. The confrontation with people from other cultures often demonstrates that these "everyday" roles also need a lot of knowledge, but a kind of knowledge that is common to all mature members of a particular society.

By generalising these well known observations we get the following definition of a social role: it consists of a set of obligatory rules of behaviour and a certain part of the knowledge that defines the culture of a society, formally a role ro = (k,r) with k being the role specific knowledge and r being the rules. In this sense a role is a two-dimensional complex: though of course the social rules of a role depend in part on the particular knowledge, which is very clear in the case of the doctor, rules and knowledge are trivially not the same. The case of deviations from a particular role makes this very plain: one may have all the knowledge necessary for a role and yet not follow the rules, as in the example of the money hungry doctor; one may on the other hand be eager to heal people and so restore their health but be unable to do this in the proper fashion, as is show by the numerous cases of well meaning quack doctors. A role assumption by someone is accepted as valid if and only if the role occupant follows the rules and has at his disposal the role specific knowledge.

The reasons for deliberate deviations from a token role may therefore be twofold: on the one hand the role actor may deviate because it is more profitable to do so in a particular situation; on the other hand the deviant role occupant may recognise that his role specific knowledge is not sufficient for his tasks and he tries to acquire more and better knowledge. The first possibility is obvious and well known; the other one is more seldom but also well known. Take for example a teacher in a society where his main educational task is to select pupils according to their actual performances. If this teacher learns about, let us say, the dependency of learning successes on social environment, he is either forced to suppress this knowledge or to change his role, i.e. enlarging his role by adding the task of compensating the environmental deficits of some pupils. In the same way, the natural philosophers of the Renaissance, because of new knowledge about the physical universe, were forced to change their role in particular in regard to the dogmas of the Catholic church. Every time some role specific knowledge becomes obsolete the role occupants have to decide whether they must change their whole roles accordingly.

Social actors therefore are social because they occupy specific roles. I stressed several times the importance of analysing two dimensions of the process when speaking of sociocultural evolution. Now we may clarify these remarks a bit. In a preliminary fashion, which I shall define more precisely in the next subchapter, both sides of sociocultural evolution are to be understood the following way: I call the social structure (of a society) the set of all rules that are held to be valid at a given time among a particular population (cf. Giddens 1984; Habermas 1981); in addition to this definition we have to take into account the relations between the different roles, which are of course rules of interaction too. Culture is the set of all knowledge that is believed to be true at the same time and by the same population (Habermas 1981; Geertz 1973). This definition of culture is a common one especially among cultural anthropologists; the definition of social structure is of course nothing other than the translation of traditional sociological concepts like institutions or organisations into terms of a theory of action. A society can then be represented as a pair (S,C) where S is the social structure and C the culture.[17]

The concept of social role as defined above as a two-dimensional complex is obviously a point of intersection of culture and social structure. The knowledge that belongs to a role, in fact constitutes one dimension of a role, must be socially believed to be true; else the role would not be accepted as part of the societal structure. Therefore the "knowledge component" of the role is part of the culture of a society. The same goes for the "rule part" of the role as part of the social structure. To be sure, "culture" and "social structure" are, from the point of view of single actors, abstractions because nobody is able to know everything about the culture and nobody is able to act according to all the rules of a given social structure. Therefore we may say that by taking a particular role as a specific vertex of culture and social structure an actor is concretely experiencing and reproducing society at his special point of action, i.e., actively occupying his/her role.[18] In this sense a society can be defined as the set of all roles, including their relations, that can be taken by members of the according population.

To be sure, a member of a society may know a lot more than his different roles demand, e.g. a merchant may be a hobby astronomer in his

---

[17] Giddens defines structure (institutions) by rules *and* resources which are not taken into account here. I shall come back to resources like power or authority in the next chapters.

[18] The well known distinction of *Lebenswelt* (life world) and system by Habermas (1981) and his thesis that in early tribal societies life world and system were extensionally equal suggests that in these societies both culture and social structure were no abstractions for the members because everybody knew the same and was able to occupy any role. Even if this was true for such societies, things changed as soon as tribal societies became more differentiated.

spare time. However, this would be his private matter: as a social actor, that is, a role occupant, it is only important whether he knows the knowledge he needs for his role(s). Therefore the accepted knowledge of a society, that is its culture, is the sum of all the knowledge incorporated in the different roles, which is the "knowledge base" of role specific actions.[19] A culture that contains knowledge nobody is able to use and/or nobody is allowed to use in a fashion society permits has, in a sociological sense, this knowledge not at all. Libraries and data banks are cultural means only insofar as concrete social actors can use the knowledge and act accordingly.

In a very general sense which will be specified in the next subchapter we may now define the concept of sociocultural evolution, that was after all the reason for these detailed considerations: *sociocultural evolution is the changing and creating of social roles by means of changing and in particular enlarging components of the culture, i.e. knowledge, and by consequently changing and enlarging sets of social rules, i.e., social structure. Therefore sociocultural evolution may be considered as the learning processes of social actors and via the actors the learning processes of sociocultural systems.*

Note that this is just a formal definition and a very general one. Nothing is said about evolutionary mechanisms and nothing is said either about conditions of these learning processes. All the reflections upon roles, knowledge and social actors just had the aim to define the subject of my analysis. However, before I fill this general definition in the next subchapter I wish to give some arguments for its reasonableness.

In Chapter 1 I dealt with the question of what the basic units of sociocultural evolution may be. In common with evolutionary materialism and the theories of rational actors I argued that indeed individual actors are the only candidates for this role. Cultural units like memes are on the one hand rather ill-defined, and on the other hand not able to bridge the gulf between culture and social structure and in particular they do not reproduce *per se*, they always need "transmitters",

---

[19] The term "knowledge base" has become quite prominent in connection with research into Artificial Intelligence (AI), i.e. so called expert systems. I use this term quite deliberately because role specific knowledge is in the same formal way the basis for actions as the knowledge base is for the behaviour of the expert systems computer programs.

i.e. actors who use them. Whether the actors use the cultural units, if there are any, or not, is not a question of quasi automatic reproduction of the units. The social sciences as *empirical* enterprises have as their fundamental subjects actors who think, believe and behave, nothing else. The question of sociocultural evolution is therefore not the quest for cultural units but the search for an answer to why people change their modes of thought and accordingly their behaviour. This is not a suggestion for the renaissance of some social behaviorism but the reminder that social sciences are empirical ones. Ideas, beliefs and cultural "units" like that are means of the actors of sociocultural evolution, not the units themselves. The same objections, by the way, must be raised against attempts at an "evolutionary epistemology" (e.g. Campbell 1988) where variations and selections of ideas are treated as processes independent of social actors. In all these theories the terms of variation and selection are mainly defined in a rather vague fashion.

Yet neither the concept of actor or rational actor nor that of individual (Sanderson) is sufficient for the problem of sociocultural evolution. Actor must always mean *social actor* and that means, as I demonstrated, a role actor or role occupant. Neither social rules nor cultural components change by themselves or by automatic operations of social systems. If there are only actors who act according to rules on the basis of knowledge and/or belief systems, then the social role is obviously not only the vertex between culture and social structure, but also the focus of society, where it becomes concrete for the individual actors: only as role occupants can individuals experience society in a concrete and in particular active manner. By role taking people learn about rules and norms, i.e., social structure; in the same way they learn those parts of culture they have to know in order to have at their disposal knowledge bases for their actions; by role taking they are able to reproduce society, that is culture *and* social structure; by role changing, and changing the relations between roles, they may change society as a whole. Therefore the definition of sociocultural evolution in terms of role theory is apparently just a consequence from the methodological postulate that the social sciences deal neither with "pure" cultural units nor with pure, that is not socialised actors. We shall see in Chapters 3 and 4 that it is possible without much trouble to construct mathematical models of sociocultural evolution based on these considerations.

At this point a parallel between evolutionary biology and evolutionary social science cannot be maintained any longer in a literal fashion. It obviously makes sense in biology to speak of the genes as *the* units of evolution, but it makes not much sense strictly speaking, to define actors as units of sociocultural evolution. Things are a bit more complicated: actors are occupants of roles and by creating new ideas and trying new rules of social interaction actors also carry out the process of sociocultural evolution. However, actors change during evolutionary processes only insofar as they acquire new ideas and new modes of social behaviour. In a theoretical sense therefore it is quite sensible to speak of ideas *and* social rules, i.e. roles, as the units of sociocultural evolution, but one has to take in consideration that the concept of unit does not mean exactly the same as in evolutionary biology. Each theory of sociocultural evolution that claims to be empirically valid must take as its basis the rule governed and belief based (inter)actions of concrete actors. Therefore we may speak about units of sociocultural evolution, but must bear in mind that the concept of units is used *logically* not in the same manner as it is used in biology.

Parsons, who in particular has stressed the importance of the role concept, has sometimes expressed similar thoughts, although he concentrated on the problem of the *reproduction* of a society by role taking and neglected the importance of social evolution by the same mechanism. Unfortunately he got caught up in the temptations of the recursive processes of his AGIL-schema. The author who is dealt with prominently in the next subchapter, Marx, claimed once that he put Hegel from his head to his feet. Perhaps these remarks can be understood as taking Parsons home from the temptations of the AGIL-sirens to the firm grounds of action theory and thus putting him to his feet again. Then the concept of social systems theory that was as important to him as it is to me may, lose all theoretical haziness.

2.2 HOMAGE À MARX: A THEORETICAL MODEL

The main critical point I mentioned in regard to contemporary theories of sociocultural evolution is that no theoretical approach systematically takes into account the two dimensions of the evolutionary process, i.e., the social *and* the cultural. To be sure, I am not the first to see this inadequacy. Durham (1991) for example criticises Boyd and Richerson (1985) for leaving out the social dimension of sociocultural processes. Yet, though he and other authors see the problem quite clearly, they were not able to fill this important and critical gap. This theoretical incompleteness, by the way, has a long tradition: one of the founding fathers of social evolutionary theory, Spencer, concentrated only on the social side of the matter by analysing just *social* differentiation and taking the mechanisms for these processes apparently for granted.

Another founding father of theoretical sociology in general and evolutionary social theory in particular, Karl Marx, developed a theoretical model that indeed contains both sides. In this respect I think that Marx is still a paradigm that must be remembered. Of course, I do not suggest to restart the endless debates for and against "Marxism", whatever that may be. Marx was obviously wrong in many respects and not only the course of history has refuted many of his assertions. Therefore I am not interested to defend his particular positions or statements. I am interested in the *general* logic of his model of Historical Materialism and what we may still learn from it, an attitude I share for example with Habermas (1976). Marx considered as well both sides of the sociocultural process as the interdependencies between them; I know of no other theoretical approach that is as complete in this crucial aspect.

In Chapter 1.2. I quoted Gould with his reference to the fact that many laymen and scientists still see Darwin as the subject of heated arguments and quarrels. The same and even more of course goes for Marx: it is very difficult to refer to him without being misunderstood as a "Marxist", i.e., someone who reads his books as holy texts. However, as Darwin's ideas are still the foundations of contemporary biological evolutionary theories, the needs for enlarging his theory mentioned in 1.2. notwithstanding, it should be a matter of course for social scientists to remember the achievements of Marx and to compare one's own theoretical attempts with the model of Historical Materialism.

Marx described Historical Materialism systematically, as far as I know, only twice in his voluminous *opus* (cf. Habermas 1976), i.e., in the "Deutsche Ideologie" (German Ideology) and the "Vorwort zur Kritik der

Politischen Ökonomie" (preface to the critique of political economy).[20] The basic ideas that I have already briefly mentioned briefly in Chapter 1.1. are roughly speaking these: central to the whole theoretical model is the concept of labour as *the* characteristic property of the human species; Marx defines labour as the material interaction between man and (material) nature; the goal of this interaction is the production of material goods or products, respectively. This interaction is conscious and intentional, i.e., unlike bees or ants, which produce great artifacts by instinct, a human artisan or architect always operates with a conscious plan and an anticipatory knowledge of the product before he/she starts with the material production process. Therefore the concept of labour always contains that of consciousness and that means, in other terms, conscious knowledge about the means and the ends of the productive process.[21]

Labour is strictly speaking a "protosociological" concept, that is it describes a property of the whole human species regardless of its social organisations. In the words of Habermas (1968) labour can be called an "anthropological constant" (cf. also Lansing et al. 1998). Social theory comes in when one takes in regard that labour must be socially organised and that the particular forms of labour organisations influence the different forms of social structure. The well known concepts of Marx for labour as the driving force of sociocultural evolution are the *Produktivkräfte* (forces of production) and the *Produktionsverhältnisse* (relations of production). The forces of production are roughly the social incorporation of the technical knowledge and skills and the material tools (including machinery) that are available in a particular society. The relations of production are the specific organisation of the production

---

[20] Being a German I read of course the original writings of Marx, which are in particular collected as MEW (Marx-Engels-Werke). In regard to readers who are not able to read German I mention only the title of these essays. Unfortunately I have no idea which English editions of Marx are to be recommended.

[21] It is quite interesting that the important role of consciousness in the concept of labour which, after all, is at the center of Historical Materialism was often neglected by partisans and opponents of Marx; the Evolutionary Materialism of Sanderson is just another example for reducing the "materialism" of Marx to the assumption that the materialistic needs of humans determine the course of history. Of course humans have materialistic needs and they try to fulfil them. However, they do so in a fashion which defines them as intelligent beings, not mere need driven automata.

processes (labour) in a society. One main assumption is that the level of the forces of production, i.e., the knowledge about nature and labour processes as well as the available tools, determines the particular relations of production in a given society.

Forces of production and relations of production together define the basis of society, that is, its economic core. The basis determines the so-called social *Überbau* (superstructure), i.e., the whole of social rules, norms and ideas like law, religion, education or polity (theorem of basis and superstructure). Therefore societies are differentiated in *one* dimension according to the distinction of basis and superstructure. In another dimension societies are differentiated into political classes, which are defined according to the different degrees of having at their disposal the means of production, that is usually the possession of tools and products. In remembrance of the famous dialectics of master and servant in the phenomenology of the mind by Hegel, Marx assumes that the labouring classes have no means of production at their disposal; in contrast the possessing classes do not labour. That defines the fundamental antagonism or contradiction between the labouring and the possessing classes.

The sociocultural evolution, or in Marxian terms the course of human history, is generated fundamentally by the continuous evolution of the forces of production. Marx apparently believed this to be an anthropological fact that did not need any explanation. The human species is characterised by its capability of conscious and creative thinking, in particular in the dimension of creating new technical knowledge about nature and how to manipulate it. Therefore human beings simply have to create new knowledge and consequently new tools and products, which in turn enable human inventors to carry on with the creative process. At this point it becomes clear why the definition of labour as a *conscious* process of material interaction is so important: the human mind as a creative instrument for understanding nature never rests, to speak metaphorically, and the solutions of some material problems always produce new problems and new solutions. Yet, as is well known, this creative process can be slowed down or even stopped.

As the creative process of developing the forces of production to higher and higher levels determines the relations of production and, in the end, the whole social superstructure, history must always go on, regardless, whether the people are conscious of it or not or whether the people wish it or not. Therefore sociocultural, and in particular technical-economical, evolution is not simply a process that is driven by the seemingly insatiable hunger of human beings for more and more fulfilment of ever growing needs. On the contrary, evolution is a process that surely serves human needs, but which is driven by human creativeness and which takes courses neither foreseen nor wished for by most of the participants. In particular humans create, in form of the superstructure, religions, arts, sciences, laws and other immaterial inventions which are only indirectly related to material needs and usually cannot be explained by just pointing to them. It is true that Marx in his analysis of industrial capitalism mainly emphasised the material, i.e., economic position of the working classes. However, the concept of Historical Materialism contains much more. Therefore approaches like Evolutionary Materialism or World Systems Theory, which concentrate on economical development and purely materialistic needs, fall back conceptually behind the schema Marx sketched already more than a century earlier.

In contrast to theories of rational egoistic actors, Marx explicitly saw the actions of individuals, which change society always embedded in a social and cultural frame. This becomes very clear when we look upon the changing forces of history in Marxian terms. The development of the forces of production, that is the ongoing effects of human creativeness, are "chained" by the relations of production if and when the forces of production develop more than the frame of the relations of productions allows. The development of the forces of production extorts the changing of the social frame, new relations of productions must inevitably emerge. But this is only a metaphor. The social and political process by which these "revolutionary" changes of the social frame happens is the "class struggle", i.e., the forcible replacement of the ruling class by the suppressed classes. As classes consist of individuals, held together by their common position in regard to the means of production, their mind or consciousness which drives them to act must be socially formed, that is the social relations determine the consciousness of the individual actors via their membership of particular classes. The famous remark of Marx *"Das Sein bestimmt das Bewusstsein"*, the being determines the consciousness, illustrates this quite plainly: the social position of individual actors, that is their class membership, determines their actions by forming their minds.

To be sure, a whole chapter could be devoted to the enumeration of the errors of this grand scheme. To name only a few: Marx assumed an automatic process by which different societies always followed the same course of development of the forces of production and subsequent revolutions. That is obviously not true, as cultural anthropology and history know of many societies that did not change over centuries, or even millennia, with no revolutions (in the Marxian sense) in sight. Further, Marx assumed a strict succession for the development of ideas. First in the technological sector inventions had to occur, which change the societal basis; then the ideas, which are part of the superstructure may change accordingly too. That has never been proven and there are a lot of counter examples, i.e., societies that changed their *Weltanschauungen,* namely religions and other forms of world views, but did not change their knowledge about the technical manipulation of nature (cf. Habermas 1976). Even the evolution of the modern, that is Western, societies did not strictly follow the Marxian model. It may be that the rise of the bourgeois class in the European countries from 1600 AD to the 19th century followed the logic of Historical Materialism and certainly Marx was inspired by these historical developments. But the next stage, which should have been the socialistic revolution, never occurred. As revolutions must happen if, and only if, the forces of production are developed more than the social frame allows, then socialist revolutions had to occur in Europe or North America. Lenin himself expected the socialist revolution in Germany. Therefore the revolutions in Russia and in China were important historical events, but they had nothing to do with the scheme of Historical Materialism. This failure of the theory has to do with another simplification: it is certainly not the case that the consciousness of social actors is simply determined by their class membership. The members of the proletariat did not develop a revolutionary consciousness as Marx assumed. Therefore as a predictive theory Historical Materialism was obviously wrong; as a theory that tried to reconstruct, and by this attempt to explain, the past it is certainly too simple because it supposes automatic historical dynamics, which cannot be found in history. In particular, with the exception of the bourgeois revolutions in Europe there are no examples of successful revolutions in

premodern societies, i.e., revolutions in the sense of Historical
Materialism, which changed the structure of societies in an evolutionary
sense.

This little list of errors could be prolonged. However, if the Marxian
theory is wrong in several of their most important aspects, why bother
with an obviously outdated theory? The fundamental answer to this
legitimate question is this: in a very general sense the theory is not
outdated at all because it still demonstrates which questions have to be
asked and which answers are to be sought for by a complete theory of
sociocultural evolution. I criticised some of the contemporary theories of
sociocultural evolution not because their results are wrong, on the
contrary, but because they are incomplete in a categorial sense. This
means as I demonstrated in the previous chapters that these theories
obviously understand sociocultural evolution only in a rather restricted
way and practically always miss the whole picture. In this *categorial*
sense Marx is still a model for a complete theory; his errors are due to his
time.

Let us therefore generalise Historical Materialism in order to learn
from it how to construct a fundamentally complete theory of
sociocultural evolution and not be led astray by its faults. Marx obviously
tried to give answers to each question with which a theory of
sociocultural evolution has to deal. First of all, he defined a general
mechanism that explains why evolution occurred at all, and why it has a
certain logic behind it. This is the capability and willingness of humans
to create inventions, in particular technological ones, in order to better
their ways of living. These new insights are passed on and taken over by
other people; as the whole knowledge of a society they become the forces
of production. Many critics have rightly pointed out that Marx probably
overestimated the sole importance of technological inventions and that
the "invention" of religious ideas, concepts of morality, philosophy and
those of law are as important for the evolution of societies. If we take
over this general mechanism without the materialistic reduction, we get
as a starter for a theoretical model the undeniable fact that humans are
creative beings who are capable and willing to produce new ideas about
nature and society, i.e., the universe in which they are living.. Some of
these ideas are useful for the improvement of production processes, some
will be used for new social organisations like institutions of law or

power, some give insights into the whys and hows of the universe itself and some are purely theoretical and/or philosophical speculations, with no apparent use for other people.

It is an open and, in my opinion, a rather fruitless question, whether human actors are egoistic and rational. They are and they are not; at least it boils down to the particular semantics one is using. However, it is a plain fact that humans are intelligent in the sense that they are able to create and obtain new ideas about their life and how to improve it. If we need a starter, and each complete theory of sociocultural evolution will need such a basis, it would be best to start with this simple fact and see how far we may come. An evolutionary theory will then deal primarily with the question, how the evolution of societies, that is of cultures and social structures, may be understood as a permanent *learning process* of actors, and via the actors, one of sociocultural systems. Learning of course means here both the creating of new ideas and the taking over of these ideas by other actors.

Creative and learning actors are not lone individuals who operate in loneliness and freedom, as was the principle of the classical German university. From Marx it is to be learned that new ideas become "social", i.e., they get transformed into social contexts. By taking over the role theoretical considerations from the last subchapter we may generalise the Marxian concepts of relations of production and social superstructure by translating them into the terms of different social roles. By this I mean the fact I mentioned above that the "sociality" of actors consists of the different roles they take during their social biography. People think according to the roles they have taken (the formal parallel of the Marxian class consciousness); they create new ideas according to the systems of ideas they had internalised when taking their roles, they learn new ideas if and when their roles demand it, and sometimes the creation of new ideas has the effect that established roles must be changed or enlarged, or that new roles must be generated. The Marxian concepts of relations of production and social superstructure may therefore be translated into ensembles of particular roles by which social actors organise processes of production, the worship of gods, the juridical judgement of deviant behaviours, the exertion of political power, the education of the young and even the generation of new ideas like philosophy and science. To put it in a nutshell: the Marxian concept of the social transformation of the forces of production into the relations of production becomes in our generalised model the transformation of ideas into roles, be it already established or new ones.

It is important to note that there is a crucial point here. People may get new ideas, but as in the case of the hobby astronomer in 2.1., these ideas are, socially speaking, not existent as long as they are the private matters of the innovators. Ideas become socially effective only if the particular society is willing or can be forced to incorporate them into the knowledge base (see above) of some role(s). New religious ideas, like early Christendom in the Germanic tribal societies, were only the private matter of some religious interested members, in particular slaves and serfs. Only when some Germanic kings like the Franks or several Viking kings established Christendom did the role of the Christian priests became a socially accepted one, and only then did the Christian ideas become part of the Germanic cultures. Accordingly, the new ideas about the mathematical structure of the physical universe during the Renaissance were the private matter of people like Copernicus and Galileo. Only when the role of the scientist became established and recognised via the scientific academies did scientific knowledge became part of the European culture, and changed it in turn (see below 2.4.).

As a first preliminary result we get that in contrast to Marx the effective transformation of ideas into social contexts is not necessarily an automatic process. Whether a particular society is willing to accept ideas and establish social roles by which the ideas become part of the particular culture and by which people are allowed to act on the basis of these ideas is by no means taken for granted. We shall see in Chapter 4, where these rather informal considerations are translated into a mathematical model, how many factors have to be taken into account. It is after all a plain fact that most of the known societies, that is the numerous tribal societies, did not come very far with the generation of *new* ideas. Given the reasonable assumption that on an average all members of the species *homo sapiens sapiens* have the same intellectual capability, that is that, e.g., Europeans are not more intelligent than Africans or American Indians by their biological heritage, this fact of different development has to be explained. I shall give some first answers to it in the following passages and in the next subchapter.

The "chaining" of the forces of production by the relations of production is a beautiful metaphor, which unfortunately Marx never explained very explicitly. The selfstyled socialistic societies in Eastern Europe took this quite seriously and claimed, in vain, as is well known, that the socialist relations of production were able to "unleash " the forces of production and by this to surpass the capitalist countries. Translating this metaphor into role theoretical concepts again we may assume that certain social roles can have a "damping effect" on the learning and discovering processes of other actors. This means that creative thinking processes as well as learning ones and in particular processes of accepting new ideas are prevented by the occupants of specific social roles. For example: the official representatives of the Catholic church obviously believed it to be their religious duty to prevent and suppress ideas that they deemed heretical, be they the ideas of the early protestants from Jan Hus to Luther and Calvin or the ideas of the early scientists like Galilei. Accordingly each autocratic ruler is interested in preventing ideas about democracy and the lessening of his power, see for example the famous speech of Cicero against Catilina. The feudal nobility in medieval Europe tried to prevent ideas coming from the cities; the mandarins in feudal China tried to suppress particular inventions (see below 2.4.) and so on. As a general statement one may safely assume that under certain social conditions that seemed to be fulfilled in most cases of human history, the occupants of certain social roles tried rather successfully to hinder the rise and acceptance of new ideas in different realms of society. I shall come back to these conditions and their consequences in the following (sub)chapters.

The same problem must be considered with respect to learning processes. Culturalistic authors like Boyd and Richerson (1985) rightly accentuate the importance of (social) learning for cultural evolution. Yet the damping effect that certain social roles have in regard to creating and accepting new ideas is, of course, also effective for learning processes themselves. The prevention of learning new ideas by other people and especially young ones, can be at least as effective as the damping of creative thinking processes themselves. Therefore the simple stressing of social learning as one or *the* important factor in cultural evolution (cf. also Tomasello loc. cit.) gives not much insight into the complex processes of sociocultural evolution. It is in particular not very helpful to give some mathematical descriptions, borrowed from population genetics, of the diffusion effects of learning, if the social conditions of learning are not taken into account. The Marxian metaphor of the chaining of the forces of production is, as often, more realistic, insofar as it does not take for granted the undisturbed creation and diffusion of new ideas but emphasises the fact that social structure may hinder both processes.

Marx as usual saw the problem in a more complete way than many of his successors, though his answers were too schematic and simplistic. The role theoretical translation of his concepts gives insights more precisely, without losing the completeness of the Marxian approach. When I assume in a generalisation and translation of Marx that the basic generator of sociocultural evolution is the combination of creating new ideas, diffusing them into society by learning processes and accepting them by incorporating the ideas into the knowledge base of particular roles, the very use of the role concept forces one to speak of social conditions which may favour, or very often hinder, these processes and thereby stop the evolutionary process. Yet even these still rather general considerations illustrate the necessity Marx clearly saw: cultural and social dimensions of evolution must both be taken into account and in particular in their interdependency.

What about class struggle as the political motor of evolution? I mentioned above that in the literal sense of the concept this assumption of Marx is simply false insofar as it claims general validity. I know of no historical example, with the exception of the rise of the bourgeois class in modern Europe, where suppressed classes successfully revolted against the ruling classes and *by this process* generated a new social order, i.e., new modes of production and new superstructures. The peasant revolts. e.g., at the end of medieval Europe or in feudal China, never had the intention to create new social orders; the famous struggles between plebeians and patricians in ancient Rome may be called class struggles but they did not end with the generation of a new evolutionary stage; the same goes for the revolts of the slaves in those times.

The reasons why these revolts and class struggles never ended by generating new social levels of evolution are easily told, in particular if one remembers why Marx assumed class struggle to be the motor of sociocultural evolution. According to Marx the working *and* suppressed classes have at their disposal the productive knowledge, i.e., the knowledge necessary to produce the material goods that are needed by society. The ruling classes in contrast do not possess this knowledge; therefore they depend in a double sense on the working classes. As they have to suppress the working classes in order to maintain their power, they necessarily chain the productive forces by oppressing those who work *and* know. That is, by the way, Hegel's phenomenology of the mind again, i.e., the dialectics of master and servant who has the knowledge the master is dependent upon. If and when, according to this scheme, the working classes revolt, their productive knowledge can develop freely, the forces of production are unleashed and a new order, that is new relations of production and a new superstructure, will emerge.

The examples of the class struggles mentioned above are very plain: none of the suppressed classes who tried political revolts. and in the case of the Roman plebeians in part successfully, had the productive knowledge that could generate new relations of production. They were working classes but they did not have cognitive skills in the sense that they incorporated the cognitive creativity of the society. Therefore even successful revolts could not result in new orders; on the contrary, all the revolts just aimed for the restoration of ancient righteous orders as the term "revolution" literally means (cf. Arendt 1963). Therefore, in particular according to the Marxian scheme, they could not be movements for evolutionary *new* orders.

By generalising these historical observations we may learn from the categorial scheme of Marx, not from his historical interpretations, that new evolutionary levels can be reached only if and when those individuals who are the holders of new knowledge become occupants of socially accepted roles, which enable them to change the society's culture and by this to change the social structure too. *Because* the bourgeois class in modern Europe was the holder of new knowledge, their revolutions resulted in the generation of new social orders; that is why this is the only example where the Marxian scheme fits. The obvious fact that none of the ancient state societies actually transformed themselves into other forms of social order (see below 2.3.) but stayed in some cases like China or Japan for millennia in the same structural state, despite permanent socio-political unrest, demonstrates that sociocultural evolution is apparently a rather improbable event and no automatic process. The question, under which conditions the generators and holders of new knowledge can change society in an evolutionary sense of the term, is obviously more difficult than Marx could have known.

Habermas (1976) remarks that class conflicts took the form of economic conflicts only in modern capitalism and that in earlier societies conflicts between classes, i.e. ensembles of role occupants, had the form of power or religious conflicts. That may be so. If my sketchy considerations about the connections between new knowledge and the evolutionary transformations of societies are correct, then obviously new ideas about religion and/or the distribution of political power are not sufficient to generate new forms of society. The reasons for the successful transformation of medieval Europe into modern capitalistic societies may additionally be found in the completeness and radicality by which the medieval European culture was transformed during the Renaissance and Reformation. The question is then, why this happened here in this way and nowhere else.

A summary of these remembrances on one of the greatest social theorists of European science yields the following theoretical model of sociocultural evolution: on the one hand we have identified an evolutionary mechanism, i.e., the creation of new ideas and their diffusion by learning processes. In a very general sense there are analogies here to the biological processes of variation, but it is not to be understood that the biological mechanisms are, e.g., in a mathematical sense the same as the cultural ones. On the other hand there are the transformations of the ideas into social structures by role generating and of course role accepting. As new knowledge functions as the knowledge base for new or enlarged roles, we have a very generalised mechanism in parallel to the Marxian transformation of the forces of production into relations of production. Thus, both sides of the sociocultural evolutionary process are taken care of. Finally we have the transformation of societies by the power of new ideas and in particular the technical-economical consequences they have, the development of the forces of production, in the terms of Marx. These transformations are, as I would like to stress again, no automatic process as Marx obviously assumed. On the contrary, it is apparently rather improbable that new ideas and inventions lead to the generation of new roles and thereby new social orders – in other words, sociocultural evolution may be a process that must have happened in the long run, but its probability is not very high. This fact was not only overlooked by Marx but also by several contemporary evolutionary social theorists like Turner (1997) and Sanderson (1995). Therefore we have not only to explain how sociocultural evolution took place by identifying the main mechanisms, but also the fact why it only rather seldom took place. After all, the capability and willingness of *all* human beings to think and create new ideas cannot be seriously doubted. I already mentioned the damping effect that certain roles may have on this process. The next subchapter gives some more tentative answers.

2.3 CULTURES, ATTRACTORS AND PROBLEM-SOLVING ALGORITHMS

The 19th century, as was observed very often, was characterised by a firm belief in the inevitability of progress; in particular both biological and sociocultural evolution were looked upon as processes that unavoidably led to higher and higher forms of complexity, with mankind as the goal of biological evolution and Western society as the goal for all other societies. I already mentioned in the first chapter that these thoughts are an heritage of the Enlightenment. However, at the beginning of the 20th century more sceptical opinions were raised, and during the 20th century the idea of progress seemed obsolete, at least in respect to its inevitability.

One of the first influential philosophers in modern times who vehemently argued against the idea of progress in history was the German philosopher Oswald Spengler with his famous (or infamous) essay *Der Untergang des Abendlandes* (The Decline of the West). Spengler, a conservative heir of Romanticism, compared the different cultures with plants: they grow, flourish and then wither with "natural" necessity. It is not necessary to reconstruct the arguments of Spengler and his certainly outdated methods of philosophy of history. The strength of his position and the reason for his world-wide fame, apart from a general mistrust of the future of Europe because of the First World War, was the undeniable historical fact that the great cultures of the past all had some phases of ascent, where they seemed to unfold their potential, they then flourished at the peak of their efficiency and then stagnated, or even declined, until they were succeeded by other cultures. These insights of course were not new; as I said in the first chapter they are the main arguments of the romantic philosophy of history. However, Spengler was one of the first who reminded of these positions after a long time of belief in progress.

Much more cautious and with overwhelming historical material, Toynbee took over these ideas in his great "A Study of History". He did not use the biological metaphors of Spengler and he did not refute the idea of progress as absolutely as his romantic (and conservative) predecessor. Toynbee argued instead that a certain progress in human history is undeniable, in particular in the realms of culture, i.e. philosophy, art and science. The basic idea of Spengler was also maintained by Toynbee: each culture has its time and then, to quote his beautiful metaphor, it passes the torch on to another, younger culture, which carries on and thus takes care of human progress in the end. In this way Toynbee's work could be seen as a union of Romanticism, with its emphasis on the multitude of different cultures, and the Enlightenment with its belief in human progress.

The fundamental question whether there is progress in human history and if so, how it is to be conceived, has by no means died with Spengler and Toynbee. Marx and his followers, e.g., are still severely criticised because of their belief in the inevitability of progress; two recent overviews of contemporary evolutionary theories just mention the fact that Habermas as a "Neomarxist" also believes in progress, which seems to disqualify him once and for all (Turner et al. loc. cit.; Schmid loc. cit.). To be sure, in the sense that Marx believed in progress, history long ago has refuted him.

Spengler, and in particular Toynbee, were certainly right when they stressed the point that cultures and the societies they are components of do not go on for ever to new heights of evolution. Neither is this the case, by the way, with biological evolution. There is no permanent progress of biological species but many species, like insects, exist for very long times without changing (Gould 1982). In this formal sense there indeed seem to exist parallels between biological and sociocultural evolution: both processes are characterised by the fact that evolution creates certain systems, species and societies, which develop in the adaptive way formally described in 1.3. and *which seem to be unable to pass a certain threshold of evolution*. The process is adaptive because the systems have to exist in a specific environment and therefore have to change their structure according to the environmental demands; but this adaptive process obviously has limits. Either the adaptive systems exist without any further changes for a long time, like insects and the mentioned cases of China and Japan, if they fulfil the environmental demands, or they wither and become extinct, if environment changes and the adaptive limits allow no further changing of the system's structures. In a formal way there is no progress of particular systems, but there is progress only by changing from one type of system to another, the passing on of Toynbee's torch.

In evolutionary biology this undeniable fact was sometimes used as an argument against the validity of Darwinism. Being no biologist I do not know whether Darwin dealt with this problem and if so how he answered it. It is important to note that particularly in the light of the modern synthesis (see above 1.2.) this problem is indeed a serious one. The generators of biological evolution are the "genetic operators" of mutation, and in higher organisms heterosexual reproduction, combined with selection. These operators always "work" on the genome of organisms, regardless of whether the species is already well adapted or not. As evolution is in this sense the blind watchmaker of Dawkins (1986), it can be understood why selection hinders species becoming less adapted: it rejects the less adapted individual organisms. However, it cannot be understood why species do not unavoidably improve, as early partisans of Darwin believed.[22]

The mathematical representation of the genetic operators and selection in form of the "Genetic Algorithm" (GA) by John Holland (cf. Holland et al. 1986) gives a general answer to this question. The Genetic Algorithm simply models the genetic operators in the way described in 1.2. and, as Michalewicz (loc. cit.) has shown, it reaches certain attractors (fixed points) with mathematical necessity. I leave the limits of the proof of Michalewicz to the interested readers (cf. Klüver 2000); the important aspect here is that this behaviour of the GA gives insights into the limits of evolutionary processes.

When we consider biological species as systems, which evolve in a space of possibilities by variation and selection, then the proof of

---

[22] A famous example for the belief in the inevitability of biological progress is the play "Back to Methuselah" by G.B. Shaw where he expressed the belief, common in his day, that *homo sapiens* would necessarily evolve to *homo superior*.

Michalewicz, as well as numerous experimental results with different kinds of GAs show that each adaptive process that follows the logic of the GA must sooner or later reach an attractor, that is a state that the system does not leave any more, or to which the system returns after a relatively short period of different states. Each biological species therefore can be considered as an attractor in a state space itself (cf. Kauffman 1992), except of course for the time it needs to reach the attractor state, the so called preperiod of the trajectory. How fast the species will reach its particular attractor state depends firstly on the initial states of the adaptive trajectory, secondly on the "rules of interaction" of the organisms of the species, that is on the complexity of the genomes, and thirdly on so called "meta parameters" (Klüver 2000), i.e., measures of the changing of the genome by the genetic operators. In this case the meta parameters are mainly the rate of mutations, and for heterosexual reproduction in addition the ratio of genes that are changed by the recombination process (crossover). In particular the initial states are, biologically speaking, the predecessors of the species in question: the successor of an already rather complex species will of course get more complex, with a higher probability than species whose predecessors were fairly simple.

By considering these mathematical aspects of biological evolution the seeming contradiction between the picture of evolution as progress to always higher forms of complexity on the one hand, and the undeniable fact of the limits of evolution on the other obviously vanishes. It is simply a question of initial states of adaptive processes that in the course of evolution some fairly complex species evolve; probability then steps in and makes higher complexity almost unavoidable, given enough time, to be sure. Yet this is not a process for any single species but only for evolution in general. Each single species sooner or later reaches its limits, that is, its attractor state in the space of evolutionary possibilities. If this attractor is suited to the specific environment, then the species will remain and no longer change, assuming that the environment does not change itself or only little enough so that the species will survive. If the environment changes more than the remaining adaptive capabilities of the species will tolerate, then the species becomes extinct. Palaeontologists tell us that more than 90% of all living species have become extinct before mankind itself added to this process.

By the way, a species being in an attractor state does not mean that it does not change at all. Genomes usually allow for some spaces of freedom which show in the difference among the members of one species. If environmental conditions change then the members of a species may bear so many differences that the species as a whole may adapt successfully by selecting the members that are better adapted to new conditions. Famous in this respect has become the so called "Red Queen Effect", which means that two competing species, e.g. predator and prey, adapt reciprocally as reactions to successful innovations of one species. Yet these processes have their thresholds defined by the limits of the genomes and the convergent properties of the genetic mechanism. Only a drastic increase of the mutation rates of species enables evolution to transcend the thresholds of single species and create new ones. However, these are purely random processes, which need time. [23]

Thus we get a mathematical answer for the puzzle why species do not evolve *ad infinitum* and why waiting for the *homo superior* (superman) is probably of no avail though the principles of Darwinism are still valid. Perhaps we may get also a mathematical answer for the parallel problem of sociocultural evolution.

In a literal sense societies, and in particular cultures, are of course no biological species and one must be very cautious when using biological metaphors in the social sciences. To be sure, mechanisms like variation and selection also play a role in sociocultural evolution but certainly not quite in the way they do in biological evolution. Therefore we have to generalise the biological parallel in order to look on a more abstract level for the lessons that this little excursion into biology may give us for our problem. At first it may be useful to consider what adaptive processes mean in a *logical* sense.

Maynard Smith, who introduced game theoretical models into mathematical biology, described the biological variations of organisms and species as "strategies" (1982, 10). This concept, taken from the mathematical theory of games, means in general that a system has to

---

[23] To be sure, this is only a rough draft. I am no biologist but a mathematical social systems theorist and these considerations stem from my occupation with mathematical systems theory in general. Yet mathematical insights cannot be denied and I often wonder why evolutionary biologists have only seldom taken into account the consequences of the mathematics of complex adaptive systems.

cope with a particular situation where the system has to behave, or act, in a manner determined by the situation. In other words, adaptive behaviour in regard to a situation can and must be understood as the more or less successful *solving of particular problems*, usually presented by the environment of the system. An adequate strategy is a behaviour that solves a problem, i.e., by developing a successful strategy the adaptive system fares better with its environment than before. Therefore we can define in general adaptive behaviour as successful problem solving by varying the internal structures of the adaptive system.[24]

To avoid misunderstandings it is important to note that the concept of problem solving is meant here in a very general sense and in particular it is not meant that the processes of problem solving have to be done consciously. This would obviously be absurd for the adaptive behaviour of most organisms and species and even in the case of problem solving human actors many, perhaps most, problem solving processes are done unconsciously. Therefore no psychological meaning is intended when I use this concept but only a *logical* one. In this sense biological species and single organisms as well as adaptive computer programs and human beings are problem solvers, sometimes good and sometimes worse and, as far as we know only in the case of humans, sometimes consciously.

Before I introduce and analyse the concept of a *problem solving algorithm (PSA)* it is again time to define the concept of culture. Following a common understanding in cultural anthropology (cf. Geertz loc. cit.) I defined the culture of a society as the ensemble of all the knowledge that is deemed to be valid in the specific society. To be sure, this is a rather cognitivistic definition that leaves out the undeniable fact that for the members, or bearers, of a particular culture it is also related with emotional and traditional aspects not grasped by the concept of knowledge (cf. Berlin 1982; Thomas 1998). I shall come back at this later. But if for the time being we accept the cognitivistic definition then it is easy to see that it is a bit imprecise and too static. Knowledge does not fall from heaven and in particular it has to be accepted by the cultural community. In a *social* sense the acceptance of new knowledge takes place by accepting the social roles of the innovators, as I previously

---

[24] Cognitive systems do this by varying their weight matrices, i.e., the strength of their synaptic connections, and their geometry (see Chapter 4.3.).

remarked; in a *cognitive* sense new knowledge will be accepted if it is created and validated by those *methods* that the society accepts as binding. These methods may be scientific ones as is the case in modern societies; they may be religious methods like the quotations of holy texts or the accomplishing of religious offerings; they may simply be methods of tradition, like the sayings of ancient people and, of course, they may be the results of technical practice as in most fields of workmanship. The famous case of the Azande, e.g., (Evans-Pritchard 1976) shows a mixture of very different methods: on the one hand a member of the Azande society obtains knowledge about what to do in the problem situation where to build a new house by invoking the oracle, that is by using religious methods; on the other hand he also has to use technical methods by choosing the right materials and planning the construction process.

Each theory of science stresses the point that scientific knowledge is valid if and only if it is confirmed by the methods that are characteristic for the different scientific disciplines. Science is, according for example to T.S. Kuhn (see below), an enterprise for solving problems. By generalising this well known fact and by remembering that of course cultures collect knowledge because it may help to solve specific problems, we may safely vary the definition of culture a bit: a particular culture is nothing more than an ensemble of accepted methods for solving those problems that are important for the society and of the knowledge, which is the result of applying the methods to problems. Social actors may then also be redefined a bit: in a cognitivistic sense they are *problem solvers* (cf. also Schmid 1998), i.e., they are applying the methods accepted in the specific society as part of the knowledge base of their roles.[25]

It is rather easy to formalise these definitions, as will be shown below, and by this to give a similar mathematical answer to the question of the apparent limits of most cultures, as was given to the evolutionary thresholds of biological species. Yet before I do this I would like to illustrate these remarks about culture and problem solving with the example of scientific progress according to the theory of scientific revolutions of T.S. Kuhn (1962).

---

[25] Schein (1985) gives a very similar definition for the concept of organisational culture which is certainly no accident as organisations always have to solve problems.

Kuhn developed his famous model in a philosophical climate that was governed by analytical philosophy of science and in particular by the heirs of logical positivism. According to these positions scientific progress was thought of as a cumulative process, i.e., better theories relieved good theories in quasi linear succession, and in this manner more and more true results were accumulated. Scientific progress has no breaks but is a continuos sequence of gaining ever more insights into the true nature of the physical universe. I exaggerate a bit but at the core this description is not much unfair. In this sense science is *the* example for inevitable progress and at the same time a decisive proof for all theories of the unavoidability of the progress of the human race.

Kuhn, as is well known, demonstrated that this schema was far too simple, and in several aspects wrong. The history of science at least since Copernicus is, on the contrary, marked by permanent ruptures that Kuhn called scientific revolutions. Instead of being a continuos sequence of succeeding theories, the course of science is characterised by the dominance of certain scientific paradigms, which define the problems with which the scientific communities have to deal. In particular the paradigms are something like an arbiter that decides in case of theory competing: a theory that is compatible with the ruling paradigms will be given preference over other theories, which are not, or not so well. The question whether one theory fits better with the known data is of secondary relevance only, as long as the paradigm itself is not in question.

Paradigms themselves are not theories that can be refuted principally by contradicting data. They are something like a worldview, that is a certain way of looking at nature. To be sure, paradigms are not arbitrary but they must be in turn supported by single theories. Yet the change of paradigms in the form of a scientific revolution is not like refuting a single hypothesis but a *gestalt switch* (Kuhn), i.e., a changing of a general way of interpreting reality. The famous example of the *gestalt switch* from Ptolemy to Copernicus illustrates this quite nicely: the conception of the earth as the center of the cosmos was changed to a model of the universe where the earth is just one planet beside others. Philosophers of Western culture have emphasised again and again what this gestalt switch meant for the whole culture. Of course, paradigm changes were usually not so dramatic, as they normally concerned only the scientific communities. For the affected scientists the effects were often deeply moving, as their professional identity was at stake. It seems very apt that Kuhn used the term "revolution" in this respect.

Critics of Kuhn have noted early that he used the concept of scientific paradigms rather vaguely and that in particular a paradigm means both a scientific subcommunity and a cognitive model for the construction and rating of single theories (cf. Lakatos and Musgrave 1970). Kuhn (1970) acknowledged this and tried to clarify, but this is another story. For our subject it is interesting how Kuhn outlined the process of paradigm changing; it is important to remember that Kuhn always thought only of the natural sciences, that is sciences that are bound together despite of different paradigms by the unchanging *general* methods of experiment and mathematical theory construction. Therefore the concept of paradigm makes not much sense in the humanities, for example.

A paradigm defines a particular field of research, i.e., a set of relevant problems that Kuhn called puzzles, accordingly the specific methods to investigate the problems and finally the criteria, which results by the puzzle solving are to be accepted or not. The process of solving the problems defined by the paradigm Kuhn called "normal science". The decisive aspect is now that the course of normal science is always the same: in the beginning the success of the paradigm becomes manifest by obtaining a lot of interesting new results and new theories, the paradigm moves to its peak. After a time of normal science, the more results are gained by following the paradigm, the more the paradigm becomes "exhausted"; less new results turn up and more "anomalies" are discovered, i.e., results which do not fit into the theories supported by the paradigm. In the end, the research steered by the old paradigm gets rather sterile because the new results become less interesting and the anomalies, which have been neglected during the reign of the old paradigm, become more important than the confirmations of the accepted theories. The old paradigm declines, so to speak, and then it is time for a scientific revolution, the creation of a new paradigm.

Several aspects of this process are of interest here. When this course of normal science is defined in a formal manner we obviously get a growth curve, which is known in population mathematics as a logistic curve: in the beginning of the process a quick growth of the paradigm in the form of many results appears and an equally fast growing number of scientists join the scientific subcommunity which is defined by the paradigm. The rate of growth then begins to decline though the paradigm is still growing by numbers of results and participating scientists. Finally the growth processes are brought to a standstill; the paradigm remains at a constant level or even regresses, i.e., the numbers of new results and participating scientists decline until they reach a lower level, where they stay. I shall deal with these growth curves more thoroughly below as there are a lot of processes that can be described in this mathematical way.

The concept of paradigm apparently has two aspects of meaning, as was noted above. Kuhn originally concentrated on the cognitive aspects in order to explain *logical* relations between different but competing theories like those of Ptolemy and Copernicus; for this task he introduced the somewhat vague concept of incompatibility. Yet a paradigm also has a social dimension because it constitutes a scientific subcommunity, which is defined by the common belief of their members in the validity of the paradigm. In this sense a paradigm is somewhat like a particular society defined above, that is a social group with a culture, the worldview and theories generated by following the paradigm, and a particular social structure, which is constituted by social hierarchies among the members of the subcommunity. Because a culture always means for the members of the particular society more than just cognitive aspects which can be taken or left, they express a *Weltanschauung* (worldview) with firm beliefs as the emotional basis for the social identities of the members (cf. Berlin loc. cit.), it is immediately plausible why Max Planck once remarked that scientific theories are not refuted but die out with their supporters. Accordingly Kuhn notes that new paradigms can be created only by scientists who are either still young or new to the specific field of research. A (scientific) culture is not simply left but remains until newer cultures, in this case newer and more successful paradigms, emerge with a fresh spirit to tackle new problems in another manner. The old paradigm, to be sure, does not vanish but its results become incorporated into the new one, e.g., Newtonian mechanics was not refuted by relativistic mechanics but was perceived as a borderline case of the general relativistic theory. In this sense Toynbee's metaphor fits here very well: new paradigms take the torch from old ones, which pass it over.

Kuhn *described* the course of science very aptly and for experts in the history of cultures the parallel between the observations of Kuhn and those of Toynbee is indeed remarkable. However, he did not explain it very thoroughly; obviously he, like Toynbee, took it for granted that historical processes just go this way. The same goes by the way for the analysis of Hart (1959) who noted without explaining it that a lot of social processes follow the logistic growth curves mentioned above.

To explain why these and a lot more processes (see below) must be described according to logistic functions it is necessary to come back to the definition of culture as an ensemble of problem solving methods. As knowledge is usually sought in order to solve problems the methods for problem solving are obviously the most important aspect; the results are in a logical sense "just" a by-product. As the concept of methods is rather ambiguous and in order to clarify our little logical analysis a bit, I like to use the concept of *problem solving algorithm (PSA)* instead, meaning with it of course the procedures that scientists and laymen use when solving problems. These PSA may be the competent use of some tools in order to build a house or to drive a car, the application of painting techniques to create a piece of art, the use of rhetoric skills in order to convince political opponents, the employment of military means to win a battle, or the use of scientific methods. In this general sense we may define a culture as the ensemble of socially accepted PSAs.

A PSA consists of several steps that have to be carried through in a certain succession. Some PSAs are "deterministic", i.e. the different steps are basically the same and they are always carried through in the same manner. The classical approximation procedures in applied mathematics and physics are examples of deterministic PSAs. Many PSAs, and possibly the most efficient ones, are "semistochastic", that is they contain both random and deterministic procedures. In other words, semistochastic PSAs proceed in a mixture of trial and error steps on the one hand and deterministic steps on the other. A rather simplified example, which was analysed by Jörn Schmidt and myself, may illustrate this.

Consider a problem that consists of finding an integer in the number space between 0 and 100. The integer itself is not known to the problem solver and he/she only knows whether one new solution, i.e., a new integer is better or not than the preceding ones. Several procedures are possible, in particular a simple trial and error one, which consists of guessing a number and if the number is wrong than guessing another until the right one is found. It is obvious that such a procedure is very slow though of course the right number will be found in the long run. Another procedure, i.e. a deterministic PSA is similar to the classical approximation procedures mentioned above: two numbers are chosen at random, say a and b. Let b be the better one of the two. One then takes the distance b - a and gets the next number c = b + (b - a). If c is better than b, one repeats the technique and gets d = c + (b - a). If c is worse than b, one bisects (b - a) and gets c´ = b + (b - a) / 2 (if c´ is not an integer one rounds up or down). One repeats these steps according to the last results until the right number is found. This technique is obviously a deterministic PSA because all the different steps are always applied in the same manner. Only the first two numbers are chosen at random and then one of two options always has to be taken in the same manner. Though this PSA is still not very efficient, it is obvious that it is much better than a pure trial and error technique.

A semistochastic technique for our little problem goes like this: again you choose two numbers a and b at random and take the better one b. Besides the fact that b is the better of the two you also know that the solution is somewhere in the number space (0,100). You then choose again at random a number c from the number space (b,100). If c is better than b, you choose again at random a number d from the space (c,100) and so on till you find a number k which is worse than the preceding number i. You then bisect the interval (i,k) which gets you (with rounding up or down) a number m, take at random a number n from the interval (i,m) and so on (I skip some technical details because they are not important). As in the deterministic case you apply one of these steps till you find the right number. This technique is a semistochastic PSA because there are stochastic steps (the choosing at random) as well as deterministic ones, that is you always knows unequivocally which of the different options is to be applied. Experiments demonstrated that the semistochastic technique is by far the most efficient one of these three, which hints at the importance of trial and error techniques controlled by deterministic frames.

This problem seems a very simple one and it is. Yet the seemingly trivial problem of finding a number in a finite number space is a representative example of problems of a much higher order of difficulty. This follows from the fact that our little PSAs may be also applied to the same problem in higher dimensional spaces, which cannot be shown here. Because it is always possible to encode each well defined problem in sufficiently complex number expressions, it is also possible to model the according PSAs with our simple ones.

For the purposes of this chapter the following considerations will be enough: with the exception of the purely random procedure, that is the simple uncontrolled trial and error technique, our little PSAs both have the characteristics of an iterative function. You always get the next result by applying one of two or more possible steps to the preceding solution and carrying on. In particular after a certain time the PSA becomes contractive, i.e., the distances between the succeeding solutions get smaller and smaller (the technique of bisecting). In the end you get the right solution as an attractor of the PSA. Typical results of the random, deterministic and semistochastic PSA respectively look like this:

Problem solving strategy	Average number of steps for solution	Maximum	Minimum
deterministic	89.7	227	21
semistochastic	19.3	27	16
random	256.0	263	246

Table 1: Results of the different PSAs

In a more formal and rigorous manner we may describe the proceedings of our PSAs like this: let $d(m,n)$ be the distance between two "solutions", that is two numbers found out by one PSA As the right solution s is not known but only whether m is nearer to s than n, we have $d(m,s) \leq d(n,s)$, which gives the next number r with either $d(r,s) \leq d(m,s)$ or the opposite. With the exception of "errors", i.e., steps which yield numbers t with $d(t,s) \geq d(r,s)$ for a preceding r, we obtain an iterative function f with the property $d(f(m), s) \leq d(m,s)$ for most of the numbers m obtained by the PSA f. As the numbers get continuously nearer to the right solution s we also obtain $d(f(m), f(n)) \leq d(m,n)$ for most of the numbers m and n. This is the definition of a contractive function first mentioned in 1.2 of which we know that it converges towards a fixed point or an attractor, respectively, in this case the solutions.

I discussed this little example in detail because it shows very clearly the main properties of a PSA in general. Its most important aspect is that it consists of a finite set of steps, which get the problem solver nearer to the desired solution, whatever that may be. It is not necessary to have an idea about the solution in advance or to know how far a preliminary solution is still away from the final one, but one ought only to know whether a new solution is better than a preceding one and of course when a solution is satisfactory. The concept of "algorithm" needs not be understood in a strictly mathematical sense. I introduced this concept in order to demonstrate that it is possible to analyse PSAn in a mathematical fashion but this analysis is of course not restricted to purely mathematical algorithms. One may safely imagine a recipe for cooking or baking with which a mathematical algorithm has often been compared (e.g. Dawkins 1986). The demonstration of a semistochastic algorithm showed that in contrast to a simple recipe the concept of algorithm also may include the neglecting of strictly fixed procedures and instead trying new possibilities at random. Therefore the general meaning of a PSA given above, as well as its formal treatment, seem to be justified.

It is now time to return to the problem of cultures and their development à la Toynbee. A PSA, if it serves to solve any problems at all, obviously has the comforting characteristic that it reaches an attractor sooner or later, that is a solution. To be sure, that does not mean that any problem that is tackled by a suited PSA will be optimally solved by it. The attractor of the PSA may be a solution but not a sufficient one because the PSA gets fixed by an attractor too early; the application of the PSA may take such a long time that any solution found by it will be quite worthless, because circumstances have drastically changed and nobody is interested in the solution any longer; the problem solvers may have tried their capabilities on such difficult problems that they become old or die before the PSA reaches an attractor. The important point is that any PSA can be defined at least theoretically by its limits, i.e., the attractors it may reach under the most favourable conditions. If we define a culture according to the remarks above as a finite set of different PSA, then *the limits of all PSAs define the limits of this particular culture*. As a first approximation of our question why cultures obviously all had limits they were not able to transcend, with the possible exception of modern Western societies which need a special treatment, we get therefore the answer: because the PSAs the cultures consisted of had just these thresholds as their particular attractors. Apparently we get, in regard to cultures, an answer which is in a formal manner practically the same as the answer in respect of biological species.

The well known example of Greek mathematics can serve to illustrate this point. In a scientific sense of the concept the Greeks *invented* mathematics, that is the science of theorems, proofs and deduction. To be sure, the Egyptians knew a lot of geometry, e.g. the theorem of Pythagoras and other results of the geometry of the plane, and the Babylonians laid the foundation of arithmetic. Neither is a creation of the Greek mathematicians. However, they were the first to systematically analyse mathematical objects for their own sake and in this way they were the founders of mathematics as an autonomous discipline and since then as the *regina scientiarum*. Yet despite their great achievements, which still serve more than two millennia later as the basis for modern mathematical education, they were not able to pass the limits of the finite. Some historians claim that the greatest of the Greek mathematicians, Archimedes, was at the brink of inventing the calculus, had not the Roman soldier slain him during the siege of Syracuse (cf. Bell 1937). Yet this can never be proved and I personally doubt it. The Greek mathematicians and philosophers had a very important cultural paradigm, i.e., the idea of the cosmos as a finite unity that can be described with the methods of finite mathematics. The Greeks knew neither zero as a number nor could they for general cultural reasons, i.e., their conception of the cosmos as a finite order, grasp the idea of the (mathematical) infinite. Therefore their great methods for creating and enlarging the mathematical universe, their mathematical PSAs, could not transcend the threshold of the positive and finite. The number zero is an invention of the mathematics of India, probably inspired by the buddhistic concept of the Nirvana; the mathematics of the infinite, the calculus, apparently needed a cultural concept of infinity which was made available by Christian theology.

The question of progress in sociocultural evolution may be answered quite similarly. I mentioned above in regard to the increasing of complexity in biological evolution that this is a question of initial conditions. A biological species that starts its evolutionary way by developing from a species comparatively far evolved, will by the laws of probability come farther than another species, which develops from a relatively simple predecessor species. The same goes of course for different cultures and societies. A culture like the ancient Greeks was able to start their cultural evolution on the foundations of ancient Egypt and partly Mesopotamia, both cultures that were far advanced already. Therefore one does not need to speculate about particular talents of the Greeks but must only note their cultural heritage, that is the predecessing cultures upon which they were based. It is certainly no accident that European culture only started its specific advance when, by the contacts with the Islamic societies, the Europeans rediscovered their lost Greek heritage. Otherwise, one may speculate, the "dark times" of the Middle Ages would not have ended in such a quick and radical manner. Only then the different PSAs of the Europeans, e.g. their concepts of infinity, could have produced modern mathematics and physics (see below 2.4.). I shall deal with the question of why the Islamic societies did not advance like the Europeans did despite the fact that the Islamic societies rediscovered the Greek culture significantly earlier than the Europeans in the next two subchapters. In contrast to the examples of Greek and European cultures, isolated societies like e.g. the Indian societies in the Southwest of the US (cf. Gumermann and Gell-Mann 1994) had no heritage they could be based on; accordingly their level of evolution remained low.

Let us return once more to Kahn's scientific paradigms. A paradigm can be compared, as I said before, to a society in the sense that both contain a particular culture with specific PSAs and a social structure. In particular we have in both cases the rise to their respective peaks and then stagnation or even decline. The reasons for these parallel developments are, of course, the same, the paradigms become as exhausted as cultures. The parallels go even further: despite the beliefs of some radical theorists of science who took Kahn's considerations and results as proof that there is no real progress in science (cf. Feyerabend 1970), no practicing scientist ever believed in that. Of course, the astronomical theory of Ptolemy was substituted by the heliocentric system of Copernicus, but since the dawn of modern science in the 16th and 17th centuries, scientific theories, which were accepted as valid became the borderline cases of the newer and more general theories, like Newtonian versus relativistic mechanics. Even the long debate about the structure of light, waves versus corpuscles, was decided in this way by quantum theory: both possibilities can be observed, depending upon the methods of measurement. One may say that the paradigms build their specific progress on the foundations laid by the preceding paradigms, and generate scientific progress not as a linear continuous succession but more in the manner of a relay of swimmers who swim in different styles. The same picture is obviously applicable to the progress of cultures: no single culture is able to transcend its particular limits, but as succeeding participants in the long development of mankind they make progress in different manners.

Kuhn is not very explicit in explaining why paradigms are necessary for scientific progress, i.e., why progress in science cannot occur in a linear fashion, because his main efforts were in proving their existence and their functions in scientific controversies. However, the general picture is clear: paradigms make available those general world views that are the cognitive foundations of specific theories. In other words one may say that the scientific *methods* of experiment and mathematical theory construction are too general for scientific research. They tell one how to do research but not what questions to ask and not what is relevant in the overwhelming set of possible research enterprises. That is the main and unavoidable function of paradigms, i.e., to give road signs for directing the concrete ways that research has to take. A paradigm becomes exhausted if there are no important questions left; the *gestalt switch* to a new paradigm means that new questions have been discovered and therefore new criteria of relevance will guide the practical research.

It is basically the same with the switch between succeeding cultures. A culture becomes exhausted when the PSAs reach their limits as in the case of the finite Greek mathematics. To be sure, very general PSAs can pass their limits if one uses them to answer new questions. That is the case with the general PSAs of modern science, that is, their experimental and mathematical methods. Therefore, in many cases the limits of culture specific PSAs depend on the problems, i.e., the questions they should solve. Given other problems the same PSAs could often give new answers, and so transcend cultural limits. However, as a particular paradigm can only generate a finite set of specific questions, and as new questions need another paradigm, a particular culture can use its specific PSAs only in one certain fashion, which brings the PSAs to their attractors. The reason for this is similar to the unavoidable function of paradigms for scientific research: a culture as a whole world view, i.e., a way of understanding nature and society, gives a necessary cognitive constraint for the otherwise overwhelming complexity of the universe. The late German social systems theorist Luhmann has often stressed the point that each complex system has to reduce the complexity its environment offers in order to cope with the environment. This necessary task is done by the frame a culture defines: it enables the problem solvers living with the culture to make a start, that is to agree upon questions to ask and to develop PSAs suited to obtain answers. The same frame operates as a constraint, which means that it hinders the problem solvers seeking for new questions, to be able to transcend the limits of the PSAs.

The German poet Hölderlin two hundred years ago described this situation once with the beautiful words "*In der geordneten Welt seid Ihr zu Hause*" (in the ordered world you are at home). A home means the possibility to live in a dangerous world without order and to reduce the unknowable complexity of the world by posing the order of its own home on the world. However, a home, as each order, is also a constraint because it hinders seeing the things outside the home. Therefore one has to leave the home, i.e. the familiar order, to see new questions and new answers. This means to leave one's own culture and try another one, which is very difficult and has to be paid with certain costs. We shall see which ones in Chapter three. That is perhaps the most important reason why cultures never transcended their PSA-specific limits but stayed within their attractors. Only new cultures, as the new scientists with Kahn's paradigms, could pass the limits of the old cultures by starting afresh and building other forms of the reduction of complexity.

To be sure, a culture also becomes exhausted in a more usual sense. When members of a society always experience the fact that there will be no new discoveries and ideas because of the thresholds of the culture, then the whole culture may go the way Downs (1967, 60 pp.) describes aptly as the inevitable fate of bureaucratic organisations: the more often the same problems are presented, the more likely formal rules for these problems will emerge that are *not open to change any more*. Cultures that become "bureaucratic" in this sense pass into the state of

"Alexandrinism", i.e., they just preserve the knowledge gained before and deem this stagnation as inevitable. History teaches us that this form of bureaucratisation seems to be the fate of practically all important cultures.

I mentioned above that apparently both cultures and scientific paradigms develop in a manner that can be described mathematically as a logistic curve. To understand why this is so we have to look a bit more precisely at this concept.

A logistic function can be expressed by the following differential equation (cf. Maynard Smith 1974):

$$dx/dt = ax - bx^2 \qquad (1)$$

The behaviour of the function expressed by this logistic equation is this: if x is small, the equation becomes approximately the exponential growth equation

$$dx/dt = ax \qquad (2)$$

and as t increases, x approaches an attractor (a steady value) in a continuous way.

Equation (1) can be expressed in quite another way, that is as a recursive function. That was done in the 19th century by Verhulst, who wrote the growth equation (2) as

$$x_{n+1} = ax_n, \qquad (3)$$

which simply means that the new unit x_{n+1} of a recursive sequence is just the product of a growth factor a with the preceding unit x_n. To take into consideration the fact that in the physical world no growth processes can go on for ever, at least not in the way described by equations (3) or (2), Verhulst added the term $(1-x_n)$ as an additional factor into equation (3), which made it

$$x_{n+1} = ax_n * (1-x_n) \qquad \text{or}$$

$$x_{n+1} = ax_n - ax_n^2 \qquad (4)$$

which is obviously, with the exception of the different factors a and b, mathematically the same expression as equation (1), the first time written as a differential equation and the second time as a recursive one. One can see immediately from these two mathematical formulae (1) and (4) that in the case of logistic developments the first phases of growth (x is rather small) are characterised by exponential functions and as x gets larger with increasing t then the growth curve flattens out until it reaches an attractor state.[26] It is well known that a lot of growth processes can be described by logistic curves; Briggs and Peat (1993) mention among other examples the growth of animal populations with dependency on the natural resources of their environment, the frequency variations of genes in a population, the spreading of rumours and the growth of knowledge during learning processes. The same goes for technological innovations (Kauffman 1995) and the famous problem of marginal utility in economics. The reasons for the mathematical equality of these different processes are always the same: first there are a lot of resources, like food in the case of population growth, which enable the population to grow faster and faster, or many people who have not already heard the rumour and which can be influenced by other people, whose number grows with each act of telling, or knowledge that the learner did not know and which he/she absorbs with a growing rate of velocity; then certain thresholds start to become effective, i.e., the rate of growing velocity slows down until it practically comes to a standstill.

Obviously we can transfer the reflections about PSAs to, e.g., the population growth. A population of animals has the problem to survive in a particular natural environment with limited natural resources. The only PSA the population has at its disposal is of course its manner of reproducing in dependency on the number of adult organisms and its death rate in dependency on the size of the resources (sometimes also a variation of the birth rate). This "PSA" apparently reaches an attractor state, i.e., a threshold of population size that depends on the size of the resources and the amount of food an organism needs to survive. Mathematically speaking it is equivalent whether we express these processes by the concept of PSA or with the more traditional concept of recursive or differential equations.

It is not difficult to imagine that this is just the case with the growth of scientific paradigms and cultures. The exponential growth of new ideas

---

[26] The asymptotic case, i.e., the approximation to a x-value, which the growth curve does not reach in finite time, is included here though strictly speaking the concept of attractor must be generalised in this case. (For such cases see for example Hofstadter 1986).

in the first phases of development is due to the fact that on the one hand there is a lot of knowledge that can be gained rather easily; this causes many people to join the enterprise of developing the culture/paradigm, which accelerates the growth once more (for the case of scientific knowledge see Mainzer 1997). On the other hand the growth of new ideas makes a particular way of creating still more ideas even more effective, i.e. the way of recombination of ideas (cf. Hart loc.cit.; Bateson 1972). Indeed, the more ideas that have been created, the more new ideas can be found by recombining the ideas already obtained. By the way, as the genetic algorithm also uses the mechanism of recombination, the number of variations between the members of a population must grow in proportion to the size of the genome, the same mathematical thing.

The thresholds of the (sociocultural) exponential growth processes are, as I mentioned in detail, the limits of the particular PSAs and the cognitive constraints of the culture/paradigm, which hinder the participants in seeing new questions and finding new answers. To be sure, cultures and paradigms can slow down their declining processes by taking over fresh questions and answers from other cultures and research paradigms. I mentioned already the importance of the contact with the Islamic cultures to the European culture of the Middle Ages. However, as we shall see in the next subchapters, there are in particular social limits to the ability of cultures to learn from other ones. It is not only a cognitive problem to leave the home of one's own culture in order to seek for new questions and answers, but also a problem of social structure. Before we turn to this additional problem it may be enough just now to summarise that the observations of Toynbee and Kuhn are apparently correct, and more, that they can be explained by mathematical considerations about growth processes and problem solving processes in general.

2.4 A CASE STUDY: THE EMERGENCE OF MODERN SCIENCE

In the last subchapter I explained the thesis of why cultures all follow the same course of development, i.e., they rise in an exponential way and then stagnate or even decline, if the members of the particular cultures lose interest in seeking for new questions and answers. I shall come back to these processes in a more rigorous and detailed way in Chapter three. In particular I hinted at the fact that there are cultural constraints immanent to each culture, which keep, so to speak, the culture's members within the frame of the culture. Before I discuss these aspects of culture in general I illustrate the problem of cultural limits with the treatment of a particular question, i.e., the emergence of modern science in Europe during and after the Renaissance. The question here is not the detailed reconstruction of this process; that has often been done elsewhere and does not need to be repeated once more. The interesting question with which I deal is why modern science developed only in Europe and not in the cultures of feudal China, Japan and the Islamic cultures, which were superior in many cultural aspects to medieval Europe. The tentative answer to this question may give some insights into the general logic of sociocultural evolution, in particular to the interdependency of social and cultural dimensions in this process. I chose the example of science mainly because in this aspect the European culture is most distinct from all other cultures; as I mentioned in regard to Kuhn, many theorists and historians of science believe science to be the most important example of undeniable human progress. Furthermore, the continuous merging of science and technology in the 20th century is not only one of the most important reasons for the contemporary dominance of Western culture, but also an outstanding example of the generative force of new ideas in the process of sociocultural evolution.

As I am no historian of science but interested in *sociological* reasons for the *Sonderweg* (special way) of the European culture, to use the term of Max Weber, I explain this question with a comparison of Chinese science and technology and the European one. To be sure, I rely mainly here on the great work of Needham, who, as is well known, gave already some answers. Because I think that Needham was basically right my own answer will be a generalisation of some of Needham's arguments.

The characteristic that makes modern science a unique cultural enterprise is the combination of experimental method and mathematical theory construction, as is generally known. Neither of these features in themselves are new or an invention of European culture. Experimental methods are basically as old as technical labour: each artisan, artist or farmer who tried new ways of solving their problems had to do experiments in their specific ways. Mathematical theories about the universe are also at least as old as the ancient cultures of Egypt and Mesopotamia, which knew a lot about celestial mathematics. The natural philosophy of the Greeks was, of course, basically founded on mathematics, as in particular the *Timaios* of Platon demonstrates. However, only the European culture of the Renaissance made the invention of combining these different ways and founding by it modern science. Why only there and not in China or the Islamic cultures, which both knew a lot about mathematics and had a highly developed technology at their disposal?

In a very general sense there are basically two answers that have been given. The first one concentrates on special features of the European culture of the Middle Ages and tries to show that even during these times the European culture contained aspects that later served as the basis for science, aspects that were not part of the Chinese or Islamic cultures. In a certain sense that is the famous answer Weber has given. This is the way too of, e.g., Nelson (1969) who analysed the rational and systematic elements in scholastic philosophy and theology which, according to his opinion, served as foundations for modern scientific theory building. As these cultural elements cannot be found for example as clearly in Chinese thinking, which Needham (1972) acknowledges himself, the answer lies in an early characteristic of European culture. We may call this type of answer a culturalistic one.

The second type of answer is more sociologically orientated and explains the rise of modern science in Europe by the general development of feudal Europe into modern capitalistic societies. Especially in the tradition of Historical Materialism, scholars like Bernal (1954) describe the emergence of science as part of the evolution of the forces of production, and therefore as an inevitable part of the evolution of modern capitalism. The rise of modern science, according to this position, had to occur in Europe because only there did happen the transformation from feudal societies into modern capitalistic ones. In a formal similar sense although with other concepts and theoretical assumptions contemporary theories of social differentiation give the same answer: modern science evolved in Europe as an autonomous subsystem because only there occurred the evolution of functional differentiated societies (cf. Luhmann 1984; Turner 1997).

Both types of answers, to be sure, just shift the question. If it is true that early European culture contained elements that other cultures lacked and which were the reason for the rise of science, then the question is why just European culture contained these crucial parts and others did not. Moreover, if these elements are sought, e.g., in the Christian conception of a law giving god (Nelson loc. cit.) and the according theology, or in the Greek heritage of systematic thinking, then the question emerges why for example Islamic cultures did not develop modern science, as they had roughly the same theological basis and were even better acquainted with the Greek tradition, in fact European culture had to relearn its Greek heritage by the contacts with Islam. Most important of all, why did the Islamic scholars not combine their own tradition of systematic thinking with the methods of experiments? According to Needham (loc. cit.) they were equally well acquainted with Chinese technology, which was far superior to European technology till the Renaissance. The classical answer of Weber to the question about the uniqueness of European science is unsatisfactory for similar reasons (cf. Spengler 1979).

The same objections hold for the sociological type of answer. It is of course true that modern science evolved as part of the evolution of modern societies in Europe, whether one calls them capitalistic or functionally differentiated. However, these theories do not answer the original question: why was Europe the region of the emergence of modern societies and why only there? Sanderson (1995) answers this general question simply: as the emergence of modern capitalistic societies inevitably had to occur somewhere it was due to some boundary conditions like climate and a particular social structure that it happened in Europe. I shall come back to this answer below in more detail. With this answer Sanderson, as a self avowed (evolutionary) Materialist presupposes a universal schema of history, which leads automatically to particular types of societies like the capitalistic modern ones. As much as I am in sympathy with the thinking of Marx, who of course is the ancestor of these theories, as much I am in doubt about the stipulation of simple universal schemas that have still to be proved. As neither Sanderson nor any other theorist is or was able to prove the necessity of the factual course that sociocultural evolution has taken, his answer too is just a shifting of the problem.

I wish to avoid any misunderstandings. It is not only that I sympathise with theories that seek for universal schemas in human history like those of Marx or of social differentiation. I also believe (and try to demonstrate in this book) that there are indeed universal features in sociocultural evolution. However, these "sociocultural universals", to borrow from other searchers for universals in human behaviour like language (e.g. Chomsky 1965), are not to be found by just declaring an observed historical development as an inevitable path that had to be followed, willing or not. The answer lies in my opinion in the mathematical characteristics of complex systems in general which already have been sketched a bit (see also below Chapter 3) and it is not to be found by just observing history and taking its course for the explanation itself. That is indeed some sort of naturalistic fallacy.

Let us come back to the question of the uniqueness of European science. Needham, who was the first to demonstrate the superiority of Chinese technology over the medieval European one never gave a complete satisfactory answer to our question, but he hinted at it, i.e., he tried to handle the problem in a *sociocultural* way. As a convinced follower of Marx Needham (1970) on the one hand believed that it was a question of political classes why modern science emerged in Europe and not in China, Japan or the Islamic cultures. In particular Needham referred to the class of merchants, which should have been the bearers of historical progress, as, according to his opinion, it was in Europe. The *social* difference between China and Europe was the small degree of political independence the merchant class had in China, in comparison to the situation in medieval Europe. Because this progressive class was "chained" in feudal China, it was not possible for the Chinese engineers and early scientists to develop a new science independently from the regime of the Mandarins. Furthermore, Needham pointed out the fact that the Mandarins tried successfully to isolate the creative inventors of new technologies from one another. Therefore they were not able to exchange their insights and results, in other words, the Mandarins hindered any mechanisms of social learning.

On the other hand Needham indicated, as mentioned above, that Chinese culture indeed lacked one important element, which in a cognitive sense may have been crucial for the development of modern science in its *theoretical* dimension. The Austrian historian of science Zilsel (1943/1976) was, as far as I know, the first to emphasise the importance of the concept of *law* for modern science. Since then it has been noted several times that the concept of laws of nature originated not by chance at the same time as the modern legal concept of law during the early Enlightenment (cf. Lepenies 1976). One of the main *cultural* differences between China and Europe seemed to be indeed the lack of this concept in Chinese science. Therefore the Chinese engineers and experimenters were not able for cognitive reasons to systematise their insights, i.e., to combine the experimental methods in which they were masters with precise, that is mathematical theory. This is, by the way, an illustrative example for the constraining force of cultural frames discussed in 2.3. Thus, both cultural and social factors were responsible for the fact that the great Chinese culture did not pass the threshold which marks the difference between modern theoretical science and successful technology.

The medieval European society in comparison, which was clearly inferior to China in the dimensions of technology and also of rational social organisation obviously had the advantages of (a) a merchant class with relatively great independence from the feudal power system and of (b) a philosophical and theological culture in which the concept of law played an important role via the concept of a law giving God. Indeed, even a superficial look at the political situation with regard to the merchants in the European Middle Ages demonstrates the differences to China: the large trading towns in Northern Italy, Flanders or Northern Germany (the *Hanse*) were not only relatively autonomous but were political powers in themselves that sometimes decided the fate of kings. The political principle in the Holy Roman Empire of German Nation *"Stadtluft macht frei"* (town air makes free) illustrates this independence very well: it means that any serf breaks free from the bonds to his noble lord when he manages to come into a city. The feudal law of serfdom ended at the walls of the free towns.

The importance of systematic scholastic theology and philosophy for the rise of modern science was mentioned above in connection with the arguments of Nelson (loc. cit.). Therefore Needham's two answers may be combined as follows: because the European medieval *culture* contained the important elements of rational law and systematic logical thinking as part of their Greek and Christian foundation *and* because the medieval European *social structure* was characterised by the extensive political freedom of the merchant class, modern science could evolve as part of the development of the forces of production. The regime of the

Mandarins in China, on the other hand, was successful in chaining these forces of production because the Chinese culture lacked some important elements crucial for the cognitive enterprise of modern science.

Zilsel (1976) described the social process of the emergence of modern science by an integration of two different social roles, that is the roles of the artisans, respectively craftsmen, on the one hand and the role of the theologically and philosophically trained scholars on the other. Neither role vanished during this process of role integration but some bearers of the two roles managed to form a new role, that of modern scientist (cf. Ben-David 1971), by taking cognitive and social components from each role: experimental operating with material nature and systematic/ mathematical theorising. Only the components of two different roles could create a new form of thinking about nature, and nowadays also about society and mind. This integration of roles during the Renaissance was possible only because the creators of the new role of scientist had the political space of freedom to do so in the relatively autonomous towns of Europe during the Renaissance.

The role theoretical considerations of Zilsel are rather important for our problem because Zilsel freed the thesis of Needham from the vague metaphor of the merchant class as the bearer of the progressive development of the productive forces. In contrast to the view of many social theorists orientated at Marx (cf. Bernal loc. cit.) it is simply not true that modern science was since its beginning a part of the productive forces. On the contrary, neither physics nor chemistry played any part at all in the rise of industrial capitalism, for the simple reason that both sciences were not applicable to practical problems, i.e., they generated important theories but were not able to solve the problems relevant to the expanding industries. This situation changed first with chemistry during the second half of the 19th century (cf. as a case study Klüver and Müller 1972) and with physics during the 20th century. Since then it has been possible to speak of science based industries, but not earlier. This being the case, there is no reason why the merchant class as a whole should have been interested in the development of modern science. In fact they were not, as the history of modern science proves: science was founded as an institutional enterprise in the form of the scientific societies and academies, which were largely sponsored by the respective monarchs (for the history of the Royal Society see for example Böhme et al. 1977).

The rising bourgeois class was interested in the evolving science for quite another reason, namely as an ideological weapon against the dogmas of the church. But that is quite another story.

Interestingly enough, Needham was not the only scholar who saw the importance of the political autonomy of the towns in Europe for the rise of modern capitalism. Other authors like Sanderson, who think that the sociocultural evolution to modern capitalism has a certain form of inevitability, pointed out that the situation in Japan was, at nearly the same time, very similar to that of medieval Europe (Anderson 1974; Jacobs 1958; Sanderson 1995). I am not able to judge the arguments in regard to economy whether in Japan there existed the beginnings of modern capitalism *before* the forced "opening" of Japan by the US navy. Instead I shall examine these positions with respect to the rise of modern science in Japan, as e.g. Sanderson (loc. cit.) not only stipulates an autonomous rising of modern capitalism in Japan, but an equally autonomous emergence of modern science too. Both processes, so we have to understand, belong together, and both had of necessity to occur sooner or later. The proof that the same process of modernisation has indeed taken place at two societies at almost the same time and independently from each other would be a strong argument for the validity of this theoretical position.

It is known how interested the Chinese astronomers were in regard to the theories of Copernicus, Kepler and Newton when the Jesuits arrived from Europe (they were less interested in Catholic dogmas). Yet despite the fact that Chinese astronomy was also well developed at this time and despite the interest of the Chinese scientists in Western natural science, it was apparently very difficult for the Chinese to accept the methodical ways of Western science (cf. Spengler 1979). Still, in 1922 Bertrand Russell noted after a visit to China that the Chinese lacked science (in the modern sense, J.K.) and mathematical abilities (Russell 1922).

In Japan the acceptance of European science was greater, and in particular during the 19th century science began to develop quite rapidly. Bartholomew summarised these developments:

"By 1800 Japanese astronomers were regularly producing telescopes and even grinding lenses. Using a telescope of his own devising, Kunitomo Tobei observed sunspots in 1835 and published a drawing of the surface of the moon; other astronomers began to do systematic observations of the planets. However, the most important development was the arrival in 1803 of a book in Dutch by the French astronomer J.P. de Lalande. Lalande was a prominent figure in eighteenth-century science, and his work was the first "advanced treatise on contemporary Western astronomy" in Japan." (1989, 17)

Sanderson (1995, 321) also mentioned the taking over of Western anatomy, studies in Newtonian physics and advanced mathematical techniques during this period. This, he concludes, is decisive proof or at least a strong indicator for the fact that in Japan similar developments in science had taken place as in Europe, *quod erat demonstrandum.*

It is not my concern to hold in scorn scholars who know a lot more about numerous historical facts than I. The similarities between medieval Europe and feudal Japan Sanderson enumerates are indeed striking; in particular noteworthy is his (and Anderson's loc. cit.) observation that the power structure of both Europe and Japan consisted of a "military feudalism", the only ones in known history, as he thinks. Though I doubt this uniqueness, Sanderson certainly has stressed an important point. Yet in the case of modern science he and his colleagues have, I fear, gone a bit astray. It is one thing to readily accept new ideas from another culture and, as was to be seen in the Chinese example, it is far from being a matter of course. Yet it is quite another thing to *create* all these ideas, in this case the cognitive revolution of modern science, in a particular culture. There is no evidence I know of that in Japan even the beginnings of something akin to modern science have been observed. The great innovations in physics, mathematics and chemistry from Copernicus and Newton to Lavoisier and Gauss (to take only the period before the acceptance of modern science in Japan) have no counterpart in Japan, not even on a small scale. The exponential growth I discussed in 2.3 is, as we saw, characteristic for any new field of enterprise, and therefore it is no accident that the development of modern science, once it was socially established, seemed to explode with geniuses and important discoveries. Nothing like that could be observed in Japan and when Bartholomew calls the arrival of a textbook "the most important development in Japanese science", everybody trained in science knows enough.[27]

---

[27] As my experience taught me that such arguments are likely to be misunderstood I wish to emphasise that I do not intend to classify Japanese scientists as inferior to Western ones. That would be quite absurd in view of the numerous contributions of Japan to science in the 20th century. I just argue against the untenable position that in Japan a similar development occurred independently in science as in Europe.

The similarities between Japan and Europe with regard to climate and social structure (military feudalism, relative autonomy of the towns) are not to be disputed. They may explain the fact that Japan was more willing to take over Western ideas than, for example, China. Therefore the obvious differences between the European and the Japanese ways in developing modern science may simply be due to differences in *degrees* of similarities. The case of Japan does *not* prove the inevitability of modern capitalism, as nobody can tell for sure how the factual development of Japan would have been without the overwhelming influence of Western culture and societies. The tale of the rise of modern science in Europe still has no parallel anywhere, and even the history of the industrialisation of Japan shows that Japan in research and education went just not literally the same way as did the Western countries. But perhaps another lesson may be learned from the Japanese case: given particular social structures and contacts with other cultures, then the culture may be able to change, that is to transcend the limits of its own attractors. We shall see in the next subchapter what kind of social structure this may be.

What after all then is the reason for the European uniqueness in developing modern science as the contemporary "most important part of the forces of production" (Habermas 1968)? The answer has something to do with recent insights into the behaviour of complex systems, in particular the fact that certain systems that are rather similar in their initial states may generate quite different trajectories in the long run. I shall try to give a general answer in the next subchapter.

2.5 THE HYPOTHESIS OF SOCIOCULTURAL HETEROGENEITY

Sanderson and other scholars emphasised the indeed remarkable fact that both feudal Japan and medieval Europe were characterised by *military* feudalism as the general power structure; in both cases the towns had some kind of political autonomy, though in the European case the degree of autonomy was certainly much greater. There was no counterpart in Japan, as far as I know, to the powerful leagues of trading towns like the northern *Hanse* or the league of Flemish towns, which defeated kings and ruled in fact whole regions. Yet the degree of autonomy of the towns in Japan was apparently much greater than in China and probably also in the Islamic societies. Neither Sanderson nor the authors who observed these facts give detailed explanations as to whether there is perhaps a connection between these characteristics of the two feudal societies, and in particular whether the social structure of military feudalism is in some way responsible for the unfolding of modern sociocultural traits. Of course nobody thinks that a military power structure of all social possibilities should be especially favourable for evolutionary processes.

Before I discuss these problems I would like to point at another example of military feudalism, which also gave rise to a brilliant culture but which is much older than the two cases mentioned. I speak of the rise of the ancient Greek culture, which in its beginning was characterised by a particular form of military feudalism, i.e., the early culture of *Mycene*. The social picture Homer and later authors show of this culture is clearly a society, which was ruled by kings who in turn based their power on a class of professional warriors. Of course, the warriors of Homer are not the same as the medieval knights, and the knights are not the same as the *Samurai*, but the similarities are nonetheless striking. In the case of Greek society this feudal order was relieved by the well known society of *poleis*, that is the ensemble of autonomous city states that became the social basis for the Greek culture. When we neglect all the obvious differences between the three cases of military feudalism, which as theoretical sociologists we may do, then we have the interesting fact that in three cases societies that started as feudal societies with the power base of professional warriors were able to evolve to a very large degree by generating a second kind of social order next to the feudal one, that is the more or less great autonomy of towns and the social class of merchants. We may notice also that in the Greek and the European cases the degree of autonomy of the towns was significant greater than in Japan.

An explanation for these observations, with the contrasting cases of China and Islamic societies in mind, has to take into account the kind of power, which can be based on a military class. Obviously, as is known from many examples of military regimes, power structures like these have several great deficiencies: on the one hand they have the problem of legitimacy, that is the voluntary acknowledgement of the citizens. Military power by itself is not able to legitimise its existence but has to look for other sources of legitimacy, for example religion. Even the famous case of Sparta demonstrated this quite plainly as the Spartan kings too needed priests to legitimise their military social order. Therefore each ruling class that exerts its power by military means alone must seek allies, that is, bearers of other social roles, which are able to give the ruling class the needed legitimacy. That is why the *de facto* ruling *Shoguns* in Japan always needed the emperor as the divine source of their power and that is also the reason why, in the Karolingian beginning of European military feudalism, Charles the Great needed the pope for his coronation as Emperor, and all his successors too.

On the other hand military rulers are not very well suited to grasp the importance of new ideas for the benefit of society. To be sure, the ruling classes are always conservative in order to maintain the social order from which they profit. I already mentioned this simple fact.[28] However, it is necessary at least to understand new ideas and whether they are dangerous for the ruling classes or whether they are necessary to cope with new problems in the natural or social environment of the society. Professional warriors are mostly unfit for these tasks and therefore the bearers of other social roles must do it, mostly priests or civil servants who were often trained by the church. In contrast to this, the ruling Mandarins in China were very well educated people who immediately understood new ideas and how to handle them socially and culturally. The mentioned fact that the Mandarins hindered the creative inventors of new technologies in exchanging their ideas in an institutionalised way, and thus prevented the emergence of new social roles, demonstrates that the Mandarins knew very well how to deal with potentially dangerous innovations.

Thirdly, but perhaps not last, professional warriors are not able to understand those ways of production, which guarantee wealth for society above the level of the elementary needs. They are mostly integrated into the social-economic order by overseeing the agricultural duties of the serfs, which are labours warriors know well from their own origins. But the more complicated labours connected with trade and manufacturing, which was done in the towns, was something the military ruling classes must needed to leave to the professional specialists, which means

---

[28] Platon whose declared political model was Sparta (cf. *Politeia*) frankly postulated as one important task of the guardians to banish new ideas because they are dangerous for the maintenance of the "ideal" social order.

bourgeois ones. This is again a question of intellectual education: the cited Mandarins of course knew not much about trading and manufacturing either, but they were intellectually equipped enough to understand those tasks in principle and to keep the bourgeois specialists in their socially low places. It is certainly no accident, as Needham observed rather early, that the merchants in China were considered to be a low class, even below the soldiers, who were not very respected either.[29] *In nuce,* these considerations about military feudalism may be summed up with a famous quotation from Talleyrand: You can do everything with bayonets, but you cannot sit on them.

The social consequences of these shortcomings of military feudalism were of course different in the three cases: in Greece the feudal order vanished and the city states became the main social structure; in Japan the feudal order did not vanish till the 20th century and perhaps some remnants of it are still to be observed, but it was weakened and therefore Japan was quite ready to take over the new ideas from the West, much easier than most other societies that had to deal with the dominance of Western culture; in Europe feudalism also vanished and the sociocultural structures of modern, capitalistic and functionally differentiated societies emerged. However, in all cases the deficiencies of military power structures had as a social consequence that besides the social roles, which defined the power hierarchy, other social roles had to be accepted as socially important, and in some aspects as equally important as the roles of social power themselves. In the cases of Japan and Europe these other roles were in particular those of the priests and the merchants.

Looking at medieval Europe with these facts in mind we get a picture of very differentiated and heterogeneous societies, the same societies the Romanticists admired for their wholeness and homogeneous order. There was the difference state versus church which lead in particular in the German Empire to violent power struggles between the emperor and the pope; there was the dichotomy between land and town, which removed the towns at least partially from the general social order of feudalism, and which finally made the towns the social places for the emergence of

---

[29] In contrast to this the social importance of the great merchants in medieval Europe is very well illustrated by the fact that the German Emperor Karl IV addressed the patricians of Lübeck, the capital of the *Hanse,* as *"Herren"* (Lords), meaning with this address that the ruling merchants of Lübeck were socially equal to the nobility.

modern societies; there was the antagonism between the scholars of the church and the secular institutions of learning and research, i.e., the universities, which were freed early from the intellectual dominance of the church; there was also the continuous competition between the different nations, which rivalled for supremacy and so on. It is no wonder that this heterogeneous structure lasted for only some centuries in contrast to the far older societies of China and Japan. Therefore we may safely call medieval Europe a very heterogeneous society.

It is important to note that the qualifying of a society as "heterogeneous" or "homogeneous", respectively, means only *degrees* of these properties. When I speak of Europe as a heterogeneous society in contrast to, e.g., China, it does not mean that China was homogeneous in all respects. China also had its differentiations both socially and culturally, for example the antagonism between the philosophy of Confucius, which was the "ideology" of the ruling Mandarins, and the Taoist philosophy of Laotse (Needham 1972). I shall give in the fourth chapter a precise definition of how to measure the degree of heterogeneity of a society. For the time being it is enough to understand that calling Europe a heterogeneous society simply means a high degree of heterogeneity whereas China is characterised by a significantly lower degree.

The Islamic societies were apparently societies with a rather low degree of heterogeneity. Though merchants were more respected than in China, they were not part of the political structure in the sense that they had political power like the merchants in the self governed large European trading towns. There was also not such a strict antagonism between state and church, as the Islamic caliphs usually were both secular rulers and representatives of the respective Islamic churches. Though things were different in this respect in the Ottoman empire, the church was no real rival to the state as the state defined itself via the Islamic faith. The legal concept of the *shariah,* the Islamic law, illustrates this relative unity of state and church quite aptly, as it means that there is only one law for mundane and religious affairs; in contrast to this in Europe there always existed the difference between secular law and canonical law, a difference that was often very important when deciding how a case had to be judged. It has been noted quite often that Islam and Christendom differ religiously in this important respect: the Islamic religion was also always a set of social norms and rules, which should guide the faithful in his daily social life; the famous quotation of Jesus before Pilatus on the other hand "my empire is not of this world" (John, 18, 36) illustrates quite clearly the fact that mundane world and the religious realm are not as united in Christendom as in Islam. Though the Islamic empires were founded by religiously motivated warriors, there can be no doubt that the Islamic societies never could be characterised as military feudalism, because of the dominating power of the religion in all societal aspects.

To be sure, we do not know much about the early Greek culture of *Mycene* and it would be therefore a bit comical to characterise it with certain degrees of heterogeneity. However, there can be no doubt that the classical Greek society, i.e., the city states, were very differentiated and heterogeneous societies, with the exception of Sparta. Political and religious roles were separated, as was the case in ancient Rome, the difference between a quasi feudal social organisation of the land and the more bourgeois structure of the towns was also to be found with a clear dominance of the towns; the roles of the intellectual philosophers, artists and scientists were well differentiated and like the ideological situation in modern societies there was no unifying bond in the form of a universal religion. This heterogeneity was observed by the Greeks themselves; it is no accident that the conservative political theorist Platon took as a model for the ideal state not his home Athens, but the rather homogeneous state of Sparta.

In terms of the theory of social roles high degrees of heterogeneity mean that the different roles are rather independent from each other. The repeated case of the European merchants shows that the bearers of this social role could act rather freely, without too severe restrictions by state or church. Of course, Christian merchants were, e.g., forbidden to trade in financial matters, that is to operate in the banking business. But when the rise of early capitalistic trade forced the introduction of financial business, nobody seriously cared when, for example, the merchant families of Fugger and Welser founded banks in the 16th century in the trading towns of Augsburg und Nürnberg, as did the Medicis in Florence. In a formal similar sense the secular scholars at the universities had a relative space of freedom to investigate those problems in which they were interested, as long as they did not interfere with the doctrines of the church. The heliocentric planetary system, e.g., could be taught if it was interpreted just as a mathematical hypothesis and not a statement about the physical world. Not least the competition among the different nations and regions often guaranteed that some scholar could continue his researches in another country, when he was forbidden to do so in his own. Very famous is the case of Martin Luther who obtained refuge against the persecutions of pope and emperor by the *Landgraf von Thüringen,* one of the most powerful nobles in the German empire. Therefore we may define the rising of degrees of heterogeneity as the rising of degrees of independency of different roles, that is the enlarging of their spaces of freedom to increase their action space.

By generalising the cases of the different societies we just considered it seems plausible to postulate a general *hypothesis of heterogeneity* as a formal criterion for the capability of societies to evolve.

The larger the degree of heterogeneity in a particular society the larger the capability of this society to evolve socioculturally, i.e., the larger the probability that this society will develop new cultural components and new social structures. In particular this means that the ability of a society to learn from other, more advanced societies is the greater the larger its degree of heterogeneity.

The observation in 2.3. that cultures by themselves always get caught in their specific attractors can be slightly reformulated: cultures are limited by their attractors as long as they have only low degrees of heterogeneity, that is, the particular roles have not much space of freedom to change their action space and to enlarge their cognitive components by adding new ideas outside the attractor. Even contact with other cultures and the receiving of new ideas by these contacts can change this fundamental situation only if the bearers of the particular roles are free to change their roles according to the new ideas. As apparently most of the known societies are rather homogeneous, in a relative sense, it is no wonder that sociocultural evolution is obviously something that happens only seldom.[30] The possible reasons for the fact

---

[30] Of all the nearly uncountable tribal societies only rather few made it to the stage of state organized societies. Though many scholars do not agree unanimously which societies belong in this category, their number is less than twenty (Trigger loc.cit.; Sanderson 1995). The stage of functionally differentiated societies was reached only once, that is in Europe. I shall come back to this fact in Chapter three.

that most societies have only low degrees of heterogeneity will be dealt with in the next chapters.

The historical cases we discussed obviously fit this criterion, but that is of course no proof in itself. A look of the development of modern societies, which will be undertaken in Chapter 5 more thoroughly, seems to confirm the hypothesis: sociocultural evolution always meant in this case that the space of freedom of different roles was enlarged, e.g. those of scientists or of judges and lawyers in relation to politics or religion. The whole theory of functional differentiation from Spencer to Luhmann (1984) can be read, and must be understood, as the reconstruction of a process by which each important social role, one after the other, enlarged their spaces of freedom till they reached a high degree of action autonomy. What after all can the concept of "autonomous functional subsystems" (Luhmann) mean if not the statement of an extensive free action space of those roles, which form the social structure of the subsystems? I shall return to these questions.

It is now possible to give a tentative answer to the question of 2.4. why only the European culture did develop modern science, that is the new combination of mathematical theory and experimental methods. To be sure, the European early scientists had to use the contributions they got from other cultures, in particular, the Greek heritage passed on by the Islamic cultures and the enlargements of Greek mathematics by the Indian number system and the invention of zero. However, these were cultural achievements the Arabs had too and they did not go the European scientific way. The Islamic cultures also had the philosophical and theological conception of infinity, as the Islam is founded on the same idea of an infinite god as the Christian religion, as is well known. According to the hypothesis of heterogeneity the answer is rather simple this: the high degree of heterogeneity, which distinguished the European societies from the Islamic ones, gave the medieval scholars at the beginning of the Renaissance freedom in a political and cultural sense to enlarge the cultural components of their traditional roles. In particular they were able to combine components of two different social roles into a new one, the social role of the scientist, which became institutionalised in the scientific societies and academies. Their Islamic counterparts obviously did not have this space of freedom though they had all the mathematical, theoretical and practical knowledge, and possibly even more, than the Europeans.

The second case of military feudalism we discussed, Japan, apparently was characterised by a rather high degree of heterogeneity too, though the case of the Japanese early scientists, perhaps only protoscientists, has not been thoroughly analysed, at least not to my knowledge. However, let us assume that the culture and social structure of Japan, which are significantly older than the European ones, also had from their beginnings degrees of heterogeneity that were only negligibly smaller than those of Europe (I personally doubt it, but I am no specialist in Japanese history). Then, as we shall see in more and technical details in Chapter 4, we need only to assume that all other factors remained equal. By this I mean that the Japanese bearers of important social roles had the same urge to enlarge their roles and change them as their European counterparts. But small differences in the degree of heterogeneity could be enough to slow or even stop the enlargement of the social roles while the Europeans succeeded in this. One may assume in addition that the Europeans just had some more cultural contacts with other cultures than the Japanese to achieve quite different developments.

The argument just sketched here is due to results of chaos theory and complexity theory. Systems with complex trajectories – see below 3.2. – are characterised by the fact that small differences in the initial states can give rise to great differences in succeeding states after sufficient time. If one assumes that social systems can be complex in this sense the different developments of Europe and Japan, respectively, despite their similar initial states, are just a mathematical consequence. This will be analysed in a formal way in the next chapters.

The uniqueness of the European way with regard to science, capitalistic economy and other autonomous functional social subsystems, is therefore no mystery at all, and certainly neither due to specific talents of the European race, if there is such a strange thing as a particular human race, nor to unique features of the European culture, whose origins could hardly be explained. The last is the position of Weber and his followers. It is probably simply a systemic consequence of the fact that for historical reasons the European societies started with initially rather high degrees of heterogeneity, which caused the differentiated structure of the Middle Ages; these seemed homogeneous only from a holistic romantic point of view. The relatively great spaces of freedom for those roles, which were changed during the Renaissance, enabled the transition from a basically feudal society to the modern kind, with all the problems, with which we still have to cope.

I mentioned critically the fact that Evolutionary Materialists like Sanderson, and in certain respects also theorists of social differentiation like Turner, take the historical developments of societies for granted in the sense that they conclude from the factual development its necessity. It is not so simple, though in a very abstract sense they are not wrong. The theoretical model developed here so far suggests a story that is a bit different: human beings try to create new ideas and when they are caught in a cultural and social attractor they are often hindered by the criterion of sufficient heterogeneity from transcending it. Therefore the development of modern capitalism and/or of functional differentiation is nothing, which *must* happen at some time with some kind of logical necessity. There is only a consequence of the laws of probability: given enough time, then a society must emerge with a sufficiently high degree of heterogeneity. Then the drive to enlarge and change established roles by creating new ideas may be successful in generating a far going sociocultural evolution. A development like the European one is also possible only if the particular heterogeneous society is able to start from a relatively high level of sociocultural evolution; otherwise it would also take a very long time to reach only the levels of the ancient cultures. This was the European case; the result then was indeed necessarily a society with independent role ensembles, the autonomous subsystems of Luhmann, including modern capitalism as the autonomous functional subsystem of economy. This necessity is a consequence of the mechanism of role changing, being enabled by sufficiently high degrees of heterogeneity. However, before I discuss these problems in more detail it is time to make these considerations more precise by some mathematical foundations and models.

3. THE MATHEMATICS OF SOCIAL PROCESSES

As I intend to translate the considerations of the last chapters into mathematical models, it seems appropriate to make some preliminary remarks about the specific concept of mathematical models I shall introduce. The main reason for these preambles is the fact that there are a lot of misunderstandings in social sciences when someone is speaking in terms of mathematics. That is not only due to the tradition of social theory, which is by and large an unmathematical one. It is also due to certain developments in the last decades, in particular to the emergence of mathematical models that have not much to do with the traditional tools of mathematical physics and strongly rely on their implementation into computer programs, i.e. they are validated by computer simulations. In 1.2. I already mentioned the Boolean networks (BNs) used and investigated by Kauffman, which can be seen as a paradigm for the new mathematical approaches to biological or social complexity.

Usually mathematical models of systems dynamics consist of ensembles of differential or difference equations like the famous Lotka-Volterra equations for the mathematical analysis of predator-prey systems, or the logistic equation described in 2.3. Sometimes the use of equations of this type is identified with the concept of mathematical model; therefore, some scholars postulate the existence of a "third symbol system", mathematics and natural language being the first two and the new computational models, which do not use classical equations being the third. That is rather misleading as it suggests that these new formal models are not mathematical ones. But if they are not a kind of mathematics – what else can they be?

Since the development of set theory and the foundations of mathematics based on mathematical logics and set theory by Hilbert and others, mathematics is generally defined as the science of all formal systems, regardless which formalisms are used to capture the particular structure of these systems. Therefore the mathematics that is commonly used in the empirical sciences, like the calculus or statistical procedures is only a part of the far greater realm of mathematics, though certainly a very important one.[31] The traditional mathematical methods have often shown their fruitfulness in the branches of empirical science, yet they were not very useful for dealing with the classical problems of theoretical sociology and the other disciplines of social complexity. Therefore it is necessary to give the concept of mathematical models in the social sciences more enlarged meanings. Some of the possibilities and results that are gained by this new approach are shown in the next subchapters.[32]

3.1 SOCIAL EVOLUTION AND THE GEOMETRY OF SOCIAL SYSTEMS

When I speak of "social geometry" I do not mean the geometry of the physical space, in which all social interactions occur. To be sure, geophysical factors often play an important role in the development of social systems, and physical barriers like mountains or oceans may be decisive for the particular paths of evolution taken by isolated societies. These are, as physicists would say, boundary conditions, i.e., they may influence the particular development of societies but have no impact on the *general* logics of sociocultural evolution, if there is such a thing. By speaking of the geometry of social systems I mean certain properties of their rules, which generate the dynamics and metadynamics of these systems (see above 1.3.), and which may be described in a mathematical manner by using some concepts of geometry. The concept of geometry is therefore used in a general mathematical sense, that is, as the description of structural features of rule systems that can be applied to physical systems as well as social ones.

In a very general sense it is possible to characterise the geometry of any set, or system, by defining a) the number of dimensions of this set and b) its topology and/or metrics. Mathematicians call a set with these properties a geometrical space which just means that certain geometrical properties can be defined according to this set. In the case of physical systems it is usually assumed that the geometrical properties of the

---

[31] These methods are of course also used in the social sciences (cf. e.g. Helbing 1995 and Gütschl 2001) and are far from worthless there.

[32] These new mathematical approaches and results are discussed in more detail in Klüver 2000. I give a short summary here because I cannot presuppose that readers interested in sociocultural evolution are acquainted with methods and results in recent mathematical social systems theory.

physical space define the geometry of these systems. In the case of social systems it is a bit more complicated.

Let us remember: in subchapter 1.3. I defined social systems by the rule governed interactions of social actors, which generate dynamics and metadynamics, respectively, evolution of the systems. The logical key concept in this definition is obviously that of *social rules* as I am speaking here only of *social* dynamics, I omit for the time being the additional importance of social roles for socio*cultural* evolution. As there is basically nothing else in social reality than social actors and their interactions and as all classical sociological concepts like structure, institutions or organisations must be understood in terms of rule governed interactions (cf. Giddens 1984), the main research question for social analysis must be the search for specific properties of ensembles of social rules, in particular such features that explain the dynamics and evolution observed in social reality. Mathematical analysis of social systems therefore means the search for mathematical features of rule ensembles that generate certain dynamical and evolutionary behaviour of the systems. It is the main thesis of this book that there are indeed such mathematical properties, i.e. parameters of different kinds, which together explain at least general features of social dynamics and evolution.

Let us first define the concept of social geometry in the double sense mentioned above. The *topology* of a set is its mathematical structure, by which the spatial relations of the set's elements are described. In particular the topological structure of a set determines if any two elements are connected, directly or by a chain of coupling elements, or if there are "holes" in the structure of the set, i.e., some elements are not connected at all. For example, two geometrical figures in the Euclidean plane are, in this sense, topologically equivalent if they have no holes or the same number of holes. Therefore the topology of a set defines measures of connectedness with regard to the elements of the set.

A special kind of topology defines a *metric* of a set, that is, a structure, which measures distances between the set's elements. A metric is formally defined by a relation $d(x,y)$ between two elements x and y with $d(x,y) \geq 0$ and which fulfils the conditions

$$(1)\ d(x,x) = 0$$

$$(2)\ d(x,y) = d(y,x) \quad \text{and}$$

$$(3)\ d(x,y) + d(y,z) \le d(x,z) \quad \text{(triangle inequality).}$$

Intuitively these concepts are clear when one is imagining the usual physical space in which we live. As we have "only" rules of interaction with regard to social "spaces" we have to translate these mathematical terms into sociological ones. That is rather easily done by use of social structural analysis (cf. Freeman 1989):

Two actors x and y can be defined as (directly) connected if they may interact with each other. In this case we define $d(x,y) = 1$. Two actors x and y are connected indirectly with each other if they can interact via a chain of interacting actors. In this case $d(x,y) = n+1$ if n is the smallest number of interacting actors, i.e. the size of the smallest chain of interacting actors (cf. the "Small World" experiments by Milgram 1967); if there is no such finite chain, $d(x,y) = \infty$. It is easy to demonstrate that these rough definitions fulfil the strict criteria of the mathematical concepts but this is not important here. As the possibilities to interact directly or via a chain of interacting actors is a question of social rules, we can obviously define some properties of social rules by geometrical concepts. For example, a worker in a factory can interact directly with his/her foreman or forewoman and therefore the distance between the two is $d = 1$. As the worker is usually not allowed to interact directly with the chairman of the firm he/she needs some interacting persons, whose number depends on the size of the firm. This number $n > 1$ defines the social distance between the worker and the chairman; the proportion between n (the actual distance defined by the rules of the firm) and m, understood as the greatest possible number of intermediating persons, defines a measure of hierarchy of the organisation (which is certainly greater in an army than in one of the Internet firms).

These topological or metrical definitions are, though not in these terms, well known to structural social theorists. We shall see in the next subchapters that certain topological features of rule systems also have consequences for the dynamics of social systems. More unusual is the use of the concept of dimensions in regard to social systems. In the mathematical theory of vector spaces, the number of dimensions is usually defined as the number of *linear independent unit vectors* one needs to describe any element of the vector space completely. The Euclidean plane has two dimensions because each point can be described by exactly two co-ordinates, which in turn are linear multiples of the two unit vectors x and y; for the same reason the physical space of our perception has three dimensions, and the strange Hilbert spaces of quantum mechanics have millions of dimensions. Well known in mathematical systems analysis are the state spaces or phase spaces whose numbers of dimensions depend on the number of (independent) variables one needs to completely describe any event of the system, and by this its trajectories.

When referring to the space of our perceptions we may understand the concept of dimensions in a more simple way, which is of course nothing more than the abstract definition just quoted. We perceive any object or event in a three-dimensional way because we always need three independent spatial indications: the event A is "before/behind me", "left/right of me" and "above/below me". By adding the indication "after/before now" we get a fourth dimension of description, which gives us the four-dimensional space-time.

By translating this rather general concept of dimensions into our sociological language of rules, actors and social roles, we get a rather "natural" definition of the number of dimensions of a social system: it is the number of distinctions necessary to describe any social event, that is mainly any other social actor and his/her actions, completely in regard to the particular society. Such descriptions may of course be very different but as we are interested in the *general* features of any given society we may safely assume that the most important distinctions are "familiar versus strange", "above versus below" and "active versus passive". In other words, if an actor meets another one and has to classify him, it is in principle enough to judge if the other belongs to one own group or not, if the other is socially above oneself or below (or equal) and if the other's role means that one is the active part in the interaction or the passive one, or if both are occupants of active or passive roles respectively. For example, a worker's interactions with his foreman are characterised by the fact that both belong to the same organisation, familiar, that the worker is socially below the foreman and that both roles are active ones. A doctor on the other hand interacts with his patients usually based on the assumption that both are strangers to one another, that the doctor is mostly socially above his patients (but not always) and that the doctor's role is an active one and the patient's role a passive.

Readers who are acquainted with the classical theory of social differentiation from Spencer to Parsons, Luhmann and Habermas, will of course immediately recognise that these considerations are a "translation" (and generalisation) of the well known distinction between three forms of social differentiation into role theoretical and geometrical terms. Segmentary differentiation means the distinction between familiar and strange, i.e., social rules that distinguish between the members of ones own group (tribe, segment) and those of others, that is, strangers. Stratificatory differentiation means the introduction of the discrimination between socially low and high roles, respectively; functional differentiation is equivalent to the *universal* difference of active roles and client roles. The principle of universal inclusion (Luhmann) states that this difference is in the same sense a structural feature of the whole society, as are the principles of segmentary and stratificatory differentiation. The statement that the three distinctions are sufficient for the classification of any actor and social event is obviously equivalent to the well validated statement that the three forms of social differentiation are sufficient for the structural description of a society.

As the theory of social differentiation is meant as a reconstruction of social evolution. i.e., a new stage of social evolution means the emergence of a new form of differentiation, we may reformulate this assertion in a mathematical way: in the beginning of social evolution societies were sufficiently characterised by one, and only one, form of differentiation, the segmentary one, and therefore these early societies can be described completely by having only one social dimension. The emergence of new forms of differentiation is to be understood as the "unfolding" of new social dimensions; modern societies, characterised by the synchronous occurrence of all forms of differentiation, can be said to be three-dimensional. It is of course an open question whether another social dimension will emerge in the future (see below).

The translation of well known sociological concepts and theories into mathematical terms is certainly not much gain in knowledge by itself. To make these translations worthwhile, i.e., to model social evolution as a dynamical and adaptive process, Jörn Schmidt and I constructed a computer model based on these considerations and mathematical concepts which I already mentioned in 1.3. (cf. Klüver and Schmidt 1999 a; Klüver 2000). I shall omit most details of this model as it is described elsewhere and shall give only the most important aspects and results.

The geometrical properties of our model were implemented into a (three-dimensional) cellular automaton (CA) which is akin to the Boolean nets mentioned in connection with the studies of Kauffman (see above 1.2.). CAs are also universal Turing machines, which principally allow one to model any real system. Basically, a CA generates a grid of cells that are in different states; the transition of the state of a single cell depends on the states of the cells in its neighbourhood and on the state of the cell itself at time t. Therefore the transition rules of a CA are like this: if the neighbourhood cells are in states x, y and z ... and the cell is in the state w at time t then the cell will pass into the state v at time t+1. Although this basic principle is simplicity *per se* it is possible to model any form of dynamics with it, in particular non-linear dynamics, which characterise all complex systems. For reasons which need not be discussed here we constructed our CA with stochastic rules which is rather unusual; most CAs described in the literature are deterministic ones.

The topological or metrical "nearness" discussed above is represented in a CA by the concept of neighbourhood, i.e., the adjacency of two cells on the grid. Two actors represented by two cells on the grid are socially close if their cells are adjacent; the distance of the cells on the grid measures the social distance between them. A social group has a high social density if all their members are socially close together; this is modelled with a CA by putting all the cells that represent the group members into their respective neighbourhoods.

Social evolution is, like every evolutionary process, an adaptive one. Therefore the CA must be enlarged by a "meta program", which changes the rules of the CA according to environmental problems. Though we were aware of the fact that the mathematical characteristics of social evolution are not the same as those of biological evolution, we coupled the CA with a genetic algorithm (GA) to adapt our formal systems to the demands of an (artificial) environment. The reason for the introduction of a GA was simply the fact that we were interested in the *general* behaviour of our adaptive system, and that the differences between a GA as a model for biological evolution and a "social algorithm" as a model for social evolution (see below 4.1.) could be neglected there. The GA operates on the CA in several ways: on the one hand it changes the probability values of the stochastic rules, on the other hand it switches rules on or off, depending on whether the states of the CA are sufficiently close to favourable values and, last but not least, it "decides" whether its own operations should take place or not (there are more possibilities in the whole program but they are not important here).

As the whole formal system is adaptive, an artificial environment must be defined that represents the problem any system has to solve in order to maintain its existence. According to our fundamental role theoretical approach, we assumed that the capability of a social system to handle environmental problems depends on the generation of certain social roles, whose bearers have to deal with special problems like food production, political and administrative tasks, producing material (and cognitive) tools and so on. We further assumed that the emergence of social specialised roles leads to stratificatory differentiation, and under conditions that had to be investigated, even to functional differentiation. Therefore the "value" of the formal system, that is the generating of states that enable the system to deal sufficiently with environmental problems, depends on the stages of differentiation, the more differentiated, the better for the system's values (for mathematical details on how this is computed see Klüver and Schmidt loc.cit.). Each new form of differentiation meant, for our mathematical system, the adding of a new dimension. The different dimensions are represented in the mathematical model by defining the state of a cell with a triple of three possible (independent) values.

Yet increasing the value of a (social) system by introducing new forms of differentiation is just one side of the matter. Because there is no such thing as a free lunch, as the science fiction author Larry Niven puts it aptly, social differentiation has a price that is mentioned by several theorists of social evolution (Habermas 1976; Sanderson 1995). Each new form of social differentiation tends to dissolve traditional social relations, which are a value themselves for the members of the specific society. Therefore we introduced *in memoriam* of the well known insights of Georg Simmel a "cohesion factor", which means that social cohesion represents another value for the system. The system therefore had the problem to enlarge its stages of differentiation on the one hand, in order to cope with its environmental problems and to maintain as much social cohesion as possible, on the other hand, in order to keep social integration.

Simulations with this formal system which we named TRISOC, three-dimensional society, usually start with a simple society that has no specialised roles and whose only form of differentiation is the segmentary one. The cohesion factor in such a society was assumed to be rather high, i.e., the members of one segment, family or clan, are placed close together on the grid of the CA. As our system is stochastic in several ways, that is, both the CA and the GA operate with stochastic rules, of course a lot of simulation runs had to be done in order to get significant results. The two most important ones are these:

a) Only with very rare combinations of parameter values, in particular the contribution values of the single roles for the system's values and the cohesion factor, can it be achieved that TRISOC transits the stage of purely segmentary differentiation at all. In most cases of parameter combinations TRISOC remains at the primordial level, which behaviour is apparently the most probable. Only if the beginning of the next differentiation level brings an *immediate* advantage for the whole system, is the new level of differentiation continued, i.e., the emergence of new social roles goes on. In any other case TRISOC either lingers with a rudimentary accomplishment of stratificatory differentiation, or even regresses to purely segmentary differentiation.

This indicates something that has frequently been described by theorists of social evolution (e.g. Habermas 1976): the transition from segmentary into stratificatory differentiated societies has very seldom happened in full degree. We know numerous segmentarily differentiated societies that became stuck on a level between purely segmentary differentiation and fully accomplished stratificatory differentiation as it were; most of the known societies did not even get that far. In comparison, the genesis of stratificatorily differentiated societies is a phenomenon that did not happen more than ten to fifteen times among hundreds, or even thousands of societies. Our experiments with TRISOC can offer some primary possibilities for a mathematical explanation here: the process depends on so many different variable parameters that the realisation of stratificatory societies seems to be mathematically rather improbable. It requires at once extremely severe environmental problems, as well as the above-mentioned favourable parameter combinations, to cause the generation of advanced social structures. As such systems can of course be understood only as stochastic systems, the coincidental occurrence of both conditions is obviously very improbable.

I mentioned before that often theorists of sociocultural evolution take for granted the evolutionary processes they analyse and hold them as nearly inevitable (e.g. Sanderson 1995; Turner 1997). It may be that some structural aspects of sociocultural evolution are indeed inevitable, *if and when evolution happens at all* (see below Chapter 5.3.). The unfolding of a third social dimension, for example, which is the mathematical expression for the emergence of functional differentiation is certainly a structural property of sociocultural evolution that also seems necessary to me. I shall come back to these problems in the next chapter. But there is no obvious inevitability for the occurrence of evolutionary processes as such as this seems to be a rather improbable event and in particular the beginning of evolutionary processes can also be stopped and even taken back. Both historical knowledge and our mathematical experiments with TRISOC demonstrate that a simple conception of inevitability is an illusion. The example of feudal Japan dealt with in 2.4. was used by Sanderson to prove the inevitability of modern capitalism. As our experiments with TRISOC showed that the unfolding of a third social dimension is even more improbable than that of a second, and that stagnations or even regressions are the rule here I see no reason why societies on the brink of modernisation, like apparently Japan, could not also have this probable fate of stagnation or regression. To be sure, nobody knows what would have happened without the interference of Americans and Europeans in Japan; but there are no reasons to assume that Japan would have *necessarily* gone the same way as Europe just because of some similarities in their development. The mathematics of probability used in our experiments with TRISOC tells us another story, in fact rather the opposite. I shall come back to this question in Chapters four and five.

TRISOC is able only to evolve if there are *immediate* advantages, as previously mentioned. To be more exact, TRISOC anticipates its future by testing different possibilities and then choosing the best one. As TRISOC can test its possible futures only for a few steps, the advantages of unfolding new social dimensions must be seen in the short run. This is certainly realistic as no social system acts according to its chances in the long run; in particular real systems are simply not able to foresee the consequences of their actions for a longer time.[33] To test the impact of the ability to anticipate its own future we repeated some experiments with TRISOC by giving it more anticipatory steps. The results demonstrate that the evolution of TRISOC is not very dependent on the number of anticipatory steps. The different factors that have to be taken into account are too many, so that a complex system does not benefit much from long runs of the anticipation of possible futures.

b) Our results with TRISOC show quite clearly that it is obviously too much for it to accomplish the different levels of differentiation, and at the same time keep up its social integration on all three levels. The levels usually split up, especially those of the segments, as soon as the next differentiation level is introduced. In fact, TRISOC always has the problem mentioned earlier: either the cohesion factor is set to a relatively high degree; then the system is mainly orientated to social integration. In that case, the evolution of the different levels of differentiation can almost certainly never occur, because TRISOC can see no immediate advantage in that – see above. Or, on the other hand, the cohesion factor is reduced so that a systems evolution takes place. Then TRISOC is forced to sacrifice social integration on the lower levels in favour of the higher system's performances. Apparently, it is impossible to achieve both, optimally efficient rules and socially dense integration, at the same time.

To illustrate these rather abstract remarks a bit, two different developments of TRISOC are shown in the pictures below. The lowest level of the three represents the state of social integration at the segmentary level, i.e., integration in respect to families, clans and/or other social segments. The next level represents the integration state at the stratificatory level, i.e., social strata or classes. The third level represents the same for the functional level, that is, for the social integration of (the same) active roles and of active ones with client roles. The first picture shows a development of TRISOC without the unfolding

---

[33] In a famous book on Artificial Intelligence, Dreyfuss and Dreyfuss (1986) mention the fact that even Grand Masters of chess are usually not able to plan their strategies for more than four or five moves.

of the third dimension and only a rudimentary unfolding of the second. One can observe that social integration is rather strong on both levels; the strength of social integration is measured, and represented graphically, with the concept of topological nearness, as I mentioned above. Strong social integration is represented therefore by a highly connected level. The third level is just a uniform plane, which means that there is no unfolding of this dimension at all. [34]

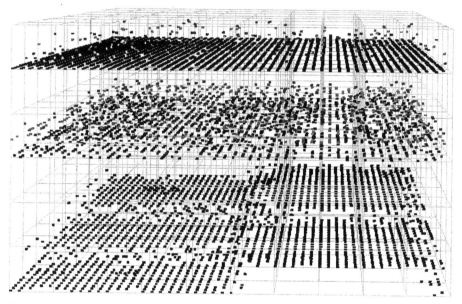

Picture a: A case of weak evolution.

The next picture shows a successful evolution, i.e., the unfolding of all three social dimensions. It can be seen quite clearly that the system paid for its evolution by obtaining only low degrees of social integration. The levels are rather disconnected and there is an obvious trend to an isolation of the single actors.

---

[34] Unfortunately these pictures do not allow a coloured vision that the original version of TRISOC contains. Therefore only the topological relations can be seen but not the different clans, classes and functionally clustered roles, which are represented by different colours. Readers interested in the original pictures which show much more details may contact the author. Soon TRISOC can be observed on the Internet.

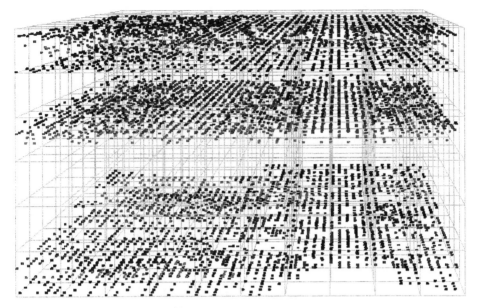

Picture b: A case of strong evolution.

The parallels of these results to the frequently noted problems of integration and splitting up, especially in modern societies, but not only there[35], are so evident that I do not need to comment on them in more detail. Our experiments teach us that three-dimensional differentiations almost necessarily lead to situations where traditional values and familiar contexts fray and are in danger of declining. It is certainly no exaggeration to point here to the famous passage from the *Kommunistisches Manifest* (Manifesto of the Communist Party), where Marx and Engels expressed just this, with an amazing far-sightedness, at the very beginning of the process of "globalisation", as one would call it today:

"Die Bourgeoisie, wo sie zur Herrschaft gekommen ist, hat alle feudalen, patriarchalischen, idyllischen Verhältnisse zerstört. Sie hat die buntscheckigen Feudalbande, die den Menschen an seinen natürlichen Vorgesetzten knüpften, unbarmherzig zerissen ... Sie hat die heiligen Schauer der frommen Schwärmerei, der ritterlichen Begeisterung ... in dem eiskalten Wasser egoistischer Berechnung ertränkt. ... Alles Ständische und Stehende verdampft,

---

[35] In his *Politeia* Platon already deplored the loss of traditional social ties for ancient Greece.

alles Heilige wird entweiht, und die Menschen sind endlich gezwungen, ihre Lebenstellung, ihre gegenseitigen Beziehungen mit nüchternen Augen zu betrachten" (MEW 4, 464).[36]

If we abstract from the specific terminology, this quotation seems to be (for me) like a comment on TRISOC; in particular, such programs can tell us to face such processes neither with resignation nor with a critique of culture, but "with sober senses" (*mit nüchternen Augen*).

At the end of these considerations on social dimensionality, the question of whether this process can (and will) go on in the same way, that is to say, if a fourth dimension will ensue, almost inevitably springs to mind. I shall not even speculate on this question here (see below Chapter 5), since it is very difficult to imagine what such a fourth dimension would be like. The only thing that is certain is that further levels of differentiation would even increase the noted problem of social integration. It remains to be seen whether modern societies will be willing to pay this price and in addition, if societies on the brink of modernisation are willing to pay the price that modern societies have already paid for their development. Mathematical analysis and experiments like those with TRISOC can at least tell us that prices like these are indeed inevitable and not only, as Marx and Engels believed, a problem of modern capitalism. The increasing of social complexity, as the unfolding of additional social dimensions, is something that is no free lunch. This is something no socialism or other "third ways" between capitalism or "real" socialism can avoid.

Programs like TRISOC are already very sophisticated and because of the rather large number of different variables it is often not easy to decide what factors were responsible for particular developments of the whole system. The results we (Jörn Schmidt and I) obtained with TRISOC are, we hope, worth the effort of constructing this model, as it is obviously possible to understand some important features of social evolution by it. Yet despite the complexity of this mathematical model of social

---

[36] The bourgeoisie, where it has got the upper hand, has put an end to all feudal, patriarchal, idyllic relations. It has pitilessly torn asunder the motley feudal ties that bound man to his "natural superiors" ... It has drowned out the most heavenly ecstasies of religious fervor, of chivalrous enthusiasm ... in the icy water of egotistical calculation. All that is solid melts into the air, all that is holy is profound and man is at last compelled to face with sober senses his real condition of life and his relations with his kind (my translation, J.K.)

evolution, it still has two fundamental deficits that make it necessary to go deeper for the task of modelling sociocultural evolution in a mathematical way.

On the one hand TRISOC is a mixture of "bottom-up" procedure and "top-down" theory. By this I mean that the *methodological* approach undertaken with TRISOC is bottom-up in the sense that the units of the model are the representations of the "units" of the social systems modelled with TRISOC. The behaviour of TRISOC is the result of "local interactions" between the artificial actors on the grid of the CA and the modifications of the rules of local interactions. However, the theoretical assumption behind the model is a macro-approach in the sense that the evolution of the system is dependent on the success or failure of just *the whole system* (and not the single actors). The value of the system's states is computed for the whole system, though it results from the number and efficiency of the different roles; the cohesion factor is defined for the whole system too, which means that social integration is again understood as a value for the system. In more technical words, the decisive parameters that determined the trajectories of TRISOC were introduced as *global* parameters. By doing this we followed a good and venerable tradition, namely that of social systems theory. However, an evolutionary algorithm in the sense that evolutionary biology got it with the modern synthesis has to be founded on a theoretical micro level, i.e., it must be based on the theoretical reconstruction and explanation of local interactions. These were either taken for granted in TRISOC or modified according to the needs of the system. Though such an approach is quite valuable, as could be seen from the results obtained with TRISOC, it is not quite sufficient.

On the other hand TRISOC models only *social* evolution and leaves out the problem of culture or takes it for granted. At the former stages of our research project of developing new foundations for a mathematical sociology, this reduction of labour was necessary in order not to tackle all problems at the same time and so get lost in the complexity of social dynamics. As I have emphasised several times in this book, the importance of taking into regard both sides of sociocultural evolution, it is time to fill in this gap. This will be done in Chapter four with the development of a "sociocultural algorithm" (SCA), which is able to complete the approach taken with TRISOC. Before I demonstrate this model it is necessary to come back again to the problem of self-organisation which was mentioned in connection with Kauffman and the limits of the modern synthesis (1.2.).

3.2 MATHEMATICAL PROPERTIES OF RULE SETS AND THE THEOREM OF INEQUALITY

The key concept for analysing social dynamics and evolution is, as I have emphasised several times, that of social rules. Specific kinds of rules characterise a certain society with its dynamics (leaving out culture again) and specific kinds of rule changing characterise particular evolutionary processes. Therefore one of the main tasks for a mathematical analysis of social dynamics and evolution is the search for mathematical properties of rule sets and, if possible, for mathematical properties of rule changes too. Before I show that the question, whether there are such properties can be answered in the affirmative, an important distinction between two kinds of rules has to be made.

Social theorists often do not use the concept of rules but that of social structure (or institutions or organisations) without defining very clearly what is meant by that. To be sure, in the sense that Giddens (1984) defines institutions by the rule concept or Habermas (1981, II) defines society as the same, most sociologists will agree with these definitions. Yet it mostly remains a bit hazy what is to be understood exactly by a "rule"; sometimes I believe that the use of "rule" in sociological contexts has a lot to do with Wittgenstein's famous *Familienähnlichkeit* (family similarity), i.e., rather different phenomena, which resemble each other only in single aspects, are subsumed under the same concept.

It is not my task here to give exact definitions of the rule concept (cf. Klüver 2000) but to emphasise the fact that there are at least two kinds of rules of interaction in social systems. Both kinds are needed to generate social dynamics and together they determine that which is often rather informally called a "social structure".

The first kind of rules may be called *general rules,* i.e., they are valid for the whole system if only in a stochastical manner and they determine part of the possibilities of social change (not evolution!). Such rules are well known in all theories of social permeability, in particular those of processes of socialisation. It is evident that, e.g., the feudal estate societies of the European Middle Ages had rather low social permeability, as it was very difficult to rise from one estate to another, in particular to a higher one. The caste societies of ancient India are an even plainer example of societies with general rules that fix conditions of social permeability for all members. On the other hand, modern societies, that is societies of the Western kind, claim to give free access to all social positions and roles for all members, though the taking over of many positions presupposes long and difficult learning processes. It is enough here to assume that Western societies have higher degrees of social permeability than many premodern ones.

The second kind of rules may be called *geometrical rules* and they represent the kind that is usually meant by social scientists when they speak of social structure. These rules determine the *possibilities of interaction;* the general rules determine what kind of interactions have to occur, if interactions are possible at all. The geometrical rules decide if two actors may interact, e.g., a serf and a king or a workman and a chairman, and if so how it is to be done. If a serf and a king interacted at all (which was possible under very restricted conditions), then of course the interaction was not "symmetrical", that is the king dominated the course of interaction, whether it would start at all, the subjects of the interaction and, of course, when and how to end the interaction. A symmetrical interaction on the other hand is up to both (or more) participants regarding its length and subjects. Geometrical rules determine these features of possible interactions and define in that way a social geometry in the topological sense discussed in 3.1. In a role theoretical sense, the geometry of a system, i.e., its topology and metric, describes the rules of role interactions. It is no accident that the use of mathematical tools like adjacency matrices for formally describing those rules is well known in social structural network analysis (cf. Freeman 1989).

There are perhaps even more kinds of social rules but certainly these two kinds are among the most important. It is a gratifying result from studies in complex systems done during the last decade that these two types of rules can indeed be classified mathematically in regard to the consequences that rule sets of these kinds have for the dynamics of systems. These results were obtained by analysing cellular automata (CAs) and Boolean nets (BNs), i.e., the universal Turing machines mentioned above. As there are often misunderstandings in respect of the universal importance of these investigations (cf. Depew and Weber loc.cit.) I would like to emphasise again the fact that universal Turing machines are models for any systems; therefore results obtained from these formal systems are valid for each system regardless of its *particular* characteristics. The mathematical properties of the rule sets of these universal Turing machines can at least be partially described by a suitable set of parameters, the so-called ordering, or control, parameters.

The first ordering parameters were discovered by analysing general rules of CAs and BNs. Perhaps the most important one is the P-parameter by Weissbuch and Derrida (Kaufmann 1992 and 1995) with regard to BNs and the equivalent λ-parameter of CA-rules (Langton 1992). Both parameters simply measure the ratio of frequency by which the different states of the units of the formal systems are reached when applying the particular rules. Consider for example a binary BN with three units a, b and c and only values 0 and 1 for their states. Let us assume that the rules f and g are the following:

$$f(1,1) = 1; \ f(1,0) = 1; \ f(0,1) = 1; \ f(0,0) = 0$$

$$g(1,1) = 1; \ h(1,0) = 0; \ g(0,1) = 1; \ g(0,0) = 1.$$

Readers acquainted with propositional calculus will see immediately that f is the logical disjunction and g the logical implication. Now let us assume that the BN is structured in this way:

$$f(a,b) = c; \ g(a,c) = b; \ f(b,c) = a.$$

Then we get the following dynamics of the BN dependent on the different initial states:

$$
\begin{array}{cc}
 & a\,b\,c \\
t & 1\ 1\ 1 \\
t+1 & 1\ 1\ 1
\end{array}
$$

This means that the state (1,1,1) of our BN is a point attractor because it will not change any more. When we consider another initial state (0,0,0) we get:

```
          a b c
    t     0 0 0
    t+1   0 1 0
    t+2   1 1 1
```

and as $(1,1,1)$ is a point attractor, as we saw from the first initial state our system reaches a point attractor again. It is easy to see, and left to interested readers, that our little system will always reach point attractors regardless of the specific initial states. Therefore we have a system with an extremely simple dynamics, or in other words, we have a system whose rules always generate simple kinds of order.

This behaviour of our system can be explained by means of the value of the P-parameter. By looking at the rules one sees that the state of 1 (of the units, not of the system) will be reached in three of four possible cases. As the P-parameter measures the ratio of reaching the different unit states we get $P = {}^3/_4$ or $P = 0.75$ for the rules of our system. If we had taken other rules, e.g. the logical equivalence and the XOR-function (exclusive or) we would have obtained $P = 0.5$ because these logical rules reach 0 and 1 with the same frequency. It can be shown that systems whose rule sets have P-values $0.65 \leq P \leq 1$ all generate simple dynamics; the nearer P is to 1 the simpler the dynamics will be. On the other hand, if P is equal or near to 0.5, uniform distribution of the values, the more complex the dynamics will be, i.e., the longer the periods of the attractors will become. In this sense P is an "ordering" parameter: its values decide whether the system will generate simple dynamics and even static order (point attractors), or complex dynamics which means that the system will get literally no rest and no static order.

Kauffman discovered another ordering parameter, which is defined as the ratio of so called canalizing function to non canalizing ones; it is not necessary to describe this parameter in detail (cf. Kauffman loc. cit.). Because these parameters are defined for general rules only, Jörn Schmidt and I also investigated the possibility of ordering parameters for geometrical rules (Klüver and Schmidt 1999 b; Klüver 2000). The most important parameter we found is the v-parameter (v for the German word *Verknüpfung* = connection). v measures the deviation from the mean value of influencing possibilities, i.e., it is a measure of the number of outputs the different units have in regard to other units, and by this, determining (influencing) the values of the other units. In our little example above all units influence uniformly all others and so v = 0 for this system. In a system of three units, where only one unit influences the others v = 1, because the deviation from the mean value has reached a maximum. We defined $0 \leq v \leq 1$. The exact definition of v makes use of the so called adjacency matrix by which geometrical rules of BNs can be represented. For readers acquainted with these techniques I give the exact definition of the v-parameter without explaining it in detail:

$$v = (\text{OD} \; \text{OD}_{min})/(\text{OD}_{max} \; \text{OD}_{min})$$

OD is the factual outdegree vector of our system, i.e. the number of outputs of all units represented as a vector, OD_{min} and 0D_{max} are the outdegree vectors, which represent the possible most homogeneous distribution of outputs and the most inhomogeneous distribution, respectively. The ordering properties of v are such that $v \geq 0.2$ (approximately) yields only simple dynamics and $0 \leq v \leq 0.2$ generates more complex dynamics. In other words, the often only informally described "structure" of a system determines the dynamics of the system as well as the properties of the general rules; obviously "structure" and "dynamics", which are often discussed as two different aspects of systems, actually belong together very closely, an interesting result *per se*.[37]

When we look at all ordering parameters together we get some interesting results, which are also of importance to the analysis of social complexity:

a) It can be easily demonstrated that all important ordering parameters measure some degree of *inequality* of the system.[38] That is quite apparent with the P-parameter, which measures the inequality in respect of the

---

[37] Recently Cohen et al. (2000) demonstrated that the geometry of a social network, defined in the sense above, also influences the dynamics of game theoretical dilemmata.

[38] Kauffman postulates an ordering parameter that is not a measure of inequality, namely K = the (average) number of *inputs* to the units. K is not a ratio but an absolute value; Kauffman asserts that $0 \leq K \leq 2$ generates simple dynamics and K > 2 complex ones. We do not doubt the experimental results of Kauffman but have our doubts as to whether these are due to the size of K because they can be explained in another way. Therefore we do not believe, for theoretical reasons and our own experiments with Cas, that K is an ordering parameter at all. However, these are questions for specialists and not important here.

possibility of reaching particular states of a unit (the permeability of the system). It is also very obvious for the v-parameter as it measures by definition the inequality of influencing possibilities. v can be understood as the difference between formal equality of a system's elements and the factual possibilities of determining the behaviour of the system by one's own actions. If v = 1 or near 1 then we have a situation where only a small minority of systems "members" can influence the system, i.e. all other members, and *vice versa*. Because the other known ordering parameters also measure other degrees of inequality (Klüver and Schmidt loc.cit.) it is rather safe to postulate a *theorem of inequality:*

The more unequal a system is in its important aspects, measured in values of the according ordering parameters, the more simple its dynamics, i.e. the more easily it will generate static order, and *vice versa*.

I shall come back to the *evolutionary* importance of this theorem below, because the ordering parameters, and the theorem of inequality, refer only to systems dynamics and not to evolution.

b) Experiments done by Jörn Schmidt and I, with combinations of different parameters, demonstrated that it is sufficient for the generation of simple dynamics that *one* parameter has values in the region for simple dynamics. Even if the other parameters have values sufficient for the generation of complex dynamics, then the system will remain nonetheless in a simple order. Furthermore, for all ordering parameters it holds that the value regions for the generation of simple dynamics are much greater than the regions for complex dynamics. Therefore it is sufficient for a system to have aspects of inequality in only one respect and only comparatively little degrees of inequality too; that will be enough to assure simple dynamics. Thus we get another consequence, i.e., the *probability of order:*

For any given system the probability of simple dynamics and therefore of (nearly) static order is much greater than the probability of complex dynamics, that is of permanent change and unrest.

c) A politically interesting consequence from the theorem of inequality is something we call the *paradox of democratic reforms*. If it is true that inequality generates order and equality tends to generate complex dynamics, i.e. permanent change, then in particular democratic reforms, which have the goal to increase the degrees of equality in a social system, tend to increase the complexity of the system's dynamics, i.e. to raise the degree of unrest. As the trajectories of the reformed system generate attractors with longer periods as a consequence of the reforms, the system will reach more different states than before the reforms. Unfortunately probability theory says that there are always more unfavourable states for a system than favourable ones; therefore the consequence of democratic reforms may be that the system will reach unfavourable states with a higher probability than before. The system then will have to be reformed again, but if by these reforms the degrees of equality are raised again, unfavourable states will be reached with even higher probability and so on. That is why we call this effect a paradox, though of course it is no paradox in a logical sense.

To be sure, if the system is reformed democratically in only one respect, the probability of order will still hold. However, reforms concerning all aspects of inequality will necessarily have the results described by the paradox. It is not my intention to argue against democratic reforms, on the contrary. Yet one must know what one does if reforms are undertaken and if perhaps additional rules must by necessity be implemented into the system to compensate the paradoxical effects of rising equality. The institution of parliaments, e.g., may be just such additional rules, as the members of parliament certainly have more influence than the normal citizens, though all of them are equal before the law and in other respects. In a democracy ruled by parliamentary institutions it certainly holds that $v > 0$.

The importance of the insights into the logic of systems dynamics for evolutionary theories is now simply this: each system has the task to reach states that are favourable according to environmental demands. If the rules of interaction that generate the system's dynamics are not able to generate favourable states, then adaptive systems can and will change these rules. Changing rules is always a complex process and the system has to pay for its enlarged values with certain costs. In the case of social systems this means social unrest, disorder and growing uncertainties about the future for all the system's members. Therefore, as can be learned from the history of revolutions and social reforms, each system has to stop the changing of rules after a time and come back to phases with constant rules, i.e., effective decision structures and planning certainty. The theorem of inequality guarantees that social structures in these phases of conservative recoveries from the strains of rule changing will generate social stability by the probability of order; in particular, insofar as social structures, of course, are also decision structures, the theorem of inequality gives a sufficient probability that new decision structures are as efficient as the system needs.

The last consideration follows from a well known distinction between communication and action that was explicitly stated by Luhmann (1984): Luhmann defined action as the "closure of communication" and meant roughly the fact that all communications that require some decisions on how to act must be closed as a result in order to be able to act practically. Communicating processes in decision structures, where all participants have the same possibilities of influencing the others, have no "natural end" but are in principle circling endlessly and never come to any practical results.[39] In other words, they reach only attractors with rather long periods. Decision structures with high v-values avoid this and guarantee practical results. Whether the members of the particular society like the results is of course quite another question.

Because the evolutionary phases of a system are costly, each system must look to keep these phases as short and efficient as possible. As in a logical sense the rule changing takes place by applying *meta rules,* i.e. rules that operate *on* the rules of interaction in order to fulfil environmental demands, the question arises whether there are also mathematical properties of such meta rules. To be sure, meta rules are not rules of interaction but *rules that change rules of interaction.* In other words: are there certain parameters for meta rules which determine the efficiency of rule changing processes? The answer is positive: there are indeed such parameters, which we (our research group at Essen) call *meta parameters* (because they refer to meta rules, of course). As in the case of the ordering parameters there are several meta parameters that we rather thoroughly investigated (cf. Klüver 2000). I shall deal here with just one of them because it is sufficient to demonstrate the importance of this second kind of parameters.

Consider a system that is characterised by a rule set with n different rules. The changing of these rules can be done in quite different ways, of course, but one important question in this case is simply how many rules the system will (and can) change at a particular time. It is obvious that,

---

[39] This is a well known fact from political or academic committees.

e.g., social systems are practically never willing to change all or most of their rules at the same time, as a lot of rules are important for maintaining the identity of the system, religious traditions, certain forms of authority, historically founded rules of conserving national identities like *La grande nation* or *Das Vaterland* and so forth. Sometimes I call this the principle of the sacred cows, for obvious reasons. This insight gives us one meta parameter r (for radicality of rule changing), which is defined simply as

$$r = m/n,$$

n being the number of all rules of interaction and m the number of rules open to change during the time of reform (or revolution).

When we (our Essen research group) did experiments with r (I skip the experimental and mathematical details) we had of course to define the term of adaptive success, as the influence of r-variations on the adaptive processes were to be measured. Adaptive success, that is, reaching systems states that are sufficiently favourable according to environmental demands, can have two meanings: on the one hand it means that the system's states are sufficiently near to some environmental goal; on the other hand it may mean that the system reaches states that are perhaps not optimal but *practically* sufficient in such a time it needs for maintaining its existence. Reaching optimal states cannot be a goal *per se* for a system if this goal can be reached only in the long run, for "in the long run we are all dead", as Keynes once remarked. Therefore the time needed for a successful adaptive process is at least as important as the degree of the system's value (for more thorough considerations in this respect see Klüver 2000).

For our experiments with r we therefore defined a constant threshold value for the system's adaptive performances and concentrated on the time the system needed to reach this threshold with different r-values. Our results are quite interesting:

Contrary to intuitive expectations the adaptive successes of our formal systems were not the better the larger r. Though our results were sometimes not quite unambiguous, a significant trend showed that the adaptive success of our systems was best in the region of $0.5 \leq r \leq 0.6$. In other words, a system that changes too many rules at one time is often not as good in an adaptive sense as systems that change only a certain part of their rules. On the other hand, systems that changed too few rules often never reached any sufficient value at all. Therefore an old wisdom may also be valid here: as much as necessary, as little as possible (see also Carley 1997 for similar results with quite different techniques).

By considering these results an explanation for them was rather obvious: if systems have a lot of different rules then the changing possibility of many rules gives the system numerous, and sometimes too many, possibilities of what and how to change. Systems that change too many rules at a time simply get lost in the vast space of possibilities. Systems which change too few rules, on the other hand may miss just those changing effects, which would have brought them to the desired goal. Therefore an adaptive system has to navigate on the sea of mathematical possibilities: finding a course between too much and too little.

We confirmed these explanations by repeating our experiments with "small" systems, that is systems with comparatively few rules (about 10). Indeed, these systems behaved in quite another way, as their adaptive success depended directly on the number of rules open to change. $r = 1$ usually obtained the best results and $0 \leq r \leq 0.6$ usually obtained no sufficient adaptive results at all. Therefore small systems in this sense indeed fare best if they are open to radical change. Social systems on the other hand are usually "large", as they have a lot of rules, which may be changed or not. For these systems the results mentioned above may be comforting: the "permanent revolution" of all social rules that Mao and his followers propagated, is from a mathematical point of view suboptimal and often even harmful for the adaptive successes of systems.

There is a lot more to be said about the complexities of adaptive processes measured by the different meta parameters, but I shall be content in this study with the final question as to if there is a general principle behind the different meta parameters as obviously is behind the different ordering parameters. According to our experiments there is indeed one, which I can just mention here: as the adaptive success of a system depends not just on different r-values but also on other meta parameters: it seems that in general an adaptive system fares best *if it keeps the different meta parameters variable; in particular the system should adjust the values of the meta parameters to the stage of its adaptive development* ("Stage of adaptive development" means here the degree to which an adaptive system is able to fulfil the environmental demands). It is a "dialectical" aspect that the stage of adaptive development of an adaptive system depends conversely on the values of the meta parameters it has had in its past.

This general principle, which means that a system should be adaptive not only on the level of rule changing but on the meta level of the mathematical properties of these changing processes themselves, can be briefly illustrated with the example of the r-parameter. Small systems, as I mentioned, fare best if they change as many rules as possible at once. If and when these systems evolve and during their evolution become larger, i.e., they get more rules, then the systems should lower their r-values. After having reached r-values in the region of about 50 % then the systems should stop their variations of the r-values and look for other meta parameters in order to maximise their adaptive successes, if the variations of r are not enough. Accordingly other meta parameters should be handled by *real* adaptive systems, although real systems, e.g., social or cognitive ones, are often not able to do so because constraints caused by tradition and other inhibiting factors operate as thresholds of their variability.

Logically this principle must be understood as a third order rule, i.e., a meta-meta rule. By introducing it one could ask if there are fourth order rules and so on; the logical paradox of *regressus ad infinitum* seems to appear. Fortunately that is not the case. Whether or not an adaptive system invokes this principle, if it is able to do so at all, depends on the adaptive success the system has reached, and that means on its particular states at a certain time. The same is true for a possible application of meta rules. Therefore adaptive systems do not need to fear the danger of infinite regresses but have "only" to take into account the relations between their rules of different order and the adaptive success that they have reached so far. We shall see in Chapter four that different logical orders like meta levels mean in reality, and in the physical reality of computer programs too, different loops the *complete* rule ensemble of the system must contain. Yet there is always only a finite number of loops in reality; these considerations indicate that even complex systems like sociocultural or cognitive ones do not need too many. By the way, perhaps it will be a fruitful possibility to measure complexity in general, which at the present time seems a rather hopeless task: the degree of complexity of a system is equal to the number of different loops the rule ensemble of the system contains. However, that is at the moment rather speculative.

Ordering parameters and meta parameters obviously allow the measurement of rule sets and by this the determination of how and why systems generate specific dynamics and obtain certain adaptive successes; they make it especially possible to analyse why particular systems cannot get stable attractors and/or why they were adaptive "failures". The task I defined as one of the most important questions of mathematical theoretical sociology, i.e. the mathematical analysis of rule sets, is for a large part solved by it. One question though remains, that is most important for the analysis of sociocultural evolution, that is the defining of a measure for the probability of evolution at all. Ordering parameters tell us what will happen if a system refrains from changing in order to recover; meta parameters give insights into the adaptive success a system will probably have *if* it starts evolutionary changing processes. However, whether a system will start such changing at all and how far it will go in this direction cannot be measured by these two kinds of parameter; therefore another type is certainly necessary in order to give criteria for the beginning of evolutionary processes, and in particular for the probable radicality of the system's evolution, measured in values of the meta parameters.

The principle of heterogeneity, combined with a "sociocultural algorithm", indeed gives us such a third kind of parameters; we may call it an "evolutionary parameter". This will be the subject of the next chapter. Before I introduce these other mathematical considerations I shall give a few additional reflections on the logical form of evolutionary theories.

3.3 SOME METATHEORETICAL CONSIDERATIONS ABOUT EVOLUTIONARY THEORIES

In 1.3. I hinted at the fact that the logical status of evolutionary theories is not always sufficiently clear. Even with the rise of the modern synthesis there still remained some doubt whether the frame of (Neo)Darwinism fits into the accepted view of what scientific theories should be (Depew and Weber loc. cit.; Dawkins 1986). As those views have orientated mainly on the concepts and logics of classical physics, the logical structure of Darwinism indeed seemed to be something else.

Even worse was (and sometimes still is) the problem with theories of sociocultural evolution. Either they relied upon the classical forms of sociological theory, which meant that they were defined in no logically precise way at all, or they declared themselves to be akin to the biological tradition of Darwinian theories and borrowed from it its unsolved logical problems, e.g. theories of cultural evolution (Cavalli-Sforza loc.cit.; Boyd and Richerson 1985). Indeed, if one identifies *scientific* theories with the postulating of universal laws like Newton's law of gravitation or Einstein's $E = mc^2$ and with the explanation of a particular event B by the classical schema " the cause A determines the occurrence of the effect B because of the validity of the universal law C", then it is difficult to see how evolutionary theories like Darwinism can be accepted as real scientific theories at all. Even the rise of stochastic theories, like thermodynamics and quantum mechanics in physics did not change this situation much, as the causal explanations "if A then B" are valid there also, though only with some probability.

In order to overcome the logical difficulties connected with evolutionary theories, Bateson (1972, 399) introduced the concept of "cybernetic explanation", which he thought to be another type of scientific explanation than the traditional ones but nevertheless as valid as the classical causal form:

> "In contrast (to the well known causal explanation; J.K.) cybernetic explanation is always negative. We consider what alternative possibilities could conceivably have occurred and then ask why many alternatives were not followed, so that the particular event was one of those few which could, in fact, occur ... In cybernetic language, the course of events is said to be subject to restraints, and it is assumed that, apart from such restraints, the pathways of change would be governed only by the equality of probability. If we find a monkey striking a typewriter apparently at random but in fact writing meaningful prose, we shall look for restraints, either inside the monkey or inside the typewriter. Perhaps the monkey could not strike inappropriate letters; perhaps the type bars could not move improperly struck, perhaps incorrect letters could not survive on the paper. Somewhere there must have been a circuit which could identify errors and eliminate it."

Bateson obviously dissociates his concept of cybernetic explanation from the classical concepts mentioned above. There is no "positive" cause A which causes the effect B of the meaningful prose that the monkey writes and in particular there is no universal law about monkeys writing prose on a typewriter. Instead of that one has to look for "restraints", or constraints as most theorists would say today, which tell us why certain effects have *not* occurred. Without such constraints, Bateson seems to think, the system would behave at random, or it would follow the laws of equal probability respectively. The constraints do not cause anything in the classical sense but they force the system to take certain paths in the mathematical space of probabilities.[40]

Bateson gives no more examples about such constraints but, in the context of explaining the logical structure of Darwinism, Dawkins (1986) also introduced a typewriting monkey (though without mentioning Bateson). The monkey of Dawkins has the task to write a quotation from *Hamlet* and as Bateson's monkey it can only strike the keys at random. Instead of constraints in the monkey or the typewriter Dawkins introduces a selection mechanism, which simply operates like this: when the monkey has written two sequences of letters (in the length of the quotation, to shorten up the process) the selection mechanism chooses the sequence, which is the more similar to the quotation. The monkey then produces another sequence which is compared with the result of the first choice and again the better one is taken. This procedure goes on until the quotation is generated; Dawkins showed that a computer program operating on this procedure could generate the right quotation in quite a short time.

Dawkins monkey obviously operated with an "external" constraint, i.e. a selective environment (and of course that was what Dawkins wanted to illustrate by this example). The logical structure, however, of the argument is just the same as in Bateson's cybernetic explanation: there are no positive causes A, which determine the evolution B of (biological) systems but there are only random processes of the system and selective constraints by the environment, which force the system into certain paths of all those that are mathematically equally probable.

---

[40] When I read this passage from Bateson I immediately remembered a famous quotation of Sherlock Holmes where he explained his methodical procedures (The Sign of the Four): if one eliminates the impossible then the remaining must be the truth, however improbable it is. The cybernetic search for constraints has exactly this function: it eliminates the impossible, i.e. that the monkey understands English and can write prose, and asks for constraints, which explain the remaining improbable events, that is the monkey writing prose.

In the last subchapter I demonstrated that things are not as easy as Dawkins and Bateson obviously thought because the processes (the dynamics) of complex systems are not simply to be understood as all being equally probable (see also above 1.2.). I shall come back to this problem below. Furthermore, Bateson's distinction between classical causal explanation and cybernetic explanation tends to suggest a wrong association: the processes inside the monkey certainly follow causal principles, or at least stochastic ones; the impression of random processes is just one of an observer who compares the monkey with a human author. A neurobiological theory of the monkey would certainly show that the monkey's behaviour "makes sense", though not in terms of literature. The same weakness of course is true for the monkey of Dawkins.

Yet despite this deficit of the two examples something important can be learned from them about the structure of evolutionary theories and the explanation of evolutionary processes: in many cases it is not sufficient to look for "positive" external causes A, which determine the evolutionary behaviour of particular systems, like geophysical or demographic factors. In particular it is mostly not very fruitful to postulate laws in the tradition of physics like "given environmental factors A_1, A_2, ... A_n then the evolutionary behaviour B will follow as a necessary consequence". Environmental factors of course are always important, not only for biological but also for sociocultural evolutionary processes (cf. Sanderson 1995) but they operate in the form of stimuli and constraints, that is they force the system to start its own evolutionary dynamics and then to choose particular paths and to neglect or abandon others. In other words, the logical structure of evolutionary theories has to consist of a) theories about the self-organising processes within the systems, internal constraints, and b) the external stimulating and constraining effects that environmental conditions have in addition.

I would like to illustrate these rather abstract remarks with the theorem of inequality and the importance of meta parameters mentioned in the last subchapter. The theorem of inequality holds that processes inside a complex adaptive system are not simply processes that are all equally probable but the possibilities of their trajectories are constrained by the values of the ordering parameters, and that means by the degrees of inequality characteristic for the system. To be sure, the processes often are causally determined and as such are dependent on their specific initial states; but whether these initial states lead to complex or simple trajectories is up to the ordering parameters and therefore to a high probability of "order", i.e., simple dynamics as described above. In Bateson's terminology we can say that the mathematics of self-organisation, expressed in the theorem of inequality, is something like an "internal" constraint for the system, as it rules out most of the (mathematical) possibilities and leaves only some (just in the methodical way of Sherlock Holmes). Therefore in most cases it is a useful way of analysing the behaviour of a system by looking for these mathematical internal constraints; having found them the next question has to be about the effects of environmental factors which operate as external constraints. The technological tools that, e.g., a society has developed are certainly due to its environment as, for example the Arctic Inuits had to invent the *kayak* in order to sail on a cold sea. The arctic environment forced the culture of the Inuits to take just one particular path of technological innovation and to exclude all others, e.g., the invention of the wheel. The social structure of a society on the other hand is most certainly due to internal constraints, that is, the generation of certain rules by social innovation and their fixation by tradition in order to solve, for example, decision problems.

The program TRISOC discussed in 3.1. is by itself an example of a formal evolutionary theory of this kind. The internal constraints are represented by the cohesion factor and the unfolding of dimensions, i.e., mathematical aspects of internal self-organisation. We could see how these factors forced the system to take particular paths, that is, only specific ways of development were left open for the system. The artificial environment acted as additional external constraints in the way that the degree of environmental pressure decided whether the system would evolve or not, and if it evolved, how much. Mathematically speaking the evolutionary possibilities of TRISOC depended on the proportion of the internal constraining cohesion factor and the external constraining environmental factor. This does not mean that all real systems evolve literally in the manner of TRISOC; it is after all just a *general* model of sociocultural evolution, which leaves out many important aspects (see above 3.1.). Yet this much can be learned from the examples of Bateson and Dawkins on the one hand and formal models like TRISOC on the other, taking them both together: instead of looking for classical causes and effects it is usually more worthwhile to analyse the internal and external constraints an evolutionary system exhibits and to try to explain the observed evolutionary behaviour by them, in particular in regard to the consequences of the combination of the different constraints. Yet it is important to keep in mind that constraints are logically not the same as causes, though evolutionary theories built on the importance of constraints can and must be as scientifically precise as those operating with the traditional cause-effect schema. TRISOC proves that such theories are possible. The classical cause-effect schema has its place mainly by analysing the *internal processes* of adaptive systems which are determined in the traditional way by the initial states; the *adaptive dynamics* as the whole picture of the system's development has to be understood in the way of analysing internal and external constraints and the role they play for the evolution of the system.

The same argument holds with regard to the meta parameters, that is to the degree of *variability* of a system. It should be not a very surprising insight that the adaptive behaviour of a system depends also on the degree to which the system is able and willing to change its structure, i.e., its rules. The values of the meta parameters of a system are certainly an effect of the history of the system which means the manner by which certain rules have been fixed and closed to variation. These are internal constraints too. The monkeys of Bateson and Dawkins obviously had no variability at all. Therefore they were utterly dependent on constraints in the typewriter or the external constraints of a selective environment. However, monkeys can learn to change their rules of behaviour though certainly not to write prose or Hamlet. If they were given tasks not totally outside their range of competence, for example using sticks in order to get bananas from the ceiling of a room, the behaviour of these monkeys can and must be explained by the degrees of variability that the monkeys exhibit as internal constraints.

Another kind of internal constraint was introduced by the hypothesis of heterogeneity. We shall see in the next chapter that the degree of heterogeneity regulates the evolution of a sociocultural system in the same way as the internal constraints just mentioned do for dynamics and meta dynamics. These considerations reinforce the methodological necessity to analyse systemic self-organisation as internal constraints.

To avoid any misunderstandings it is important to make one additional remark. Although I stressed the point that evolutionary theories should not be constructed according to the schema known from physics and chemistry, the systems these scientific disciplines deal with are usually no evolutionary systems at all, the explanations done by cause-effects schemas and those that operate with constraints do not exclude each other mutually, in a logical or factual way. The supposition that rules of interaction inside a system are deterministic ones is, after all, equivalent to the supposition that the interactions are governed by causal principles, i.e., they can be described by causal schemas (e.g. Markov chains). Therefore each complete theory of evolution that is structured principally by the interdependency of adaptive self-organisation on the one hand (internal constraints) and the effects of the environment on the other (external constraints), must also contain parts where classic causal principles are assumed. It is an empirical problem how important these are for the explanation of the whole system.[41]

Last but not least I would like to make some final remarks about the question of sociocultural evolution as an *intentional process* which is explainable only by looking for the goals of evolutionary change. To be sure, this cannot mean the revival of the old arguments about teleology; these should have been buried for good. Yet it also cannot be denied that human beings do act intentionally, that is they orientate their actions to goals, which are in the future. As social systems consist of human beings in their roles as social actors, in an abbreviated sense one can say that social systems act intentionally as well, i.e., they orientate their dynamics to the goals, which are obligatory for the majority of their members, or all of them. Yet classic causal explanations and related ones operating with constraints are not able to integrate the future as cause or constraints because these factors are only effective in the system's past; therefore the undeniable fact of intentionality seems to be an absolute limit for all precise theories of sociocultural evolution, and of all social processes, in fact.

---

[41] It is also possible to describe this theoretical situation the following way: one can *theoretically* assume that the whole process of adaptive development is causally structured, but it is *methodically* not possible to describe (and explain) the process by classic cause-effect schemas. Therefore it is necessary to introduce the concepts of internal and external constraints.

Fortunately things are not so bad. Let us come back to TRISOC once again in order to clarify this point. TRISOC, as I mentioned, is able to anticipate its future in the sense that it undertakes different simulation runs on the basis of some initial state and then decides which of these courses it should choose. In other words, TRISOC constructs several *possible* futures for itself and then the chosen path becomes the "real" future. The only goal TRISOC has is to do best under the circumstances, which are given to it. The possible futures are no mystery at all but simply *a part of the state of TRISOC at a certain time.* For an observer who knows nothing about the mathematical principles of TRISOC it may seem that TRISOC orientates itself to some future, but that of course is impossible for a program. TRISOC just makes its development dependent on the state in which it is at a certain time, and a part of this state is the generation of possible futures; therefore the next states are a (deterministic or stochastic) consequence of the present state and nothing else.

To be sure, as I conceded in 1.3., the fact that it is possible to construct mathematical models and computer programs like TRISOC is no proof by itself that intention in cognitive or social systems is just the same mechanism as that in TRISOC. Of course there are much more complicated processes of goal orientation than those modelled by TRISOC. However, the general argument remains valid that literally all modes of intentionality can be modelled this way and that therefore there is no need to assume that processes of intentional goal orientation are basically something other than the processes just sketched. The orientation at a goal is always a part of the system's state *at the present time* and the decision for some particular course of action is a consequence of this partial state and other parts. A theory of evolution that contains intentional goal orientation does not need to add structures other than those mentioned. Therefore, as evolutionary biology has become for a long time an accepted part of the sciences, so should it be with theories of sociocultural evolution.

A lot more could be said on a meta theoretical level about evolutionary theories. However, as always it is much more convincing to construct such theories and test them against historical knowledge than just to speculate about them. "Who can, does it, who can't, criticises" as G.B. Shaw once remarked. Therefore let us just do it.

4. A MATHEMATICAL MODEL OF SOCIOCULTURAL EVOLUTION

The mathematical models and principles discussed in Chapter 3 refer mainly to *social* evolution only, which I already conceded in connection with TRISOC. In addition they are basically macrotheoretical ones, as they analyse systems as a whole and take (artificial) actors just as variables with different states. Both deficits now have to be filled in order to sketch at least the principles of a theory of sociocultural evolution. The main model in this context is the sociocultural algorithm (SCA), which is the subject of the next subchapter and which I constructed together with Jörn Schmidt. However, speaking of sociocultural evolution also contains the problem of individual learning and that is cognitive ontogenesis. When Habermas (1976) speaks of the learning of social systems he is of course aware of the fact that this is only a metaphor. In a strict sense only individual actors learn and the learning processes of social systems are on the one hand the sum of individual learning processes, determined by individual *and* social factors, and on the other hand the impact of these learnings on the society as a whole. How this interdependency of individual and "systemic" learning is to be understood is the core of the SCA. However, to get a precise understanding of the logic of cognitive ontogenesis I shall (together with Christina Stoica) sketch a preliminary model of it and give some aspects of the dependency of individual learning on environmental factors, and vice versa. A complete understanding of the manner in which *social* actors learn, generate new ideas and construct new roles according to new ideas and in this way realise sociocultural evolution is possible only if one has at least some ideas about the logic of individual learning as well. In this general sense sociocultural evolution has to be understood as the learning process of the human species.

4.1 THE SOCIOCULTURAL ALGORITHM (SCA) (TOGETHER WITH JÖRN SCHMIDT)

4.1.1   The meaning of algorithms

In 2.3. culture was defined as an ensemble of problem solving algorithms and the logical meaning of the concepts of algorithms in general was sketched accordingly. As the mathematical model of sociocultural evolution that we explain in this subchapter is called an algorithm, it is useful to consider the theoretical meaning of using algorithms as mathematical models for dynamical processes. Mathematical models, as has been mentioned at the beginning of Chapter three, are usually identified with sets of equations that describe the behaviour of dynamic systems. As those equations usually are t-invariant (independent of the time direction), it is possible to explain the past behaviour of the system as well as to make some prognostications about its future behaviour; nevertheless, there are a lot of systems where this assumption cannot be made (see below 5.2).

Such equation models are usually seen as contrary to algorithms, which serve as procedures to solve problems. However, the use of computer programs has demonstrated that the seeming difference between mathematical laws, expressed in the form of equations, and algorithms, is a bit superficial. The simulations, e.g., of astronomical systems by computer programs use as their mathematical basis usually the well known equations of celestial mechanics, including those of general relativity theory. However, because the simulations shall capture the dynamics of these systems the equations have the function (as basis for the programs) to *generate* the transitions of the system from one previous state to the next. In this sense the equations are nothing more than the mathematical formulation of a "generator", which drives the system along its trajectory of different states. In the program therefore, the equations function as an algorithm for determining the succession of states and for realising them. When dynamics was defined as a rule governed succession of different states, and evolution as the additional changing of rule ensembles in order to cope with environmental demands, then algorithms are simply the mathematical expression for this unfolding of a system's dynamics and evolution.

We would like to illustrate this point with the example of evolutionary biology. It is a well known fact that important characteristics of biological evolution can be captured with differential equations which, e.g. Eigen demonstrated in his famous hyper cycle (Eigen and Schuster 1979), for the subject of prebiotic evolution. It is equally possible to use the mathematical tools of Game Theory as Maynard Smith (1982) showed. And of course one can very efficiently use Holland's genetic algorithm, which models *directly* the generating mechanisms of variation and selection in regard to the genome. In particular the last model captures the generative forces of evolution in a very clear manner, as it refers to the mechanisms themselves, which are known from evolutionary genetics. Therefore the use of an algorithm as a mathematical model is the most suitable way if one wants to capture the generative mechanisms that drive evolution. It is not by chance, by the way, that often Darwin's greatest achievement is said to have demonstrated that biological evolution must be understood as a complex algorithm (Dawkins 1986: Dennett 1995).

Because the theoretical model postulated in this book is founded on the assumption that there are basically only actors who think, believe and act on the basis of these belief systems and generate by these actions the dynamics and evolution of sociocultural systems, we take an algorithm as a mathematical model too. The units of this model are artificial actors who take roles, or sometimes not, who learn and invent new ideas, who create new social roles or abandon them again and who are generating in these manners an artificial sociocultural evolution. The model of course is rather simple compared to real sociocultural evolution. However, even with this simple model quite interesting insights into the principles of sociocultural evolution are possible.[42]

---

[42] In the last years models like these are often called "multi agent systems" (MAS) or the modelling of "intelligent agents". We leave it to the readers whether the term "agent", which makes sense in the natural sciences, is very appropriate in the social sciences. As sociology has long ago introduced the concept of actor, we prefer to speak of artificial actors instead of agents.

4.1.2   The model SCA

In the sense of the "generative" modelling of biological evolution by the genetic algorithm, though not with the same model, we intend to model sociocultural evolution in a similar generative aspect: we attempt to model sociocultural evolution as the result of actions and interactions of social actors as problem solvers. These actions generate a culture as well as a particular social structure, defined as a set of roles with certain relations. The social structure emerging from these actions in turn determines the individual actions, i.e. problem solvings. Thus, at least basically, our model, termed sociocultural algorithm SCA, comprises both sides of sociocultural evolution.

The SCA operates in an artificial society typically consisting of 400 individuals. The "world" incessantly confronts the individuals with problems to be solved by them. The society has a (virtual) environment, which requires certain achievements of the society in order to maintain its existence. These achievements are differentiated according to a certain number of categories; these categories may be understood as an attempt to model real achievements of a society, like production of food, production of material goods, integration by law and so on. For practical reasons the model is confined to 5 categories, represented by a so-called "environmental vector" U with real components between 0 and 1; we leave these categories abstract because their content is irrelevant for our model. We assume that these restrictions, like various others in our model, though admittedly severe, will not impair the generality of results.

The environmental vector is applied as target vector and is compared with a corresponding vector L equally with 5 categories containing the actual achievements of the model society (see below); the degree to which the artificial society meets the environmental demands is defined as a measure of its adaptivity. Since absolute measures for different categories of achievements are meaningless, we have normalised both vectors so that the sum of components amounts to 1; thus adaptativity in our model refers to the relations of different achievement categories or an appropriate balance of different achievements. The basic measure of adaptive performance of our system is defined as deviation from environmental requirements sys, with

$$sys = \mid L - U \mid$$

being the distance between the two vectors.

Environmental requirements are modelled as problems that are posed by the environment and have to be solved by the society. For our model it was sufficient to represent problems by a number and the ascribed allocation to one of the 5 achievement categories which, in this respect, may be interpreted as different areas of knowledge. The complete set of problems of the "world", with assigned achievement categories distributed corresponding to the relative sizes of the components of the environmental vector, is held in a special set of typically 5000 problems initially, growing over time so that new problems continuously emerge; the increase or historical dynamics of the number of problems in this set is determined by an appropriate parameter. Other parameters can designate a range of "standard problems" (typically problem numbers < 2000) which are posed with higher frequency.

Posing of problems is modelled by a second pool, the actual problem pool, of typically 600 problems randomly chosen (in case of the existence of standard problems with emphasised frequency of the latter) out of the whole set of problems. Out of this actual pool the individuals of our artificial society have to take the problems that they want to solve; after each time step the actual pool is filled up according to the same distribution as described above. The individuals take on problems assigned to their own area of knowledge with priority, or the first available problem (with consequences for the ease of solving) in case the actual pool does not contain appropriate problems.

Whenever an individual has solved a problem the "solution", i.e. the problem index number, is stored in the individual's memory. Furthermore, any solution reached by any individual is stored in a memory termed "memory of the society"; the number of these solutions is evaluated as the knowledge of the model society and may be interpreted as a quantitative indicator of the culture of the model society.

Individuals possess a certain life span and die at a predefined maximum age (typically 50 - 100 time steps); the program starts with a population of equally distributed ages. If an individual dies it is substituted by a new individual with age 0. A fixed knowledge area out of the 5 categories is attributed to each of the individuals. An individual can take a role out of 5, corresponding to this knowledge area, according to certain conditions explained below. Moreover, 4 individual strategies of problem solving – defined as time steps counted from picking up a new problem from the actual pool to its solution – are assigned to the individuals, referring to the 4 cases resulting from the properties: role taken or not and problem within area of knowledge or not. The individual values are scattered around global average values of typically between 10 and 40 time steps.

Individuals are embedded into a social interaction network, which is mathematically expressed by an interaction matrix: potential interactions between individuals are defined by a value of 1 for the corresponding matrix element, other elements being 0. For practical reasons – convenient graphical representation in order to observe the dynamics and especially clustering effects in our model system – we applied the homogeneous interaction structure of a cellular automaton (MOORE neighbourhood, i.e. each individual interacts with 8 surrounding individuals), although our program permits application of very general, even asymmetric or real interaction matrices; this interaction structure can be understood as representing an essentially egalitarian, but strictly locally organised society. The social structure or the *social environment* of an individual influences several processes, namely (a) the assignment of a certain knowledge category for a new individual, (b) the process of role taking, (c) the process of learning from interacting individuals, (d) the intra-role enforcement, i.e. the acceleration of the individual's problem solving process by interaction with individuals of equal roles, (e) the inhibition of technical by cultural roles, and (f) the dissemination of inhibitional effects from cultural roles to neighbouring individuals, termed "infection".

Whenever an individual reaches its predefined maximum age, it is replaced by a new one, whose knowledge area is statistically determined by means of a roulette method from a vector Z with 5 components (referring to the 5 possible knowledge areas in our model), which, in their part, are calculated according to

$$Z = a * X + (1 - a) * Y,$$

where a is a predefined parameter, the components of X are the normalised frequencies of the occurrence of the 5 areas in the *social environment* and Y is the normalised vector $D = (L - U)_{korr}$ of the difference between the system's performance and environmental requirements, where D_i is 0 if the difference is ≥ 0; thus, X measures the weight of areas of knowledge in the social environment, Y expresses the deficits of the society against its environment, and a the relative influence of the social (endogenous) *versus* exogenous environment.

Role taking requires a minimum amount of knowledge, i.e. a certain minimum number of problems, solved or learned, in the individual's memory. The probability of an individual taking a certain role is then given by

$$p = (p_{ex} + p_{en}) * N_k,$$

with N_k being the *relative* number of individuals of the same knowledge area within the social environment,

$$p_{ex} = p0_{ex} * D_k$$

with $p0_{ex}$ a parameter and D_k the appropriate component of the environmental deficit vector, and

$$p_{en} = p0_{en} * NR_k$$

with NR_k the relative number of roles k within the social environment, and $p0_{en}$ a second parameter; the ratio $p0_{ex} / p0_{en}$ reflects the exogenous *versus* endogenous influence.

At a given time step, the individual performs four different actions: (1) It takes over, as already described above, a problem from the actual problem pool. (2) It attempts to learn from individuals in its social environment, i.e. it scans the memory of the "best" (in the sense of the highest number of solutions contained), and in case of no success the memory of the second best, neighbour with the same knowledge area for problem solutions that are still unknown to itself, beginning with the latest solutions; the number of attempts is a variable parameter (typically 2 or 3 attempts). Moreover, the individual adopts problem solving strategies that are more effective (in the sense of less steps) from any interacting individual with the same knowledge area.

If an individual has taken a role and there exists at least one equal role in its social environment, then the remaining, still necessary steps s until the problem actually dealt with is to be solved, will be decreased according to

$$s = s_{old} * (f_{intra})^{NR},$$

where $0.5 \leq f_{intra} \leq 1$ is a parameter (intra-role enforcement factor) and NR is again the number of roles equal to the individual's within the social environment.

Two of the 5 roles of the model, defined as "cultural" or "moral" roles, can *inhibit* the other roles in their environment; inhibition means that an inhibited individual cannot perceive – and consequently cannot take on and solve – problems of higher "modernity", i.e. with problem index numbers higher than a certain threshold index (an adjustable parameter). Inhibition is calculated as probability from a constant parameter value (out of a 2∗5 matrix, the so-called inhibition matrix, part of the cultural matrix mentioned before) and a factor calculated from the frequency of members of the two cultural roles and of "infected" individuals (see below (f)).[43]

The cultural roles can – with a certain probability p_{inf} – "infect" other interacting roles "with their ideology"; infection means that infected individuals may inhibit other roles in their social environment as do cultural roles, except with lower effect (typically $^1/_2$).

Achievements or cultural status of our model society are evaluated by a number of properties, the most important of which are the total knowledge of the society or the "memory of the society" (see above), i.e. the number of all problems ever solved by individuals of this society, and, in addition, the number of solutions for each of the 5 knowledge areas divided by the actual number of its individual members $K_{rel} = (K_i)$, i = 1...5. The actual achievement vector L, as used for the calculation of the system's adaptive performance sys, or systems value (see above), is the normalised (i.e. divided by the sum of its components K_i) vector K_{rel}. As has already been pointed out, L, as well as sys, are exclusively mapping *relations* between the achievements within the 5 categories or vector components; the value of sys therefore measures how far the performances of the populations assigned to each of the 5 categories are balanced.

---

[43] The details of the according expression, like several other details not crucial in the context of this study, may be obtained from the authors. The factor takes values from 0 to a maximum of 1 (in case of the highest possible frequency of cultural roles in the social environment).

In summary, one can say that the population of our model society is unceasingly busy with solving problems and thus increasing the knowledge of their society and coping with the demands of their environment. The effectiveness of a member's actions depend on its individual competence *and* on its role occupation. Interaction in our artificial world means chiefly social learning, i.e., taking over past solutions of problems from other problem solvers and also "learning" better strategies for problem solving, that is, imitating more successful individuals with whom it is interacting, i.e. with individuals in the neighbourhood. In addition an individual that has no role as yet will take a role according to the majority of role occupants in its social neighbourhood.

The logic of the social action rules, basically embedded in the interaction matrix, is plain: social learning can take place only when there are individuals from whom one can learn; in particular the adoption of a role by a young individual will be influenced if not determined by the example of adult role occupants in the social environment (children of doctors tend to become doctors also, in premodern societies children were literally born into the class of their parents and so on). It is well known that associations of people with the same role favour learning success and that these associations can stabilise the members against external influences. It is not by chance that rulers at all times and in all societies tried to hinder the generation of associations of their subjects. Needham for example (1976) emphasised the fact that the Chinese Mandarins, the ruling class, successfully hindered the Chinese scientists and inventors uniting and forming institutions of their own.

Individuals in the same neighbourhood, occupying the same role, can reinforce one another in the sense that they solve problems more effectively. Last but not least the neighbourhood, i.e., the formal representation of the social environment of an individual, offers reinforcement in an additional sense: the more occupants of the same role are in the neighbourhood of an individual, the less sensible the individual is against the inhibiting effects of the culture, which the occupants of cultural roles exert.

The reinforcement factor refers to a well known fact, namely the possibility of reciprocal encouragement and increasing the motivation to learn and discover new ideas by strong social associations. The aforementioned example of the importance of scientific associations for the emergence of the role of the scientists illustrates this quite clearly; other examples are the strong connections between philosophers and scientists in ancient Greece like the Platonic Academy, and during the Enlightenment.

Relations *between* different roles may be inhibitory. Inhibition means the reduction of effectiveness of problem solving on the one hand, and the inability to perceive new problems. An individual can be "directly" inhibited by occupants of cultural roles in its neighbourhood; individuals without cultural roles in their neighbourhood can be "infected" with the consequence of acting similarly to cultural roles.

Local inhibition rules and reinforcement can be formally represented by a cultural matrix, part of which is the inhibition matrix previously defined. This matrix is a formal expression of the fact mentioned above that cultural limits will have effects on individuals only if these limits are "embodied" and transferred by the occupants of respective roles. Alternatively, it would also be possible to define certain variables for each artificial culture as global system parameters and study their effects on the different problem solvers. However, because we intended to model the evolutionary societal processes – as it is in social reality – from a strict actor's or micro-sociological perspective, we expect the inhibiting and reinforcing effects on the whole society as an emerging phenomenon, i.e. as a product of local interactions and not as an initial boundary condition. After all, when human beings start to develop their society there are no cultural boundary conditions from the beginning but they construct these like any other aspect of their social reality (Berger and Luckmann 1966).

In our model, the generation of social roles in an undifferentiated society or development of new roles in addition to old ones is regulated by exogenous and endogenous parameters. The exogenous parameters are dependent on the degree of adaptation of the system to its environment The endogenous parameters depend on the number of individuals in the neighbourhood that are linked to the same category. The assumption behind these parameters is on the one hand that the situation of the society as a whole influences the generation of roles in order to increase the "competence" of the society, i.e. its ability to tackle problems, which are important for the system; on the other hand we have again the contention that decisions of individuals are dependent upon their social environment.

Because the problem solving strategies of the individual actors predominantly operate "endogenously", that is, they are mainly driven by the wish of the individuals to solve problems that are *subjectively* important for them, it might well be that the whole system reaches performance or systems values that are higher than the target value of the environmental vector. The individuals – and that means finally the whole society – produce a cultural surplus, to speak in economic terms. This assumption seems to be realistic, too: the philosophical and mathematical achievements of the ancient Greeks, for example, can hardly be explained by environmental demands. What environmental pressure could have forced Euclides to think about the infinity of prime numbers or the existence of parallels? In our model, a cultural surplus is simply without further influences.

An interesting possibility of systems development might be regression. If one component of the environmental vector becomes very large, leaving the other components unimportant in relation to it, established roles will literally die out; that is when new individuals are "born" they will not take the roles associated with unimportant categories; those roles are extinguished with the death of the old role occupants. It is important to note that the process of regression is also a mainly local one. The endogenous parameters *generally* cannot maintain the generation of roles against the exogenous one in a significant manner, with some exceptions (see below). However, it is always possible that occupants of unimportant roles remain though the whole situation for the society has changed drastically. We think this to be a realistic assumption too.

In nuce, the SCA obviously models the interdependence of the cultural and the social dimension of the evolution of societies on a strictly local or micro level, that is, by introducing actions and interactions of individual actors exclusively. In this we follow the classical insight of theoretical – and empirical – sociology that basically there is nothing else in social reality than actors that "socially construct their reality", to again quote Berger and Luckmann. That this is fundamentally a "dialectical" process, in the sense that the constructed reality in turn influences the further actions of construction, has also been principally known since Marx. Therefore the SCA is basically nothing more than a formal model of those theoretical insights, which constitute one of the few unifying properties of theoretical sociology.

4.1.3   Discussions and results

We wish to avoid a possible misunderstanding: the model is not intended to offer a *complete* representation of sociocultural processes. In the next subchapter we describe an important extension of the model in regard to "internal evolution", that is, the evolution of some of the evolutionary factors just explained as internal processes of a society. Yet other aspects of sociocultural evolution are not even captured with the extended model.

To name only two: the environment of a society has of course important influences on the ways the development of a culture will take. Not only material tools like the wheel or the *kayak* of the Inuit, mentioned above, are cultural achievements generated in response to the demands of the physical environment of the respective societies, but also religions and other world views are without doubt strongly influenced by the environment. The invention of astronomy, e.g., was possible only in an environment where the stars, including the sun, could be continuously observed as was the case in Egypt and Mesopotamia. Inhabitants of tropical rain forests or the arctic regions, with their long darkness, were literally unable to create such forms of views of the universe. The same goes for particular religious creation myths, which becomes evident when one compares the Biblical Garden of Eden with the Ginnungagap of Nordic mythology. Therefore detailed modellings of cultural developments should also incorporate the factors of particular environments as an initial boundary condition (see above 3.3.). We shall come back to this problem below. However, as we are interested in the modelling of *general* principles of sociocultural evolution regardless of particular developments and environments, we omitted this aspect. It would be quite interesting (and not very difficult), though, to classify environments with respect to these questions.

By the way, the SCA-model rather easily explains an interesting fact, which a lot of scholars in the field of sociocultural evolution have observed (cf. Trigger loc.cit.): the numerous different societies we know from history differ mainly in the cultural dimension, where great differences can be observed; the social dimension of different societies is a lot more similar. As culture is produced in our model by the ideas that problem solvers have, it is easy to understand that many of these problems are posed by the physical environment, as mentioned above. Individuals are not only social beings but, of course, also members of material ecosystems. As physical environments differ greatly it is no surprise that cultures differ in the same way. Social structure, on the other hand, always has to solve the same problems everywhere, i.e., the ordering of social affairs, deciding conflicts and so on. That is why theorists like Brown (1991) speak of "human universals" in this respect. Obviously the SCA captures these aspects.

The other important aspect we left out is the emergence of social hierarchies and particular decision structures. To be sure, the model could have been extended rather easily in order to capture these aspects of social evolution by taking generalised Boolean networks instead of the geometrically simpler cellular automata. We decided not to do so because we had already dealt with this problem in specific studies (see above 3.2.). To sum up these experiments once more: the emergence of social hierarchies, from a mathematical and systems theoretical point of view, can be rather easily explained by the theorem of inequality. Inequality, as we showed, leads to simple attractors and that means, in case of decision problems, to effective decision structures; we also saw that inequality is a very probable outcome of processes of rule changes. In particular social hierarchies mean the existence of decision structures with point attractors, i.e., the efficient transformation of decision processes into common action. A point attractor of communicating processes, that is to say, signifies the fact that the social group does not change any more with respect to the different opinions of the members; if this is reached then communication can be finished and transformed into action, as especially Luhmann has frequently pointed out, though not in these mathematical terms. Therefore the emergence of social hierarchies is mathematically speaking an evolutionary effect, which is unavoidable insofar as social inequality is one of the outcomes of social transformations. The empirical fact that all evolutionary advanced societies, regardless of their particular culture, were politically organised in the form of more or less strict social hierarchies confirms these mathematical considerations. That is why we decided to omit this problem in our model and to concentrate on the interdependency of cultural and social evolution.[44]

When discussing the results of our experiments with the SCA we have to distinguish between the *cultural* development of our artificial system, i.e., the growth of knowledge, and its *social* evolution, that is the generation of social roles and their distribution among the members of the society. To be sure, these processes are mutually dependent, as we have emphasised several times, but they are not the same. It is quite possible to get the same growth curves of knowledge with very different role distributions. In all simulations the artificial society starts with no roles at all, which can be imagined as an undifferentiated tribal society.

a) The *cultural* development is dependent, as we showed, on external factors on the one hand, i.e. the difference between the environmental demands and the cultural states of our society, and on internal factors on the other hand, that is the influence of social milieus on the cognitive "ontogenesis" of our artificial actors. Although there are various parameters that influence the growth of knowledge, our results are quite plain. The main determining parameter is the relation between inhibiting and reinforcing effects, which are expressed in our cultural matrix as the relation between the mean values of the components c_{ij} with $i \neq j$ and of the components with $i = j$, regardless for example of different topologies of social milieus (neighbourhoods) and other factors. In other words: the significant aspect that decides upon the cultural evolution of our society is the proportion between the *intra role relations IAR* (relations between occupants of the same role) and *inter role relations IER* (relations between occupants of different roles). Four different cases of cultural development are shown to illustrate this main result.

---

[44] In the meantime one of our students is developing a model that contains the SCA *and* cognitive ontogenesis (see below). In this model the CA of the SCA is substituted by a Boolean net, which also captures the emergence of social hierarchies.

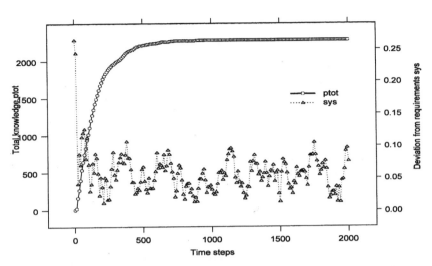

Figure 1: A typical development of the model system with high inhibition and low intra-role reinforcement; ptot describes the accumulation of knowledge in the model society, sys the variation of the system's value.

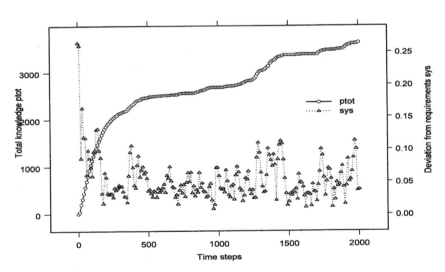

Figure 2: The same model system as in Figure 1 with equal parameters, except for a considerable increase in endogenous orientation (role generation probability). The system is now able to transcend the threshold limiting the development in Figure 1.

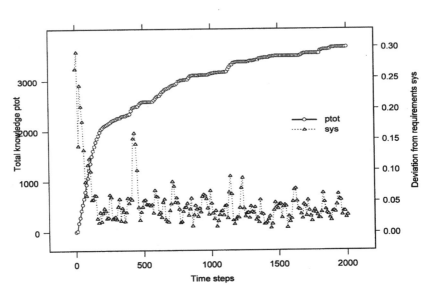

Figure 3: The model system with high inhibition and high intra-role reinforcement, other parameters retained as in Figure 1. The level of ptot is considerably higher than in Figure 1, but clearly lower than in Figure 2.

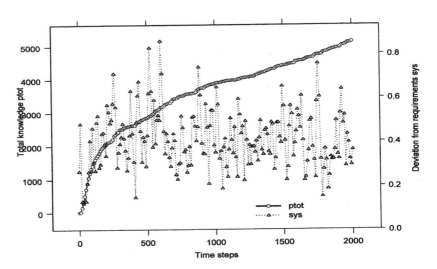

Figure 4: A typical development of the model system with low inhibition and very high intra-role reinforcement, other parameters retained as in Figure 1. Note that the level of ptot is much higher than in Figure 1.

In the first case the culture is developing rather rapidly during the first 500 time steps but then the cultural acceleration is rapidly slowing down and the development is stopped at a threshold level of 2000 (= the number of solved problems). The explanation for this growth curve is this: in the beginning of our culture all members are solving problems and their strategies of problem solving become better by taking particular roles, i.e. by specialising. As there are high environmental pressures and only few cultural roles, the external factor for role generating favours the growth of knowledge and the inhibiting effects of the cultural roles are not spread out over the whole society. Furthermore nearly all problems presented to the individual members are new ones and learning, in the sense of taking over problems already solved, is only seldom possible. This is typical for growth curves, as was mentioned in 2.3. As the value of the society increases the environmental pressures decrease, a lot of problems are also already solved, so that many individuals do not tackle new problems all their time and, last but not least, the high inhibiting effects of the cultural roles become effective. The culture stagnates on a comparatively low level.

A variant of this development is shown in figure 2, where the effect of endogenous orientation can be seen. The threshold of figure 1 is transcended but not much.

In the next case the cultural growth in the beginning is also very fast for the same reasons as in case one. In nearly the same time the growth slows down and the inhibiting factors determine the development. Then the high IAR values become a "counterpoise", i.e. a compensating factor, which again rises the cultural acceleration. At this time occupants of the same roles have formed associations. The growth curve is not so smooth as in the first case because both factors – IAR and IER – operate against each other. Sometimes the IER factor forces the system into stagnation but in the following time steps the IAR factor allows the culture escape it. Finally the culture becomes captured by a threshold which it cannot leave any more because the society has exhausted the possibilities of forming of associations, and then the inhibiting effects stop the evolution for good. Yet the culture has reached a significantly higher level than the first one which is only due to the IAR values – the environmental vector is the same in both cases and also in the third.

The last case is obvious after the interpretations of the other cases. The initial development is again similar and even in this case a flattening out of the growth curve can be observed after 500 steps. Then growth of the culture continues steadily though not in a linear fashion. The curve is a bit smoother than that of the second case because the effects of the IAR values override those of the IER ones. At level 5000, after 2000 time steps the cultural growth still continues although it has slowed down. Yet 5000 is no attractor because longer simulations demonstrated that this level is also transcended. The fact that the growth slowed down is due to the simple fact that all (adult) members of our society now have a lot of knowledge; new members can learn, i.e. take over solutions already found by others, with a much higher probability than during the phases of lower cultural levels. As all individuals only have a life span that enables them to solve about four new problems on average, it is clear that learning from others takes time and only fewer new problems can be dealt with. In other words: cultures that are already far advanced can only maintain a steady growth of knowledge if they "import" new, additional individuals. With a constant population as in our experiments, only increasing life span would solve this problem if the culture is not able to forget.

We want to analyse this aspect a bit more thoroughly. Without a doubt even the third culture would come to a standstill despite its high IAR and low IER values because as knowledge would grow even more, then at some time all new born individuals would practically only learn solutions that have already been found and they would have no time to deal with problems new for the whole society (and not just subjectively new for them). This is simply an effect of the limited life span: because new individuals first look to see if there are solutions to the problems posed to them and if the society has at its disposal more solutions than a new individual can learn from others, then this individual (and all others after it) spends its whole life with just learning solutions new to it but not new to society as a whole. Although many individuals would be able to recognise new problems they simply could not deal with them. The cultural effect on this society would be a kind of "Alexandrinism", i.e., a culture that only reproduces knowledge already discovered by former generations.

To be sure, there is an obvious answer to that problem, which could carry such a culture over any limits. The culture could forget, that is it could decide that it does not need certain solutions any more which had been found in the early stages of its development. The new individuals then would not have to learn all solutions that had been found already but only those that had been found in the, e.g., two last generations and would have time to deal with new problems. That is exactly the case in societies like the Western ones: no pupil learns, e.g., the arts of staying alive in a wild forest and how to make fire without a lighter (or if he does he is on a survival trip or in the army). Instead he learns the new achievements in science and technology that have been invented during the last century.

b) The *social* development, i.e. the generation and distribution of the different roles is a bit more complicated. The generation of roles is also regulated by two main factors, an external and an internal one. The external factor is again the influence of the environment which partly determines the emergence of roles and by it the cultural success of the society. The internal factor is the social milieu, i.e. the neighbourhood, that regulates the generation of roles in the beginning of role differentiation as well as the role taking of young individuals. However, in contrast to the cultural development that is characterised by a tension between the *two* internal factors, the factors of social development do not oppose one another but work together. Interestingly enough there are quite different developments with different combinations of the two parameters.

If the influence of the external parameter is high in relation to that of the internal one, the system has to adapt continuously, i.e. it tries to steer the taking of roles by young individuals to those categories that exhibit the highest differences between systemic values and environmental demands. The social milieu is less important. The next figure shows a typical social development under these conditions.

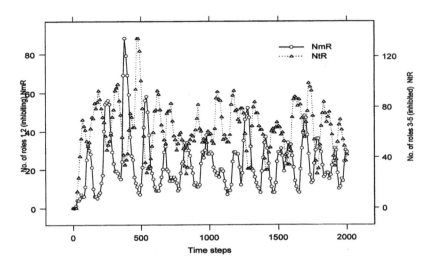

Figure 5: Dynamics of the inhibiting and inhibited roles in a model system with an extremely exogenous orientation (orientation with regard to environmental requirements); other parameters as those in Figure 1. Note the strong variations in role populations due to an overreaction of sorts when the system is compelled to re-adapt.

The growth curves for the different roles demonstrate that the society always tries to adjust the number of different roles according to the environmental demands for each category. We make the assumption, by the way, that no individual leaves the role he has taken at the beginning of his social career, which is certainly realistic for premodern societies and even in modern societies not improbable.[45] By continuously adapting, our system never comes to rest but has always to improve its social states. The reason for this unrest is well known to all economists and planners of educational organisations: if one needs for example more engineers, then you have to motivate young people for this profession and train them for a certain time. Having succeeded with this, other young people start this profession as well and you get more engineers

---

[45] Even in societies like the US where the switching of professional roles is more usual than in, e.g., Germany, many professional roles need much time for training. Therefore no society can adjust the number of professional roles continuously but only with a certain time lapse.

than you need; as a consequence there are not enough medical doctors. You then start the whole process again with training doctors, which gives you the same effect for other professions and so on. Either you have too few or too many of the different professions. Not even the socialistic societies of Eastern Europe, which tried to cope with these problems by central regulations, managed to have always the right number of professionals in the different fields. We think that growth curves like these are rather typical for modern societies; readers who are acquainted with predator-prey systems and the typical Lotka-Volterra dynamics will recognise quite similar developments to those in our curves.

The last figure is a trajectory of the whole system in a state space with the dimensions "cultural roles" and "technical roles" (for the sake of simplicity we call all roles that are not cultural ones "technical roles" borrowing this term from Habermas (1976)). We observe again that the system does not reach simple attractors or asymptotes as was the case with cultural evolution but only regions of the state space, which the trajectory does not leave. That picture exhibits something like a "strange attractor" though not literally because we operate with finite systems.[46] A strange attractor defines, roughly speaking, a region of the state space towards which the trajectory is attracted but in which the trajectory moves in complex manners. That is also typical for Lotka-Volterra systems.

---

[46] Finite systems are always periodic though in the stochastic case with certain local fluctuations and often with very large periods. This has been principally known since the famous "theorem of eternal return" by Poincaré but often neglected in descriptions of chaos theory and complexity theory. In a strict mathematical sense finite systems have no strange attractors.

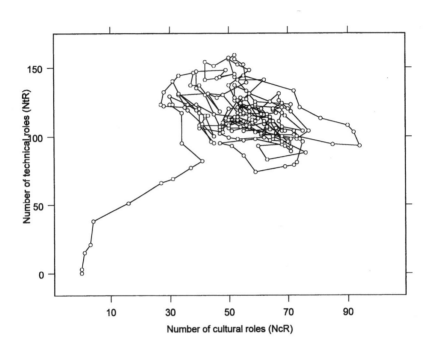

Figure 6: SCA with predominantly exogeneous generation of roles; the attractor of the trajectory between technical and cultural roles appears to be much more dispersed.

If we reduce the influence of the (environmental) external parameter, i.e. make the system in some sense more casual about its environment, and rise the internal parameter value then we get different developments. The next pictures show typical growth curves for the different roles and again a trajectory with the state space dimensions cultural/technical.

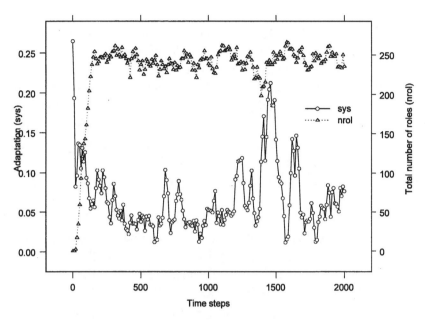

Figure 7: A typical result of an SCA run with predominantly endogeneous generation of roles: high number of roles and poor adaptation.

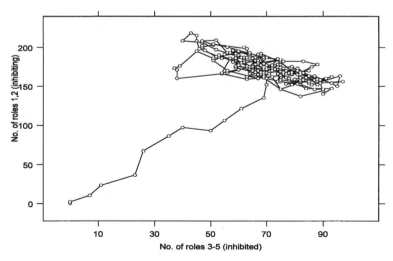

Figure 8: Dynamics of the two types of roles (inhibiting and inhibited) in a model system with highly endogenous orientation in a trajectorial representation.

Before we introduce some important extensions to our basic model it is useful to give a preliminary summing up. Our experiments demonstrate that and how sociocultural systems always have to account for different factors that regulate their dynamics and evolution at the same time. The *social* dimension of development depends on the interplay of internal and external parameters; if a society concentrates on the external factors, i.e., if it mainly accentuates adaptation to environmental demands, it will have difficulties in obtaining social order in the sense that it maintains certain social states over longer periods of time. On the other hand, if the society concentrates mainly on internal factors, it will achieve stable states but will pay for it by maintaining states that are not necessarily satisfactory with respect to its (physical and social) environment.

When looking at history it seems that at least most of the premodern societies chose the option of favouring internal parameters. Social stability was preferred to an optimal development of the society; even material needs of the majority of those societies like hunger and insufficient housing or clothing were tolerated. The sociocultural "values" about social welfare were apparently such that social rest and order were looked upon as the most important value, and successful adaptation to environmental problems was only secondary. Our mathematical model demonstrates that one cannot have both, that is, successful adaptation *and* social rest and order at the same time. Because our model also demonstrates how difficult problems of adaptations are even in an artificial world, it is rather understandable that traditional societies did not want to take the risk of permanent social unrest without any guarantee of adaptive success.[47]

The *cultural* development apparently depends on the proportion of relations between roles, i.e. the relative autonomy of roles *versus* the integrative and inhibiting forces between the different roles. By looking at history again we may conclude that most societies preferred rather strong integrative forces to role autonomy, which explains the fact that all known cultures – with the exception of the Western one – sooner or

---

[47] In Chapter 3.2. we mentioned the theorem of inequality and its consequence for the probability of social order. To avoid confusion we would like to remind that this holds only for systems with constant rules, i.e., without adaptive and evolutionary dynamics.

later became "chained" (Marx) by a cultural attractor. That is understandable too, at least in hindsight: Platon's worries in the *Politeia* about the disintegrative consequences of unrestrained thinking are not merely the usual conservative opposition against something new but seem, at least to us, to anticipate the problems that modern societies have with the loss of traditional integrative relations. As there is nothing like a free lunch, premodern societies possibly saw and tried to prevent the dangers of losing inhibiting relations between the different roles. In addition, our experiments demonstrate that only with particular combinations of IER and IAR values is the transcending of cultural limits, in general, possible; in most cases our artificial cultures were caught sooner or later in an attractor. Therefore mathematical probability seems to be against the frequent occurrence of *real* sociocultural evolution.

One final remark is in order to clarify our use of the concept of "social rest and order". Several theorists of social evolution, e.g., Sanderson (1995) and Turner (1997) argued that the agrarian state empires, like for example China or ancient Rome were in permanent social unrest, revolts of peasants, slaves etc., and that therefore these societies had inevitably to vanish to give rise to modern societies (Sanderson loc. cit.). Apparently these authors think that modern societies are more stable. Apart from the fact that some of these empires like China or Japan have existed for much longer than the Western societies so far, we think that in a *structural* sense the agrarian state societies were rather stable: no revolt seriously threatened the fundamental social order and no political struggle changed the society as a whole –neither in a social nor in a cultural sense. This fact was already mentioned in Chapter 2. On the contrary, all these societies had obviously reached particular sociocultural attractors and no evolutionary factors existed that took the societies out of it. When speaking of social order we only mean this structural meaning of the term and in this sense our model is obviously able to reconstruct and explain the evolutionary fates of these societies.

4.2 SOCIOCULTURAL MATRICES AND EVOLUTIONARY PRINCIPLES

The basis of our model consists, as we explained, of the two matrices which regulate social interactions, defined as learning and role taking, and the cultural growth, dependent on the relations between the specific roles. To be sure, the "external" parameters, which represent the influence of the environment, are also important as the analysis of the *social* dynamics demonstrated. Therefore no sociocultural evolution can be understood if it is not modelled in terms of adaptive dynamics. Yet history teaches us that sociocultural evolution may occur in rather different environments and that, apart from extremes like tropical rain forests or arctic snow regions, the difference between specific environments may be neglected if one looks for *general* features of sociocultural evolution. Therefore it seems safe to concentrate on the characteristics of sociocultural systems themselves when trying to explain the logic that may lie behind the historical processes. In the mathematical sense of the term we can say that these general characteristics can be represented by matrices of the kind described above. Of course, there are other important properties of social systems that are not represented in our matrices, as for example, those kinds of social rules that regulate social change defined, as the possibilities of leaving old rules and taking up new ones, or the problem of social hierarchies mentioned above. Because these aspects of social dynamics are not important for our task here and as we have dealt with these problems elsewhere (cf. Klüver 2000; Klüver and Schmidt 1999 b), we may assume that our matrices contain all the relevant information necessary for our analysis.

The "inhibition" or "cultural" matrix is of particular importance here because it defines not only *social* relations between the roles but also relations between the components of the *culture*. The reason for it is of course the definition of a social role (see above 2.2.) as a pair (r,k) with r being the social rules specific for the interactions of the occupant of a role with other social actors and k the knowledge, which is characteristic for the role. The relations between roles therefore are also *per definitionem* relations between cultural components. In this sense the cultural matrix defines the structure of the culture as well as particular social structures, although this becomes a bit complicated by the influence of the social geometry: if there are no social interactions between occupants of different roles then the inhibiting factor is not effective at all. Therefore the cultural matrix strictly speaking determines the effects of *possible* interactions; social geometry, i.e., the distribution of actors in a space of possible interactions determines if the inhibiting and reinforcing factors become effective.

Some additional considerations are necessary. At least since Lévy-Strauss (1958) it was thought in cultural anthropology to be a truism that there exists some kind of "isomorphism" between culture and social structure, although this originally mathematical term was never explained very exactly. Culture "mirrors" social structure and by analysing culture it is also possible to understand the social structure, and *vice versa*, of course. Though this assumption was often criticised (cf. Turner 1969; Eder 1991) most cultural anthropologists and evolutionary sociologists still maintain this opinion, although it was not very often substantiated.

I believe that this assumption goes back basically at least to the Marxian criticism of ideology, most famously expressed in *Die Heilige Familie* (The Holy Family). Marx and Engels explained the conception of the Holy Family in Christian religion, as is well known, by the interests of the ruling classes to establish certain social structures, like family, as given by God himself and thus legitimising them. As according to Marx all beliefs represent nothing more than social interests according to the specific social structures it is self-evident that culture and social structure are isomorphic. By generalising this approach, sociology of knowledge stipulated that all belief systems and world views reflect the social structure of a society because they are nothing other than the attempt of the members of that society to understand the world by transferring their social experiences to other realms, like the physical universe.

These explanations may be true or not which is not my concern here. It is neither necessary to use the Marxian concept of class interests nor the rather socio-psychological explanation of sociology of knowledge for our tasks but it is sufficient to assume that all knowledge, *which is important for the whole society* becomes institutionalised in social roles as soon as the society differentiates into different roles. In this sense our problem is not the same as that of cultural anthropologists, who often deal with undifferentiated societies. It is then certainly a truism that in evolved societies the role structure is *eo ipso* also the cultural structure and *vice versa*. Therefore the degree of role differentiation is "mirrored" as the degree of knowledge differentiation; hierarchies between different roles mean also *societal* hierarchies of knowledge components; social equality between different roles means a cultural equality among the respective knowledge components like, e.g., those of a physicist and of an art critic.

It is important to note that the term "cultural structure" does not necessarily mean the ensemble of *logical and/or semantical* relations between cultural components. It just means that cultural components are connected or separated in the same way as the according roles. Hierarchies between different concepts, e.g., may also represent logical hierarchies: in religious world views the concept of God was certainly thought to be the highest category in a logical sense; the famous logical proofs of the existence of God are an illustrative example for it. However, the main point is that the role of the priest was thought to be superior to that of the secular scholar and that is why the logical relation between the concept of God and all other cognitive concepts was considered as a hierarchy. To the extent that the role of the scholar was separated from that of the priest the concept of God was no longer held as logically superior to concepts describing the physical universe.

Our inhibition matrix therefore represents the cultural structure as the societal definition of the relations between different ensembles of cultural components, that is, components of knowledge. Therefore it is methodically sound to assume that certain characteristics of our matrix represent characteristics both of the social structure and of the culture of societies. No additional assumptions about social interests and/or human reasoning are necessary.

After this little excursion I can go back to our matrix. It could be demonstrated that the main factor for the development of culture is the relation of IAR and IER, i.e., the reinforcing relations between occupants of the same role and the inhibiting relations between occupants of different roles. For the sake of brevity let us call this relation EP, which means "evolutionary parameter". Apparently the cultural evolution will become higher the lower the IER-values and the higher the IAR-values. A possible definition can be EP = IER - IAR, using the mean values for all components of the matrix for IER and IAR, which is consistent with the results given in 4.1. We then get that the evolutionary level of a culture is higher the smaller EP and *vice versa*. Therefore a society will have the best chance to evolve culturally – and by this socially too – if it starts with comparatively low EP-values. If we can confirm the assumption that the relation between the two factors can be represented by a simple parameter EP as in the example, obtained by a suitable algorithm from the matrix elements, then we obviously get a mathematical formulation of the hypothesis of heterogeneity of Chapter 2.5. in terms of matrix representations.

By translating these results into common sociological language we see that this is basically very similar to the well known concept of differentiation. The experimental results of our model must be understood as the statement that societies with comparatively high degrees of role differentiation (= low EP-values) in their beginnings have better chances to evolve and reach rather higher cultural levels than those that are more integrated, i.e., have moderate or even high EP-values. The cases of Europe and China or Japan and the Islamic societies obviously fit this explanation: the Middle Ages of Europe were characterised from their beginnings by a rather high degree of differentiation, in contrast to the other societies.

I believe that this principle of differentiation, though not necessary in this particular form, is typical for evolution in general – not only for sociocultural evolution. The "symmetry breaks" that astrophysicists hold responsible for the evolution of the universe (cf. Barrow 1991) are logically nothing more than the beginnings of differentiation of energy and matter. Of course, the mathematical principles are certainly quite different from those presented in the last subchapter, but the principle is the same. Accordingly biological evolution needs heterogeneous, i.e., different structures as well, which can be easily demonstrated by experimenting with the genetic algorithm of Holland. Evolution apparently needs differences to succeed, regardless of whether it is physical, biological or sociocultural evolution. The condition of the possibility of evolution, to quote a well known concept of Kant, is the existence of differences as large as possible from the beginning. Indeed, if we assume that the physical universe as well as life and sociocultural systems were quite homogeneous in their very beginnings, i.e., nearly totally undifferentiated, then the first step to evolution must have been the introduction of differences – one way or the other.

Apparently this argument goes even further. If the conclusions are valid that those sociocultural systems that have the best chance to evolve rather far are differentiated to a high degree in the manner described above, then evolution is in a certain sense a self-reinforcing process. By this I mean that favourable initial conditions for evolution, i.e., a high degree of differentiation in the beginning may not only lead to rather high evolutionary levels by themselves, but that the very evolutionary process generated by the initial conditions can alter those in turn and as such reinforce its own development even more than the initial conditions allowed. To explain this consideration I shall make a little digression to social and cognitive ontogenesis.

Researches in the ontogenesis of social competence (Bateson 1970; Schwartzman 1978) and verbal competence (Andresen 2002) give strong evidence that the development of these competences is always accompanied *and reinforced* by the development of a *meta-competence,* i.e., a competence to change the rules which comprise the social or verbal competence. Basically this idea goes back to Mead (loc. cit.) who emphasised the importance of game and play for social ontogenesis: in games and plays children learn to vary the social rules that they have learned so far and to enlarge their repertoire of roles. In the terms of Bateson children use the different social games and plays to enlarge their social competence by developing and applying a meta-competence. In the same spirit Andresen (loc. cit.) demonstrated that verbal games are decisive for verbal ontogenesis because children learn to vary verbal rules like those of meaning and different speech acts. Therefore it is apparently necessary to develop meta-competence at the same time as competence in order to succeed with social and verbal ontogenesis. From this it follows, though the authors mentioned do not say so explicitly, that as competence grows by applying meta-competence, the same goes for meta-competence itself because at least principally, variations of verbal and social rules are certainly easier for competent speakers and occupants of social roles than for social and verbal beginners. By the way, meta-competence is not necessarily the same as consciousness: the children observed by Schwartzman and Andresen were all kindergarten kids who applied their meta-competence without conscious thinking.

By generalising and formalising these thoughts as well as applying them to sociocultural processes we get the following considerations:

At least the processes of human ontogenesis and sociocultural evolution are not exclusively dependent on favourable initial conditions, i.e., comparatively high degrees of differentiation, but they are also characterised by a continuous interaction of competence and meta-competence in the sense that each conditions and reinforces the other. Low competence at the beginning is increased by an equally low meta-competence, which enables the evolving system to vary and enlarge its competence. This leads to higher degrees of meta-competence, which in turn accelerates the process of developing more competence, which leads to more meta-competence and so forth. In other words, we have a classic case of positive feedback. To be sure, this mutual reinforcement by feedback does not go on forever but has, in the case of ontogenesis, an absolute threshold in the biological capacity of the brain; in addition the whole process can be slowed down or even stopped by negative influences of the physical and/or social environment of the ontogenetic process. Ontogenesis, after all, is a learning process that needs favourable environmental conditions and positive responses, that is the learner must succeed with his tasks of problem solving. The limits of sociocultural evolution, to remind of the second case we are dealing with, by certain attractors have often been mentioned in this book.

In contrast to the usual feedback mechanisms studied in cybernetics and systems theory we have here a feedback process that operates on two logical levels; developments on one level cause developments on the second, which in turn cause developments on the first and so on. Usually feedback processes extend to only one level, like, for example, the famous case of the thermostat. However, the interaction of at least two different logical levels is characteristic of adaptive systems in general, as I recently demonstrated (Klüver 2000). The mutual interdependency of the development of competence and meta-competence is a special case, which is obviously one fundamental feature of ontogenetic learning processes.

To be sure, this "two level" interplay does not mean that these learning systems are totally independent of initial conditions. Children who are physically handicapped in the brain, for example, will never evolve as far as physically normal children. Therefore we have to assume that successful evolution is dependent both on favourable or at least "normal" initial conditions *and* the succeeding interaction of competence and meta-competence.

The interdependency of competence and meta-competence was observed and analysed so far for ontogenetic processes. When applying these considerations to the field of sociocultural evolution we have to transfer those concepts, of course. In order to do this we have to consider what the term "meta-competence" means in a general fashion.

Bateson, who introduced this term, was strongly influenced by Russell's logical theory of types; the concept of meta-competence has its origins in the tradition of "metamathematics", which was founded and named by Hilbert (cf. Tarski 1956). The idea behind this is the assumption of different levels of thinking where the higher levels are used to analyse the lower ones. However, the very concept of "level" is a formal reconstruction of processes that in fact have no levels. Neither in the brain nor in any other real system are there levels of different orders; the same holds, e.g. for computer programs like our SCA (cf. Klüver 2000). Instead of levels we have different loops that the system traverses in different time steps: one loop is used for solving certain problems and another loop is used to analyse and value the operations of the first one. Let us call the first type of loops first order loops and the second type second order loops (in complex cognitive and social systems there are without doubt more than two types but two are enough for this discussion (see below 4.3.)). It is now easy to imagine that during cognitive ontogenesis the development of loops of both types occurs as a positive feedback of the following kind: in the beginning there is just one loop of the first kind and one of the second. The first loop solves problems but after a certain time its capacity is exhausted, i.e., it meets problems it cannot solve. The second order loop "analyses" the situation and causes a second first order loop to be generated which operates in a different manner. This causes the generation of a second "second order loop" which analyses the new first order loop and perhaps the generation of a third first order loop which in turn stimulates the generation of a third second order loop and so forth. I shall analyse these processes more thoroughly in 4.3, though these rough sketches are sufficient here.

The decisive points in this process are these: on the one hand the environment of our cognitive system has to set rather different problems in order to get the whole process started. If the environment is homogeneous in the sense that all problems are of the same kind, there will be no need for our system to develop different loops of both orders. On the other hand, the system must be able to perceive the difference between problems and it must have at its disposal initial conditions that allow the generation of different structures, i.e. cognitive loops. In other words, our cognitive system must have at its disposal certain differences in its structures at its beginning, or at least the capability to differentiate its structure as soon as environmental problems require it. In particular, there must be an initial difference between the two loops of the first and second order and both have to be different from the rest of the system. I believe, by the way, that these little formal considerations capture the essence of the famous model of Piaget, with his distinction between assimilation and accommodation; Piaget himself analysed the difference in cognitive ontogenesis between children in both a homogeneous environment and a heterogeneous one (e.g. Piaget 1975).

After these formal clarifications it is rather easy to transfer the ontogenetic considerations of Bateson to our field of sociocultural evolution. As the formal parallel to individual competence we define the knowledge a society has at its disposal at a certain time, that is the sum of all solutions to problems, respectively, its culture. The generation of this "societal" competence basically follows the same logic as was demonstrated in the ontogenetic case: as the environment sets problems of different kinds the society is forced to differentiate between different kinds of problem solvers, i.e., occupants of different roles. The formal equivalent to the individual meta-competence can be defined by EP, the evolutionary parameter, which is in principle the degree of sociocultural differences between the specific roles. The reason for this definition is the fact that EP both measures on the one hand the degree by which a society is able to enlarge its knowledge, and on the other hand generates, so to speak, the enlargement of knowledge *if the problems set by environment or by cultural development are of different types* (that is why EP is a measure). Indeed, if the environment is very homogeneous and sets only problems of one kind and in particular always the same problems, as in the case of tropical rain forests, then no specialised problem solvers would be needed - the society could remain undifferentiated. On the other hand, a heterogeneous environment that sets problems of different kinds forces the society to generate specialists, that is, occupants of different roles who must have a minimal degree of autonomy. This degree is measured by EP and that is why EP is also a measure, or the societal parallel to individual meta-competence. As in Bateson's considerations meta-competence is used to value, and if necessary to vary, rules of social competence, the values of EP decide upon the variation of knowledge production, i.e. the rules of enlarging societal competence.[48]

The general reflections on the continuous interaction between competence and meta-competence suggest that EP and the development of the culture are mutually dependent. In other words, the values of EP are not constant for a certain society but variable. Therefore we may conclude that the values of EP at a certain time are themselves the result of the evolution of this particular society. A casual look at European history confirms this: the degrees of role autonomy have certainly changed during the last millennium and in particular they have grown. Although the European societies had apparently rather favourable EP-values at their beginning for the reasons stated in 2.4. and 2.5., these values of course would never have been enough to generate the culture of modern societies, with the strong autonomy of methods for problem defining and solving in all important parts of the culture. Therefore these values must have been the result of the evolution of European society itself; the further the sociocultural evolution developed, the greater the values of EP became, which in turn forced evolution further and faster and so on. The theory of functional differentiation (e.g. Luhmann 1984) tells us just this story but without real evolutionary explanations and only as an informal reconstruction.

From our basic model we know that the development of a culture C is dependent on the values of EP. If we designate the set of rules formally represented in the inhibition or cultural matrix and in the social interaction matrix as a function f, then we have

---

[48] Bateson did not use these terms and his considerations are, despite his orientation to formal logic, rather informal and difficult to read. In particular he used only the concept of meta-competence as something that is there or not. We can see from our considerations that it is necessary to define meta-competence or its formal equivalents by degrees – which is the usual definition of all concepts in the natural sciences.

$$C = f(EP).$$

The considerations just explained mean that EP is also dependent on C, i.e., the level that C has reached, measured as usual by the sum of all problem solutions. The formal rules that represent this second dependency will be given below; if we name these rules as a second function g then we get

$$EP = g(C).$$

We have to bear in mind, of course, that these equations always mean the values of EP and C at a certain time t. By designating the values of C and EP respectively at time t_n as EP_n and C_n, we get the general recursive equations

$$C_{n+1} = f(g(C_n)) \tag{1}$$

$$EP_{n+1} = g(f(EP_n)) \tag{2}$$

which I like to call the general sociocultural equations.

We may visualise a society as a web of roles that are connected in different ways and that regulate the actions of the social actors on the one hand and are changed by these actions on the other. The equations describe this mutual dependency: the cultural achievements that the actors produce influence the social geometry, i.e. the topological/metrical relations of the web; these relations in turn determine the cognitive and social actions of the actors.

The similarities of these equations to the simple growth equations of Verhulst in 2.3 are of course not by chance because they express the universal logic of developmental processes. These equations are more complicated not only because societies are more complex than simple populations but mainly because the equations express the differences and mutual interactions of the two sides of sociocultural evolution. In particular the equations represent not just the changing of states of a system like the usual growth (logistic) equations, but they describe (and explain) the growth of cultures on the one hand in dependency on the degree of role differentiation, and on the other hand the variation of just these differentiation values in dependency of, the cultural development.

The mutual dependency of two variables is, by itself, nothing new and for example expressed in the predator-prey equations by Lotka and Volterra, which describe the changes of population size for both species.

In contrast, the sociocultural equations describe the changing of the state of a culture C in dependency on a regulating sociocultural value and the changing of this value in dependency on the states of the culture. If we borrow once again from Bateson the concept of two different logical levels, then we may say that the usual equations describe the mutual dependency of two or more variables belonging to one and the same level, i.e., states of a system; our equations describe a mutual dependency of variables on two differing levels: the first represents the states of a cultural system, the second expresses the "state" of the social rules that regulate the dynamics of the state succession on the first. Obviously this is the formal expression of the considerations made above about competence/meta competence and loops of different orders, defined for the case of sociocultural evolution. This interaction of two levels also describes the interdependency of the cultural and the social dimension of sociocultural evolution: cultural development determines the social structure and *vice versa*.

It is important to see that although the concept of levels is a metaphorical one, the sociocultural equations describe an evolutionary dynamics, which is indeed two-dimensional and therefore not to be mixed up with usual feed-back processes like those expressed in the Lotka-Volterra equations. EP defines a *structural* feature of sociocultural systems, i.e., a relation between social roles. C on the other hand expresses the level of a culture, that is, a quantitative measure of cultural achievements. The relations between these two logically quite different aspects of societies that are expressed in the sociocultural equations are *mathematically and logically not the same* as the relations, e.g., between different populations whose sizes vary in mutual dependency. This is a relation on one logical level because we have just the interdependency of two variables of the same kind. The sociocultural equations, as well as the ontogenetic equations described in the next subchapter, express the interdependency of structural and quantitative features as well as the interdependency of two different *analytical* dimensions of sociocultural systems.

In a certain formal sense this reminds one of a game player who changes the rules of the game according to his winnings or losses. Yet in contrast to a game where the sense of it is in playing always according to constant rules, else it would be no game at all, evolutionary processes are just characterised by their ability to change their rules according to their evolutionary success. The importance of selection in biological evolution is to be understood in exactly the same manner: genomes as rule systems for the epigenesis are changed if and when the environmental circumstances require it.[49]

Discrete mathematical representations of systems that generate their states recursively, i.e. generate state S_{n+1} according to certain rules from state(s) s_n, s_{n-1} and so forth, are also called Markov chains, which have been examined rather thoroughly. Rather famous has become the "Fibonacci-sequence" $x_n = x_{n-1} + x_{n-2}$, which can be used for the computation of population growth under certain conditions (Hofbauer and Sigmund 1984). In our case we obviously have a "two-dimensional" stochastic Markov chain, which makes the matter a bit more complicated although it can be treated in the same way as "normal" Markov chains.

It is quite possible that the principle of the continuous interaction of competence and meta-competence holds not only for cognitive and sociocultural systems. Biological systems for example may be treated in just the same way. Competence for these systems may be defined with a generalisation of the fitness concept: the degree of fitness is measured by the number of *different* problems with which an organism or a species can deal. As the ability to deal with many problems clearly gives a species more reproductive possibilities than a species that can deal with only few this definition is obviously closely related to the classical definition of fitness or perhaps even equivalent. Meta-competence then is measured by the degree of physiological differentiation that the species has at its disposal, in particular of course the differentiation of the brain. It then seems quite probable that biological evolution can also be defined as a self-reinforcing process by which the fitness of a species is dependent upon its degree of differentiation and in turn the growth of fitness enlarges that of differentiation. Unfortunately I know of no

---

[49] To be sure, a correct statement is that variations of the genome are evolutionariöy successful if and when the environmental conditions favor the according phenotype. By the way, the whole principle is a mathematical expression of a famous story, that of the lying Baron von Münchhausen who, according to his own tale, managed to pull himself and his horse out of a swamp by his hair. In Klüver 2000 we referred to the similiarity of this improbable story to the logical structure of adaptive systems in general. Perhaps Münchhausen was no liar at all.

evolutionary biologists who have analysed biological evolution this way, in particular with the use of mathematical models. As a biological layman I can only suggest this idea to a related field of research.

If these biological speculations are not valid then at least we have here a principle that obviously holds for the cases of ontogenetic development and sociocultural evolution. According to these considerations we enlarged the basic model of the last subchapter by adding the following algorithms, which define the g-function.

(1) If EP is sufficiently high, then the increasing of the number of occupants of the same role in one coherent cluster will also increase the local EP-value, *dependent on the level of knowledge acquired by the members of the cluster.* In other words, the association of occupants of the same role will increase their ability to discover and solve new problems because either their particular IAR-values are increased, or their IER-values are decreased, or both, if their knowledge has reached a certain level. Note that these effects are only locally defined, i.e., the EP-values might differ in different parts of our artificial society.

(2) If a cluster of occupants of the same role is sufficiently large and if the IER-values are sufficiently low in relation to the IAR-values (if EP is sufficiently high) and if the level of knowledge in the cluster is sufficiently high, then actors who are in the neighbourhood of this cluster and who occupy another role, may take over the role of the cluster with a certain probability.

(3) If a cluster according to (1) and (2) is sufficiently large and EP is sufficiently high and if the knowledge has reached a certain level, then new individuals may take over the role of the cluster with a certain probability, regardless, which other roles are in their neighbourhood.

(4) If there is at least one successful cluster for which rule (1) is valid then occupants of another role who are in the neighbourhood of this cluster and whose knowledge has reached a certain level may also generate a cluster containing occupants of this role; for this cluster rule (1) becomes valid even if the new cluster is not as large as the first one.

In terms of sociological concepts rules (2) and (3) mean that successful clusters, i.e., clusters that are rather advanced in regard to knowledge acquisition, will attract adult and new individuals to join this social association. Rule (4) means that one successful cluster may serve as a positive example for changing the whole structure of the society.

It is important to note that the rules (1), (2), (3) and (4) are logically independent. One may introduce rule (1) but not the other three and accordingly one may introduce rules (2) and/or (3) but not (1). To be sure, if (1) is not valid then neither is rule (4). In this case the forming and enlarging of clusters will have no effect on the evolution of the society because the EP-values will not change by local processes. "Sufficiently high", and "certain probability" mean of course that these are parameters whose influence on the development of the system has to be investigated.

I call this kind of dynamics that varies its own *structural initial conditions* in dependency on its own progress *third order dynamics,* a concept that will be explained in detail in Chapter 5.

Several additional remarks are necessary:

(a) Dynamics in the sense just described, i.e., a two-dimensional positive feedback, will happen obviously only in the case rule (1) is valid. If the generation of local clusters has no effect on the EP-value, then even a society that allows the associations of occupants of the same role will not transcend its particular cultural attractor if its EP-values are not high. By the way, that may have been the difference between feudal China and the Islamic cultures: in China associations of occupants of the same technical role were practically forbidden, as Needham observed (see above Chapter 2). Therefore no increasing of local EP-values by local associations was possible, and that meant the stagnation of Chinese culture because of their low initial EP-values. In regard to Islamic societies on the other hand I know of no regulations against the forming of associations, i.e., geometrical clusters in our model. Yet these clusterings apparently had no evolutionary effect for these societies, probably because the homogeneous impact of the Islamic religion was so great that the EP-value always stayed low. In terms of our model that means that rule (1) was not effective despite the possible validity of rules (2) and (3). Of course rule (4) was not valid either in this case.

(b) Rule (1) in particular demands as one condition "sufficiently high EP-values". Only societies that are already differentiated to a certain degree at their beginnings will have a chance to evolve according to third order dynamics, i.e., that kind of dynamics, which regulates the system's evolution by changing the structural initial conditions (see below 5.1), via introducing rule (1) and the other three.

I discussed in Chapter 2 the similarities and differences between the cases of feudal Japan and medieval Europe and noted the fact that the development of two systems with rather similar initial conditions may differ greatly in the long run. It seems very probable to me that the initially small differences between feudal Japan and Europe may have been differences in the EP-values, that is sociocultural differentiation. The degree of sociocultural differentiation in Europe was just large enough so that third order dynamics could happen, with all its evolutionary consequences; in Japan the degree of differentiation was just a little smaller so that third order dynamics could not unfold. Mathematically speaking the g-function of the sociocultural equations had in this society the form g = const. or g = id. Japan stayed in its particular attractor and Europe evolved dramatically. According to the results of preliminary experiments done by Jörn Schmidt and I with these rules, we assume that even small increasings of the initial EP-values will have large effects for the society, that is, if third order dynamics becomes effective or not. I discussed in Chapter 2 the similarities and differences between the cases of feudal Japan and medieval Europe and noted the fact that the development of two systems with rather similar initial conditions may differ greatly in the long run.

(c) Rules (1) to (4) are all locally defined. Therefore, as was mentioned above, the effects of these rules may change the local geometry of the society in the sense that different EP-values, and that means different kinds of interaction, will take place in different regions of the society. EP is defined in terms of the cultural matrix but the additional rules may change the interaction matrix too, because the generation of clusters and the changing of the relations between roles will have effects on the conditions, which role occupants interact with which other actors. It is too early for us to give precise results in regard to the geometrical effects of the rules, as we are still analysing the total impact of them on our model. But one interesting observation can already be made:

Mathematically speaking the social space of a system with third order dynamics that unfolds locally has astonishing parallels to a so-called Riemann space which Einstein used in the General Theory of Relativity. In both types of space, in our case the topological/metrical connections of the societal web, the local geometry is dependent upon the local "mass concentration" which means in a social space of course the forming of clusters of occupants of the same role, i.e., local concentrations of "social masses". We cannot describe yet social spaces in terms of Riemann geometry in an exact manner, but I do not think that these mathematical parallels are by chance. It may well be that we have here a very general and very abstract case of an "evolutionary universal". However, before I consider these problems in detail a bit more, it is time to make some remarks about the problem of cognitive ontogenesis, that is, ontogenetic evolution.

4.3   A MODEL OF CREATIVE COGNITIVE ONTOGENESIS (TOGETHER WITH CHRISTINA STOICA)

Sperber (1996) articulated one of the main objections against too simple concepts of cultural units like "memes" and the like, namely that those concepts do not take into account the undeniable fact that intelligent actors "construct" actively the concepts and cognitive categories they use for world representations (and problem solvings). Even learning processes by which people take over concepts from other people are no simple imitating processes, but rather complex constructive ones, whose results are dependent on the individual learning biography of the learners and the social context in which they take over the new concepts. Therefore, in a strict sense, no two persons have the same concepts in mind (or brain), although they may use the same symbols for it. The cultural transmission hypothesis usually neglects this fact. A similar objection was raised by Durham and Weingart (1997) by referring to the linguistic theory of Lakoff (loc.cit.): concepts and categories are not independent units but are always embedded in semantic fields and clustered around "prototypes"; yet these embeddings and clusterings are again the results of an active acquisition by the learner and not of a passive taking over in the form of imitation (see above 1.4.). Insofar as these arguments are common knowledge in the cognitive sciences, the cultural transmission theories are based on a too simple concept of learning that was abandoned some time ago.

We are reminding of these objections already discussed in 1.4. because they emphasise the necessity to have a closer look at the way humans learn and, in particular, create new ideas. To be sure, a theory of sociocultural evolution does not necessarily need a special theory of cognitive ontogenesis but could leave that to the cognitive sciences; after all they have reached important results in this area. However, because in this book the importance of creative and learning social actors has been stressed again and again and because there still is no generally accepted *mathematical* model for these processes, we would like to sketch some mathematical foundations for such models. The following considerations are rather preliminary as this part of the whole "evolution project" at the University of Essen is still in an early stage. However, we are quite sure that each attempt to construct the foundations of mathematical theories of sociocultural evolution will not be fulfilled without an exact model of some principles of cognitive ontogenesis, and therefore we shall develop a basic model for this task.[50] In other words: it is not a matter of indifference for the social sciences in which precise manner the socio-individual processes of knowledge acquisition and knowledge generating operate; without taking these processes in regard theories of sociocultural evolution will remain incomplete in a very important aspect and will have to go along with vague and hazy assumptions about their own foundations.

There is still another and even more important reason for looking for principles of cognitive ontogenesis. In the last subchapter a rather special type of dynamics was introduced, which seems to be particularly important for sociocultural evolution and which may be a special common characteristic of both cognitive ontogenesis and sociocultural evolution, that is, the evolutionary development of cognitive and sociocultural systems. If this is the case then it is even more important to investigate *how* this particular dynamics regulates evolutionary development in both kinds of systems and whether there is not only a formal parallel in this respect between cognitive and sociocultural systems but also a causal relation: the dynamics of sociocultural systems may be an effect of the ontogenetic one. We shall see that this is indeed the case and that it is possible to extend the sociocultural equations to general sociocultural-ontogenetic equations.

In the SCA-model described in the last subchapters the problem solving strategies of the (intelligent) actors were simply defined as

---

[50] Christina Stoica is writing her *Habilitation* (second and advanced doctoral thesis) about this subject and will give more considerations and results therein.

different numbers of time steps in which the actors had to reach an index number – the symbol of the problem. Strictly speaking that is a "black box view" of the actors because they were just defined as simple finite state automata that operate according to specific rules and change their states –their knowledge thereby. From a purely sociological point of view this definition can be justified because sociologists deal primarily with social structures and their impacts on social actors; these can be treated accordingly as finite state automata (but only from this point of view). However, an approximately complete theory of social processes that bears in mind the objections by Sperber and Durham/Weingart as well as the importance of problem solving actors that is emphasised in this book must go a bit deeper and try to model cognitive processes as well. By doing this it will be possible to analyse these processes in dependency on the social environment by computer experiments in the same way as we did with social evolutionary processes, via the SCA. Therefore we have to look, in a manner of speaking, *into* the intelligent actors.

The mathematical model we wish to describe is by no means complete and in particular it is not a basis for an Artificial Intelligence, whatever that may be. It just captures some of the numerous cognitive processes, which we all mean when speaking about intelligence. It is up to the experiments we have to do with the model to decide if those processes modelled by our algorithms are important (and sufficient) for our purpose, i.e., the analysis of creative thinking and learning in dependency on particular environments. To be sure, we know ourselves that the model must and will be extended.

Since the first discussions about artificial intelligence (AI) in the fifties, two differing paradigms of mathematical models of intelligence were postulated and developed. The partisans of the first paradigm saw intelligence as an ensemble of rule governed operations, and developed accordingly rule based or knowledge based systems as formal models for intelligent behaviours; these systems became famous under the misleading headings of "expert systems". In a very rough sense these systems had the purpose to model some operations of the conscious mind; because the rules of these systems were defined and constructed as symbol manipulating ones, the whole approach was also named as "symbolic AI".

The second paradigm became known as "subsymbolic AI" (Hofstadter 1986), which meant that the formal units of the operating systems are not necessarily symbols but that symbols are stored up in the systems in a "distributed" way: the systems contain the symbols with which they operate only implicitly, i.e., distributed over the whole structure of the system. The main modelling techniques used in this approach are artificial neural nets, which serve as a mathematical approximation for cognitive processes of the brain (not the mind, which is thought to be a symbol processing device). Artificial neural nets, NN in the following considerations, are constructed roughly according to the basic architecture of the brain: the units of the NN are meant to represent the neurons in the brain; the synaptic links between neurons are represented by "weights", i.e., real numbers, which reinforce or lessen the values of the units states (excitatory or inhibitory links). Specific rules –the activation rules –regulate the changing of these states in the net; additional "learning rules" make it possible that a NN changes its structure – the matrix of the weights – according to special learning tasks (cf. as introductions to NN Stoica 2000; Mainzer 1997). Because the intelligent operations are modelled this way by an ensemble of different units that are connected as one or several nets, this approach was also labelled as "connectionistic".

To be sure, it is possible to model learning and knowledge generating actors with both approaches. Rule based systems can be constructed in a way that they are able to learn too, e.g. by coupling them with genetic algorithms (cf. the "classifier systems" in Holland et al. 1986). In a very general mathematical sense each rule based system can be mapped onto an equivalent NN and *vice versa*, that is, each learning process can be modelled by using either a learning rule based system or an appropriate NN. For our purpose we decided to undertake the modelling with NNs for several theoretical reasons, of which the most important one is that the modelling of heterogeneity or differentiation, respectively, which was discussed in the last subchapter, can be done with NN in a rather elegant manner; another reason is that we are interested in a general theory of meaning and communication for which, in our opinion, NN are suited best. A lot of operations that we call intelligent are done rather unconsciously without using symbols explicitly; therefore a subsymbolic approach is more general than a symbolic one.[51]

When modelling intelligent operations like learning and the generation of new ideas one has to consider of course many different aspects, which we cannot all capture in our still rather simple model. We therefore had to decide which operations our model should represent as a starter. According to our knowledge about cognitive operations, we selected the following ones, which certainly belong to the important activities any learning system has to be able to do. By the way, when we use the term "concept" in the following paragraphs we mean it in a very general sense to designate different forms of the synopsis of information in a cognitive system –brain or mind. A concept can be the verbal symbol for a class of animals like "dog", it can be the explanation for a process like the cause of an effect, and it can be part of a world view like "Athene" in Greek theology.

a) Learning is done, at least by humans, in two ways: on the one hand learning occurs in a supervised manner, i.e. the learner receives an immediate response (valuation) when having solved a problem. The classical example for supervised learning processes are interactions in the classroom between teacher and pupils, when the teacher values each answer to his questions with "right" or "wrong". Other examples are the orientating processes of little children, when they have to learn the difference between hot and cold things by touching them.

On the other hand there are learning processes that are not supervised, which means that the cognitive task has to be fulfilled by applying particular schemas, which the learner has previously learned. Usually these processes are done without immediate responses, or valuations, respectively, by the environment. A classical example that we also use is the construction of semantic networks (cf. Lakoff loc. cit.), i.e., the ordering and structuring of concepts learned independently from another – the accommodation process of Piaget. This process usually has to be done without immediate response.

---

[51] It is possible to describe approximately the relation between symbolic and subsymbolic systems in the manner that symbolic systems are the result of subsymbolic operations.

In a general sense all learning processes are supervised because even the highest cognitive achievements in theoretical science or philosophy are finally valued by the environment of the thinker. If, for example, a child has constructed a semantic network about animals and, after having seen the TV-series about the dolphin Flipper, it places the concept of dolphin into the category "fish", the child will be corrected sooner or later. Therefore it would be more adequate to distinguish between learning processes with and without *immediate and direct* responses. However, because the concepts of supervised and nonsupervised learning are generally used, we shall also use them.

b) Each cognitive system has not only to learn concepts, including solutions of problems, by other people but it also often has the problem of creating its own concepts. This creative operation is, of course, not done arbitrarily but mainly by formation of analogy. In other words, if a learner has to create new concepts by himself without supervision he/she will rather often (perhaps not always) do so by applying the logic he/she has previously learned when learning concepts from other people. A student of mathematics, e.g., who has learned the technique of constructing proofs by contradiction, like the famous proof of Euclides about the infinity of prime numbers, will without doubt try this technique when he is confronted with a new problem. This ability is certainly more than learning in the sense described above because the cognitive system has to enlarge its knowledge without the aid of other experienced people. To be sure, the results of these operations must and will be valued by the environment too but not necessarily by others who already know the "right" solution. "Formation of analogy" therefore is basically nothing more than the application of a certain technique of problem solving to a new problem [52]

c) Last but not least, concept formation occurs not only on one level but on different ones. A child learns the concept of dogs by seeing (and hearing or smelling) different examples of this species in the same way it

---

[52] It is quite reasonable, by the way, to imagine that the creation of a new *technique of problem solving* often also occurs by using formation of analogy, though on a higher level. The mathematical proof by *reductio ad absurdum* for example may have been invented by applying the "negative" principle to avoid contradictions by all means to the "positive" task to prove certain mathematical statements and enlarge mathematical knowledge.

learns concepts like cat and horse. It also learns concepts like butterflies, fish and frogs. These concepts may be called for our rather pragmatic purposes "first level concepts". The next level will be reached when the child learns what concepts like dog and cat have in common, in contrast to concepts like fish or butterfly. This cognitive experience of conceptual difference the child will usually treat with the formation of a "second order concept", in this case the concept of mammals. Accordingly, it is possible to generate third order concepts and so on. In particular this process may become quite far detached from empirical observations and by that acquires a logic of its own. Some of the greatest achievements in mathematics and philosophy, e.g., were reached by processes like this; the extension of the number concept from the integers to abstract entities in multi-dimensional spaces like the space of the quaternions is only one example. Integers and the handling of them by the simple operations of arithmetic were almost certainly discovered by manipulating, i.e., counting sets of physical objects; in contrast to this concepts like real numbers or complex ones are defined by referring to characteristics of integers, and *not* to those of physical objects.

To be sure, these operations are certainly not the whole of intelligence and therefore the model described below is not to be understood as a model of intelligence in general. However, a model of these operations is certainly a starter which, enables us to examine important cognitive operations in dependency on particular environments.

The model consists of several neural nets of two different types. The first type, which is used for the modelling of supervised learning and the generating of new first and second order concepts, is a so-called "bi-directional associative network" (BAM); the second type, which is used for the modelling of the generation of semantic networks, is a "Kohonen feature map", which is able to learn in a nonsupervised way.

BAM-networks operate in the following way (for a detailed description see Kosko 1987 and 1988 or any textbook on neural nets): the net receives pairs of patterns, usually coded as binary vectors $X = (x_i) = (1,-1,-1,1, \ldots)$ and $Y = (y_i)$. The task is to learn the connection between the two patterns, i.e., when receiving just one vector to generate the other. (The term "bi"directional means that a BAM-net is able to do this in both directions: when receiving (x_i) the net remembers (y_i) and *vice versa*. For our purposes it is useful to understand (x_i) as the representation of a set of information, e.g., visual ones and (y_i) as the "concept" that belongs to the X-set of information. Therefore, learning the connection between the two patterns is a formal model of learning the connections between, for example, sensual information and the concepts, which belong to them. This is an example of supervised learning because both patterns are given to the net by its environment.

When having received the two patterns –usually several pairs of patterns – the net constructs a "weight matrix" W by performing some algebraic operations, i.e. by using a particular form of vector multiplication X * Y. We will skip these technical details and refer to the literature about BAM-nets. The matrix W is the decisive point, that is, its construction is the formal model of the learning process: when a BAM-net receives just the vector X after having constructed W, it performs another operation of vector and matrix algebra and reconstructs Y – it "remembers" Y by using W.[53]

Readers not familiar with artificial neural nets may be a bit astonished when they get some algebraic operations as the formal model for learning processes. This book is not the place to argue if perhaps just these operations are a well suited model for the "active" construction processes of the brain. It may be enough for our interests here to note the general aspect of all models of learning processes done by connectionistic approaches: learning is principally defined here as the construction of an appropriate weight matrix, that is a matrix that represents the different connections between the units of formal nets. This is done either in a supervised way or in an unsupervised fashion. The final weight matrix W is literally the knowledge gained as the result of the learning process. In other words, the learned knowledge is not accumulated as a set of symbols in a special store, but is represented in the matrix W. That is why we operate here with a subsymbolic approach. To be sure, this is exactly the case with the brain, which contains no special stores of symbols either but just particular connections between its neurons. In a very abstract manner of speaking one may say that the "computational

---

[53] For readers who are acquainted with learning neural nets we add that BAM-nets are not trained in the way usual for supervised learning nets. The BAM-net does this by "itself", i.e., by performing the algebraic operations. It is possible to extend the BAM-model described above by using real numbers instead of just 1 and -1. These "dynamical" BAM-nets must be trained in the usual fashion.

brain" (Churchland and Sejnowski 1992) performs its learning processes by constructing a mathematical pattern in itself. Therefore our BAM-net approach is not as strange as it may seem at first sight.

The particular advantage of BAM-nets for our purposes is its bi-directionality, which we can use for the formation of analogies. The basic idea is that a BAM-net uses for this task a matrix W, which has already been constructed by another net. This is done the following way: when a BAM-net receives a vector, i.e., a pattern X without the matching Y it has to construct Y by itself. To do this it examines all vectors X_i that have already been learned by itself or other subnets together with matching Y_i. The net chooses the vector X_k which is the most similar to the new vector X. This is be done by using the so-called Hamming distance definition which is a simple measure for the similarity of different vectors. Then the net takes over the weight matrix W_k which represents the connection between X_k and its "counterpart" Y_k and it constructs a new vector Y, which is the counterpart of the new vector X. Obviously this is a formal representation of the formation of analogy because now the connection between X and Y is defined as the connection between the pair X_k and Y_k or in other words, the construction of Y is done by the same logic that had been learned for the connection between some similar vectors.

By using BAM-nets in this way it is apparently possible to model two of the operations mentioned above, namely the (supervised) learning and remembering of the connections between information and concepts on the one hand and the generation of new concepts by formations of analogies on the other. We also use BAM-nets for a third task, i.e., the "invention" of second order concepts. However, because this can be done only when the whole cognitive system has learned to construct semantic networks, we have to first describe the second type of neural nets with which our cognitive system operates, that is the Kohonen feature map (e.g. Kohonen 1987).

A Kohonen feature map (KM) is the best known example of unsupervised learning. Its operations also start with different pairs of vectors which are again the representations of some sets of information, e.g., sensual ones and the concepts associated with them. An illustrative example has been given by Kohonen and Ritter (1989): when a child sees animals like dogs, cats or cattle, it learns to attach different sensual information to them like "small versus big", "barking versus meowing", "feeding on flesh" versus "feeding on plants" and so on. This information is again coded in the form of binary vectors X; the same is done with the assigned concepts which form vectors Y. The KM now operates on the X-vectors, i.e., it constructs clusters of them according to their similarity. If the X-vector of "dog" is more similar to the X-vector of "cat" than to the X-vector of "cattle" or "bird" the KM associates the first two vectors and therefore their Y-counterparts, and distinguishes them from the other vectors; these form other clusters until all concepts have been associated in specific clusters. The KM reaches an attractor, i.e., it does not alter its ordering operations any more, when each concept has been put into one special cluster. The resulting ensemble of clusters is the formal representation of a semantic network. We again skip the mathematical details because it is sufficient here to understand the principal logic of a KM. The following picture shows the result of the operations of a KM, i.e., the clustering of concepts for different animals.

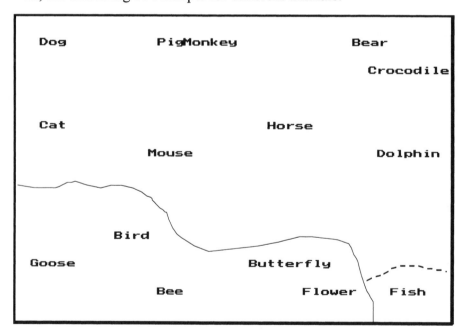

Picture 1: A semantical network as the result of KM operations

Like BAM-nets a KM is a deterministic system without stochastic components. Yet like most complex deterministic systems a KM is crucially dependent on its initial states: mathematically speaking the KM has to solve an underdetermined problem which means that there is usually more than one solution. It is always possible to argue whether a dog is more similar to a pig, both are domesticated animals, than to a fox which is a wild animal. The result of one run of a KM depends in this case, simply speaking, on whether the KM started its ordering operations with the fox or with the pig. We think that this is not a disadvantage of KMs but that in reality the construction of semantical networks is also dependent on the order of succession that human learners become acquainted with different concepts. To be sure, sooner or later the learner has to understand that there are types of clusters that are socially more accepted than others –the "right" clusters of biological concepts are defined by the science of biology. This is an example of the fact mentioned above that in the long run there is no unsupervised learning in a strict sense, but only such learning that is performed without immediate response by the environment of the learner.

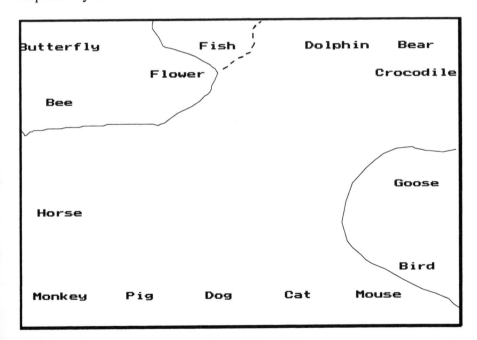

Picture 2: A semantical network with the same concepts but another starting concept

For our purpose of constructing a model of cognitive systems that can perform different cognitive operations, one or more KMs are coupled with the BAM-nets. The KM takes over the pairs of vectors that the BAM-nets have learned and arranges the Y-vectors by constructing clusters. The same goes for the new Ys that the BAM-nets have constructed by formations of analogies. In this way our whole system is able to generate and enlarge semantic networks on the foundation of unsupervised learning and the "creative" invention of new concepts.

The mentioned effect that the result of KM-operations depends on the initial state, i.e., on the concept with which the KM started when forming clusters, shows that the generation of semantic networks is in an important way dependent upon the environment of the learning system. Children who get to know animals rather early will form other clusters *with the same concepts* than children who later became acquainted with animals. The two pictures above demonstrated that the results can be quite different when choosing different initial concepts. However, a culture is defined as the knowledge *common* to all members of this culture and therefore the social environment has to evaluate the different semantic networks that children have generated, depending on their different environment. This is done in our model in the following way:

The topological space of the different clusters is transformed into a metrical one by placing the concepts into the cells of a grid, similar to the grids of cellular automata. A distance d between two concepts X and Y is defined simply by the following convention: $d(X,X) = 0$; $d(X,Y) = n$ if n is the smallest number of cells between X and Y, that is, the shortest way on the grid between X and Y. One can easily show that d defines a distance in the strictly metrical sense of the word (cf. Klüver 2000).

The distances between the concepts of a semantical network of the magnitude m give us a m * m matrix, which defines the connections between all concepts. The valuation of this semantical network by the environment occurs simply by presenting another (or the same) m*m matrix, which is compared with the first matrix, constructed by our cognitive systems. This is done by writing both matrices as m*m-dimensional vectors whose differences are measured by the Euclidean distance. The cognitive system then has to change its own matrix according to the size of the difference.

It is now possible to generate second order concepts by again applying the operations described above. To do this, a "second order BAM-net" receives one cluster of the semantic network that the KM has constructed as a "second order X-vector". Note that this second order vector consists of the different Ys that the KM has put together in one specific cluster. Because this second order X-vector is also encoded in a binary fashion, it is possible to compare it to the first order X-vectors that the different BAM-nets have used for learning and generating the associated Ys. The second order BAM-net again takes the first order X-vector that is most similar to the second order X-vector taken from one cluster, uses again the associated W-matrix and constructs a second order concept Y', which is again generated according to a logic which has been successful in the (cognitive) past of our system. Another KM, also a second order one, takes over and generates a second order semantic network following the same logic as the first order KM. We leave to other cognitive scientists if it is more appropriate to connect the second order semantic network with the first order one, or if the two semantic networks would be better separated.[54]

Obviously the construction of second order concepts is done by formation of analogy. Though we cannot state the reasons for this assumption in detail here, we believe that this is just the way second order concepts are generated: they are formed according to the logic that the cognitive system has found appropriate for problems on a lower logical level. To be sure, it is quite easy to generate third order concepts in this way and so on.

Apparently our cognitive system is now able to perform the cognitive operations described above. The whole system can be illustrated by a graphic overview.

---

[54] In an informal manner Flohr (1991) has also proposed to model cognitive processes by arranging a cognitive system in layers or loops, respectively.

The coupling of different cognitive operations

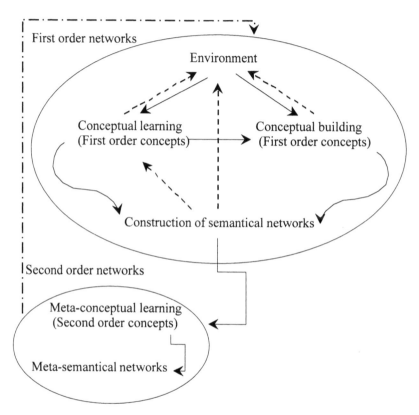

Figure 9: The model of cognitive ontogenesis

The usage of the terms "first order" and "second order" might not be understood in the way that we mean with them a strict sequence in only one direction from lower to higher orders. In 4.2. it was emphasised that adaptive systems are characterised by a continuous interdependency among all "levels" or orders, respectively. The same holds of course in this case: second order concepts may be used to correct some clusters in the first order semantic network if the environment of the cognitive system produces negative responses to second order concepts gained by the first order network. In the culturally "right" way a dog belongs in the same cluster as the fox and not in the cluster of the pigs, because biology, as the culturally accepted arbiter in such questions, does not generate clusters of animal concepts along the distinction "domesticated versus wild". The "right" second order concept in this case for dogs and foxes is therefore "predator". For these reasons all lines in our little picture have to be understood as bi-directional connections.

Our artificial system becomes a model of ontogenesis via the following developmental assumptions: the beginning of the ontogenetic process is the generation of first order BAM-networks, which are only learning supervisedly. The next ontogenetic step is the generation of a KM, which allows for the construction of simple semantic network consisting of different clusters; this network is evaluated by the environment. Thirdly new first order BAM-networks are generated which are able to use analogies in order to construct new concepts. The fourth ontogenetic step is the construction of second order BAM-networks, which generate second order concepts; finally, a second order KM is generated, which gives the whole system a second order semantic network. Though our experiments at present go no further, it is of course easily possible (at least in principle) to elongate this ontogenetic process in the same way.

Our model obviously now allows to apply the general principles of (sociocultural and cognitive) evolution. We already mentioned in 4.2. that terms like "competence" and "meta-competence" must be reformulated by using the general principle of heterogeneity, that is, the evolution of difference by the evolution of competence and *vice versa*. "Difference" in our model means *the difference of the clusters* the semantic network consists of. This is measured in the following way: the clusters consist of concepts, i.e., pairs of (X,Y) vectors with components x_i and y_j, respectively. The program constructs for each cluster the intersection of the components x_i and y_j of all the cluster concepts and orders them in a vector (intersection x_i, intersection y_j). This is done for all clusters. The program then computes the differences between each pair of clusters, measured again with the Hamming distance. *The measure of heterogeneity of the semantic network, and that means of the cognitive system, is the mean value of the differences of all cluster pairs.* We call this measure EP_O as the "ontogenetic evolutionary parameter".

The cognitive competence of our cognitive system is of course defined by the number of different concepts the system has at its disposal at a certain time. The meta-competence of our system then, defined by its heterogeneity in regard to the clusters of the semantical network, is the generator of the system's competence: the more different clusters the semantical network consists of the more differentiated the perception of the system becomes, i.e., the more different BAM-networks have to be generated in order to learn new X and Y vectors. The reason for this is the fact that comparatively different clusters in a semantical network force a cognitive system to consider even small differences between new sets of information, new X-vectors, and old ones. Rather similar clusters allow the cognitive system to handle small differences in a rather neglecting manner, that is to overlook the differences between the new information and that already learned. In this case the cognitive system does not have to store new concepts for the new information. In cases where the clusters are already very different, even small differences between new concepts, i.e., small differences in the x- and y-components, cannot be neglected and new concepts have to be generated. In this sense the enlarging of meta-competence causes the enlarging of competence, i.e., the number of different concepts. In our artificial model we take this in account of by defining a rate of the generation of new BAM-nets in relation to the degree of heterogeneity among the (evaluated) clusters.

The same holds in turn for the dependency of the meta-competence on the degree of competence. The more different concepts a system has at its disposal, the more difference the system is able to perceive, and the more heterogeneity the system will generate. To illustrate this, let us imagine the cognitive ontogenesis of a baby, which literally has only the difference between "me" and "the world", usually represented by its mother. In the sense of Piaget's theory the baby assimilates all information into this simple dual schema. The baby then learns to distinguish between "me" on the one hand and "mother" and "not mother" on the other hand – again a binary schema. The same procedure can be imagined for the concept "me", e.g., different parts of the body. Obviously its competence *and* its meta competence have been enlarged, because a concept or cluster "not mother" contains more different components to the different subconcepts of "me" than only the concept "mother". Another process of using analogies now becomes effective: by learning that things that had until now been perceived as identical are different the child presumes that this may also hold with other things previously perceived as identical. Then accommodation in the sense of Piaget steps in, i.e., the child enlarges its cognitive structure by introducing, e.g., the difference between "things that can be eaten" and "things that cannot" into its category "not mother". Because the environment evaluates this accommodation as valid, the child establishes this new difference and tries by the same process new differentiations of the category "not mother". If these are successful, i.e. confirmed by successful assimilations of information, then the child will go on until its biological limits, which are defined by the capacity of the human brain, have been reached. In this sense we have again the enlargement of meta-competence by the (growth of) competence of the system.

By the way, it is easy to translate this definition of heterogeneity into neurobiological terms, that is the "language" of the brain. "Difference of clusters" can be understood as the degree of strength of connections between neural clusters, which "represent" connected sets of concepts in the brain. Similar clusters in our artificial semantic network represent neural clusters with strong connections, different clusters correspond neural ones with weak connections. Apparently our model is neurobiologically well based; the parallels between the sociocultural definition of heterogeneity and the neurobiological one are certainly not by chance.

It is of course dependent upon the information that the environment gives our cognitive system how fast the process of the mutual reinforcement of competence and meta-competence will be: the more heterogeneous the environment, i.e., the more different the X-vectors presented to our system, the more different clusters the semantical network(s) will contain and *vice versa*. The "dialectical" relation between cognitive competence and meta-competence will become effective only if the environment contains "enough" heterogeneity. This crucial importance of environment for cognitive ontogenesis has been observed very often; the same holds of course for sociocultural evolution, as mentioned above.

To be sure, this process is neither automatic nor without limits. The biological limits of the human brain as an absolute threshold were previously mentioned and it can be noted that the same goes for sociocultural systems; they can evolve in this manner only as far their material means allow, i.e., the material wealth that enables the system to contain individuals with no contributions to the material reproduction of the society. Besides that the role of the environment becomes crucial here: an environment of our hypothetical child, which does not offer much different information will slow down or even stop this process, because the child has no "external" reasons to try new forms of differences. This important environmental factor certainly also explains some differences between the paths of evolutionary development of sociocultural systems (see below). In particular one must assume that the capabilities represented in our model are not literally the same in all individuals. Yet we believe that this *general* logic of the interdependency of competence and meta-competence explains a universal feature of cognitive ontogenesis; in particular it can explain why the cognitive progress of children in their first years with regard to language and other skills, is as fast as was often noted by researchers in children acquisition processes – children are "natural geniuses" (cf. for language acquisition Pinker 1994).

By systematising these considerations it is again possible to express them in the form of the same schema of equations as was done for sociocultural evolution. If we call the heterogeneity of our cognitive systems EP_0, the evolutionary parameter for cognitive ontogenesis measured by the mean difference between the single clusters at a certain time t, the competence of our system again as C, the number of different concepts the system has at its disposal at the same time, the dependency of C on the state of EP with $C = f(EP)$ and the corresponding dependency of EP on C as $EP = g(C)$, we obviously get the same equations as in 4.2. The "function schemas" f and g have been described above as the mutual dependencies of cluster difference and the number of concepts.

It is important to note that f and g are very different functions in the two cases of sociocultural evolution and cognitive ontogenesis; the common evolutionary principle is a *schema* of equations, not particular equations in the usual sense of the word. The "universality" of evolutionary processes is not to be found in the specific rules that govern these processes in different fields, but in the general principle expressed in the equation schemas.

In the beginning of this subchapter we mentioned the fact that this part of the "evolution project" at Essen is still at an early stage. Therefore we dispense with other results, which could at the present time be only preliminary. The mentioned *Habilitation* of Christina Stoica will demonstrate the possibilities of this cognitive model quite fully.

Let us now come back to the relation between cognitive ontogenesis and sociocultural evolution. The particular sociocultural dynamics that was expressed in the equations in 4.2. can and must be understood as a kind of dynamics that makes itself in an important sense *independent from the system's environment.* This will be analysed more thoroughly in 5.1.; the meaning of this consideration can be illustrated here by referring to the great cultural achievements of different cultures in philosophy, religion, art and finally science. The Greek invention of irrational numbers, e.g., cannot be understood by adaptive behaviours of the Greek culture, that is by the necessity of solving problems posed by the physical or social environment of the Greek *poleis.* These and other achievements must be due to a sociocultural dynamics, which has emancipated itself from the pure adaptive behaviour characteristic, e.g., for biological systems.

Apparently, the cognitive foundation for this capability of sociocultural systems is just the capability of cognitive systems to generate not only first order but also second order concepts, and even those of higher orders. We have already mentioned that this means an emancipation of the information that the physical or social environment presents to the cognitive system, i.e., the cognitive system enlarges its competence (the number of different concepts) by referring to and varying its own conceptual foundations and immanent logic. The statement often articulated by neurobiologists (cf. Roth 1996) that the brain mostly deals with itself, now gets a very elaborated meaning: from a particular stage of development on cognitive operations consist, to a large degree of processes, which refer mainly, or sometimes only, to results of earlier operations and no longer to environmental information. We may safely assume that this is just the source of the rather autonomous sociocultural evolution just emphasised: the cognitive emancipation from direct environmental information of the individual learner and problem solver results, via the SCA, in a cultural development with exactly the same effect. In this sense there are not only parallels between sociocultural evolution and cognitive ontogenesis but the latter is also the cause of the first development and *vice versa*.

The last consideration has to be examined a bit more thoroughly. We already mentioned the importance of the environment for cognitive ontogenesis: only differentiated environments enable cognitive systems to unfold their capacities by using third order dynamics. That is of course not only true for physical environments but in particular for sociocultural ones. A sociocultural milieu that gives no positive reasons for a cognitive system to develop itself will force the system into stagnation, sooner or later. Yet from our analysis of sociocultural evolution it can be learned that those societies offer most favourable conditions for cognitive development that are differentiated to a large degree themselves, and that means they evolve according to third order dynamics (see below 5.1.), that is, that kind of dynamics that evolves itself by changing its initial structural conditions. Therefore sociocultural dynamics is the most important condition for ontogenetic dynamics. On the other hand, obviously, according to the logic of the SCA, only those sociocultural systems can unfold third order dynamics, which contain individuals capable of ontogenetic third order dynamics. We again have a case of positive feedback, which now contains in total four dimensions – the social, the cultural, the cognitive differentiation and the level of individual development, i.e., the number of learned and created concepts. This "four-dimensional" feedback can be formally expressed by a *general sociocultural-ontogenetic equation.*

We remind the reader of the sociocultural equations in 4.2. and of their counterparts for the ontogenetic case. Let K_t denote the individual level of knowledge, i.e., number of concepts in the general sense defined above at time t. The ontogenetic equations are then

$$K_t = f_0 \left(EP_{0,t-1} \right) = f_0 \left(g_0 \left(K_{t-1} \right) \right) \quad \text{and} \tag{1}$$

$$EP_{0,t} = g_0 \left(K_{t-1} \right) = g_0 \left(f_0 \left(EP_{0,t-1} \right) \right). \tag{2}$$

A culture C_t at the same time is nothing more than

$$C_t = \sum K_t, \tag{3}$$

meaning the sum of all individual knowledge in this society (not counting the same knowledge components more than once). Formally speaking the increasing of this sum is dependent upon an average value of the ontogenetic parameter EP_O.

Let us call f_S and g_S the function schemas for the sociocultural case, and accordingly f_O and g_O the function schemas for the ontogenetic one, as was done in equations (1) and (2). By substituting the ontogenetic equations into the sociocultural ones, according to the considerations about the mutual dependency of both cases of evolution, we obtain the general equations

$$C_t = f_S (g_S (\textstyle\sum K_{t-1})) = f_S (g_S (f_O (av.EP_{O,t-1})))$$

$$= f_S (g_S \textstyle\sum (f_O (g_O (K_{t-1})))), \qquad (4)$$

av. EP_O meaning the average degree of ontogenetic heterogeneity, and

$$EP_{s,t} = g_S (C_{t-1})) = g_S (f_S (av.EP_O)) = g_S (f_S av.(g_O ((K_{t-1})))$$

$$= g_S (f_S av.(g_O (f_O (EP_{O,t-1}))))). \qquad (5)$$

In a rather abstract way these equations illustrate how ontogenetic dynamics causes sociocultural dynamics and *vice versa*; in particular one can see that heterogeneity on both levels as well as growth of knowledge on individual and societal level, increase themselves by basing their developments on the other dimensions of society and individuals respectively. The whole process may then be understood as a particular form of four-dimensional Markov chains. Of course, these processes may stagnate or even regress if one or several of the different evolution functions f and g are the identity function, or constant functions.

We now can also describe the effects of inhibition and reinforcement in a bit more in detail than was possible only on the sociocultural level. The effects of inhibition were defined both as the decrease of problem solving capabilities and the inability to recognise new problems outside the limits of the cultural attractor. Decrease of problem solving competence is represented in our model as reduction in generating new concepts by formations of analogies on all levels, which obviously means a decrease of the enlargement of the system's competence. The inability to perceive new problems is represented by the "disturbed" transfer of concepts from the BAM-networks to the KM (the Kohonen feature map), and by the incomplete perception and consideration of x- and y-components in the (X,Y) vectors presented by the environment or created by formation of analogies. In the case of inhibition the KM simply ignores some concepts or components and does not insert them into the semantical network, or only incompletely. In a certain sense these concepts do not exist at all, or only incompletely for the cognitive system though the system has learned and/or generated them. The theoretical idea behind this definition is the assumption that a cognitive system has at its disposal only those concepts that are not isolated but are connected with all or most of the concepts the system has learned and generated so far. We think that this is a rather safe assumption. A similar problem arises for the cognitive system if it perceives and processes concepts only incompletely. Although these concepts are connected with the rest of the semantic network, they are not very satisfactory and exist therefore only partially for the cognitive system. Inhibition means in this case that the semantic networks are "reduced", i.e., they do not contain the knowledge that the cognitive system could get from its environment or by its own operations (formation of analogies, generating concepts of higher order). Reinforcement of course is simply defined by reverse rules and effects.

We connect the sociocultural and the ontogenetic levels of the evolutionary process not only for theoretical reasons and the search for mathematical generalisations. One of our students, Rouven Malecki, is presently (Spring 2002) constructing a program that contains the enlarged SCA, together with the model of cognitive ontogenesis described in this subchapter. In other words, the complete program will consist of an SCA where the individual cells are not just finite state automata but those combinations of neural nets that we have just described. Results of experiments with this rather large program will be published in due time.

As the main subject of this book is the analysis of theoretical and mathematical foundations of sociocultural evolution, we shall not describe this model further as this will be done in other publications. The goal of this subchapter was to demonstrate that it is indeed possible to model cognitive ontogenesis as precisely as sociocultural evolution, and that the former is not only a parallel to the latter but also a causing foundation for sociocultural processes and *vice versa*, as was expressed in the general equations.. To be sure, sociocultural evolution cannot be completely reduced to cognitive ontogenesis; that would be another form of reductive fallacy, which ignores in the same way the importance of social structure, as do the theories of cultural transmission. The SCA takes this into account. Yet the SCA would also be incomplete as a mathematical model without the *formal* foundations of cognitive ontogenesis. We believe that our model is at least a beginning for solving the problems that Sperber (loc. cit.) and Weingart/Durham (loc. cit.) mentioned in regard to cultural transmission theories.

5. CONCLUSIONS: THE LOGIC OF EVOLUTION OR ARE THERE SOMETHING LIKE HISTORICAL LAWS?

5.1 THE THREE ORDERS OF SYSTEMS DYNAMICS

In a certain sense this essay deals mainly with the question of the special evolutionary path of Western societies, which started in the beginning of the Medieval Ages, i.e., the classic question of Max Weber. The reason for this concentration on the European way is, of course, not the Eurocentric opinion that history had its goal in the development of these societies. In the usual meaning history, like all evolutionary processes, has no goal at all but follows the logic of its evolutionary algorithms. Therefore it would be logically meaningless to speak of any historical goals and, in particular, it would be quite absurd to take the Western societies as an "end of history" (Fukuyama). The "end" of dynamical processes is, mathematically speaking, either a simple attractor, which means that by operating with *constant* rules the states of dynamical systems do not change any more, or it is a state that is reached and not left because the important rules of state changing are "switched off". In addition, mathematically things are even more complicated because systems with operating meta rules may also reach an attractor if the meta rules force the rules of interaction into a "meta attractor", i.e., a state of the rules of interaction where the rules do not change any more and generate attractors of the system (cf. Klüver 2000). Yet neither case can be observed in contemporary Western societies; on the contrary, rules of interactions are nearly permanently changed, and attractors are left by rule changing in an equally permanent manner. Whether the evolutionary *logic* that characterises the emergence of the Western societies is an ultimate stage of sociocultural evolution is quite another question, and I shall deal with this problem below.

My concentration on European evolutionary development has, of course, its reasons in the conviction that the emergence of European societies is founded on the unfolding of the particular dynamics that was the subject of the last two subchapters. To be sure, earlier societies were also evolutionarily regulated by "weak" kinds of these dynamics, where sometimes, and only locally, self-reinforcing processes of cultural evolution occurred. Only in the European case were the initial evolutionary conditions, the values of the evolutionary parameter EP, such that the third type of dynamics could become effective and generate the European evolution, which could only lead to modern societies because it functions as the described feedback mechanism *which, among the effects described above, also accelerates its own velocity.* In *this* sense the Western societies are the most advanced of all societies that human history has produced, and in this sense other societies have to adapt to this kind of dynamics, not necessarily to all features of the Western societies, or become mere peripheral secondary regions, as World Systems Theory would call it. As any theory of evolutionary processes has to demonstrate what kind of logic generated the most advanced levels, i.e., to reconstruct the evolutionary processes from their preliminary end, it is rather unavoidable to concentrate on the European case, when trying to develop the foundations of a theory of sociocultural evolution.

The question if there are laws in history is, to be sure, mainly the question if there are principles of sociocultural evolution that explain the historical processes that we know empirically. In 4.2. and 4.3. I dealt with such principles, which were also analysed for the case of cognitive ontogenesis. Before I try to give an answer about the relations of these principles and some theoretical explanations of the processes we know empirically from history, it is necessary to have a more general look at these principles.

In 1.3. I gave a general definition of evolution and described it as a particular type of dynamics, i.e., a *meta dynamics* in the words of Farmer (1990) or *adaptive dynamics.* A dynamic system regulates its own development by adaptive dynamics if the system is able to vary its rules of interaction *according to the demands of its particular environment.* A "simple" dynamics, which is characteristic for most of the systems physics and chemistry are dealing, is characterised by the fact that the system changes its own states by applying its rules of interaction recursively on the preceding states and holding these rules fixed. To be sure, this kind of dynamics is "simple" only in the logical sense that the rules of interaction are not changed; physics and chemistry have shown many times that neither empirically nor mathematically is this dynamics simple in the case of systems that are interesting for research. Let us call this kind of dynamics *first order dynamics*.

In Subchapter 3.1. it was demonstrated that it is possible to classify first order dynamics by the ordering parameters, i.e., mathematical properties of the rules of interaction. Generally the different types of first order dynamics can be classified and explained by the theorem of inequality: the more degrees of inequality a system contains the simpler its first order dynamics will be, that is, its trajectories are characterised by simple attractors and therefore by a stable order.

Adaptive dynamics can be described as *second order dynamics*. Adaptive systems not only change their states according to their rules of interactions, but also their rules themselves if and when environmental conditions are such that the system's states generated by the rules of interaction are not favourable in regard to these conditions. In particular adaptive systems can vary the ordering parameters that characterise the rules of interaction and thus generate new kinds of first order dynamics. Therefore systems that are capable of second order dynamics always have some kind of meta rules, which regulate the changing of the rules of interaction; Holland's genetic algorithm is an example of such meta rules. Yet second order dynamics is always dependent upon environmental conditions: although the varying of rules often happens without regard to any environmental conditions like, for example, mutations of the genome, the environmental selection decides whether these changes are successful, and will therefore remain or not. In the same sense adaptive variations of social structures will often occur as a reaction of a social system to environmental conditions that have, e.g., changed; if the variations of social rules are successful then the system returns to first order dynamics and with great probability to simple attractors, i.e., social order.

It is quite possible to describe and explain the greatest part of sociocultural evolution by an interplay of first and second order dynamics. Sociocultural systems have to maintain their existence in a particular environment, which demands certain achievements in both cultural and social dimensions. If an early society is not able to get along in a particular environment with first order dynamics, then second order dynamics will bring the system into other trajectories, i.e., the generation of new forms of social structure and of new cultural concepts as the competence of the system. If these new achievements are sufficient then, as in most known historical cases, evolution will stop, i.e., the system returns to first order dynamics and it will remain in the according attractors. This was obviously the case not only with early tribal societies but also with most of the agrarian state empires. In particular these systems were not differentiated enough to allow the processes described in 4.2. become effective.

The dynamics described in the preceding subchapters can be called *third order dynamics*. Systems that are principally capable of this type of dynamics, like cognitive and sociocultural systems, contain of course the capability of the "lower" forms of dynamics too, i.e., they generate stable order by producing trajectories with fixed rules and they are able to change their rules if environmental conditions change. However, under certain conditions they can do more, that is, they can generate their trajectories by a dynamics, which is a permanent feedback mechanism between the system's development and the evolutionary conditions that regulate just this evolutionary development. I named this dynamics with a mathematical term, a two-dimensional Markov chain; in a more colloquial way one may describe this kind of dynamics as "the Münchhausen Principle" because the system regulates its dynamical development by applying its own evolutionary logic to its initial states and the initial values of its evolutionary parameters, like the lying Baron did in his story of pulling himself and his horse out of a swamp by his hair. The effect of this Münchhausen Principle is a systemic evolution, which under favourable conditions accelerates its own development and finally, is able to change almost all cultural and social features; mathematically speaking sociocultural systems capable of third order dynamics change the very geometrical conditions with which they started by varying the relations between roles and generating new relations and roles.

Third order dynamics is not *directly* dependent upon environmental selection like second order dynamics, but in a certain sense defines its own criteria of success. The evolution of Western culture cannot be understood mainly as answers to some environmental problems, but only by the logic characteristic for particular problem solving algorithms, which were no longer inhibited by cultural thresholds. Therefore we may say that adaptive systems, i.e., systems of second order dynamics, are in a relation of *coevolution* with their environment, that is a mutual interdependency; systems characterised by third order dynamics are, in contrast, not directly dependent upon their environment but they determine and change it. Third order dynamics depends mainly, as the equations in 4.2. and 4.3 have shown, on the recursive sequences of structural conditions, level of cultures (or cognition) and the feed-back relations between them. To be sure, systems with third order dynamics also have to maintain their existence in a particular environment and must therefore generate states that are favourable with regard to environmental demands. That holds in particular for cultural achievements and political decision structures. However, the development of such systems has an additional logic of its own, which operates not in regard to environmental constraints, as purely adaptive systems do, but takes its own course, *provided basic environmental demands are fulfilled.* The exponential evolutionary rise of Western culture can be explained only in terms of such a kind of logic: cultural, and social, progress fed, so to speak, themselves and changed the physical and social environment of Western societies in the way we all know.[55] In a certain sense, systems characterised by third order dynamics define their own criteria for evolutionary success.

Therefore we have a certain form of "dialectical" relation between the three types of dynamics: first order dynamics operates independently from its environment insofar as these systems are "blind" to environment and follow only their own logic. I presume that the famous term of "autopoiesis" by Maturana and Varela means just that, i.e. a certain blindness with respect to environment (cf. Luhmann 1986). Adaptive systems, on the contrary, take environment into regard and adjust their structure according to environmental conditions. We may understand first and second order dynamics as thesis and antithesis.

Third order dynamics then seems to be the synthesis, in the sense that it contains both characteristics of the first two kinds of dynamics. Like adaptive systems, the systems capable of third order dynamics can

---

[55] I am quite convinced that the development of the so called "axial cultures" (Jaspers) must also be understood at least partially by a certain kind of third order dynamics. Yet apparently the conditions of initial heterogeneity were not favorable enough so that these early cultures (compared to Europe) stagnated in the end in their particular attractors.

change their structure, but, similarly to first order dynamical systems, they do so only partially as reactions to environmental demands and mainly as a characteristic of their own internal development.

To be sure, speaking of these three types of dynamics does *not* mean that the capability of generating its evolution according to, say, third order dynamics, is a property a complex system either has or has not. *Natura non facit saltus,* nature does not make jumps, is a statement that also holds true here. Sociocultural systems like cognitive systems all have this property in principle. It is a question of the initial values of the EP whether a system unfolds this capability or not; in addition it is a question of the *absolute* evolutionary level at which a sociocultural system starts whether third order dynamics can become effective at all. Societies on a low cultural level, i.e., without much knowledge of how to deal effectively with the natural and social environment, must take these environmental conditions much more in regard than evolutionarily higher advanced systems. Therefore, early societies simply could not unfold third order dynamics like later ones: the early European societies were not only much more differentiated than their contemporary rivals (see above), but in particular they could take over from Islamic and Chinese cultures a lot of achievements, which they did not have to invent themselves. In this sense European societies were just lucky in two aspects, namely as a "follow up" culture and a society with a high initial degree of differentiation.

Generally, we must understand the properties of exhibiting the different types of dynamics as *evolutionary degrees* which are *more or less* manifest or latent respectively in a certain society. This much can be learned from the natural sciences, that the question with problems like these is not whether a certain property is there, but to which degree it is manifest, i.e., what values the according parameters obtain. Therefore the European case is special not because only these societies were capable of third order dynamics *in principle,* but only because they contained favourable evolutionary conditions at their very beginnings.

The degree of third order dynamics, and that means its probable effectiveness at the evolutionary beginning of a sociocultural system, must be measured by the degree of EP, and that means by the degree of heterogeneity.[56] In sociological terms of course this is the degree of sociocultural differentiation, as demonstrated. The same holds for the case of cognitive systems, as was sketched in 4.3. Apparently third order dynamics can be found only in these two cases in a more or less high degree; neither pure physico-chemical nor biological systems seem to contain the capability for this kind of dynamics. Yet the emergence of this highest form of dynamics is, of course, no mystery at all, but an effect of a general evolutionary principle, which again is an abstract form of the principle of heterogeneity.

In subchapter 4.2. I have already mentioned the fact that apparently the evolution of the physical universe must be understood as the occurrence of certain symmetry breaks (cf. Barrow 1991) as random processes. Physical laws usually express symmetries, which by themselves cannot explain physical evolution. This must be understood as the additional effect of symmetry breaks, which generated higher and higher degrees of heterogeneity. Theorists of biological evolution, in particular of the emergence of life from prebiotic systems, seem to agree that physico-chemical systems must reach a certain degree of "complexity", that is a degree of heterogeneity and, of course, a minimum size to unfold adaptive behaviour as second order dynamics (Dawkins 1986; Kauffman 1995 and 2000). The basic idea behind these considerations is that systems with a high degree of differentiation are able to deal with more different aspects of their environment, and therefore are better equipped to maintain their existence than simpler systems. The evolving of higher degrees of heterogeneity of course is just the result of random processes, which had to occur in the long run. Therefore the step from first order dynamics to the second type is on the one hand a consequence of the rising of degrees of heterogeneity, and on the other a necessary effect of probability.

It is easy to see that the step to third order dynamics can be understood in the same way. The evolution of the human brain can be described in particular as the rise of degrees of heterogeneity in relation

---

[56] The analysis of EP that we have done so far indicates that one must distinguish between a *general* EP-value that is valid for the whole society and which is defined by the cultural matrix, and a *factual* value, which results from the general EP-value and the geometry of the system, i.e., the distribution of the individuals, which decides who may interact with whom.

to subhuman organisms, which enabled human cognitive systems to develop the cognitive third order dynamics, which was sketched in Subchapter 4.3. This cognitive development in turn enabled human societies to become more differentiated, as was modelled by the SCA; these degrees of heterogeneity generated the high cultural levels of the ancient cultures of the Axial Age civilisations, to quote the famous term of Jaspers (cf. Eisenstadt 1998), and finally, under favourable evolutionary conditions, third order dynamics could generate sociocultural trajectories with the known results of modern societies. Therefore we may postulate another abstract principle of heterogeneity: *the rising of degrees of heterogeneity, mostly started by random processes and then accelerated due to the effects of the particular dynamics, generated in this succession first, second and third order dynamics as the evolution of universal dynamical complexity.*

It is important to note that something akin to the concept of third order dynamics has been discussed in biology and biochemistry during the last twenty years. The perhaps first and certainly most famous attempt to explain the origin of life by the model of a selforganising system that generates an increasing number of different molecules, thereby overcoming certain information thresholds, is the hypercycle of Eigen which won him the Nobel prize (Eigen and Schuster 1979; for an improved model done with a CA see Boerlijst and Hogeweg 1992). A similar approach was undertaken by Kauffman (1992, 1995 and 2000), who developed an "autocatalytic system" which is able to evolve by increasing its "diversity", that is the number of different types of molecules. Bagley and Farmer (1992) constructed a mathematical model of autocatalytic systems and showed that it is quite possible that prebiotic evolution followed this course. Not by chance they mentioned in this context the famous definition of evolution by Spencer in his "First principles": "a change from an incoherent homogeneity to a coherent heterogeneity" and explained it as the dependence of evolution on diversity. In 2000 Kauffman enlarged this idea to the conception of a whole biosphere, which literally organises its own evolution, i.e., its increase of complexity, by enlarging its diversity. Third order dynamics, so it seems, is even more fundamental than "only" being a characteristic of rather late emerging systems, like cognitive and sociocultural ones.

Yet again a great *Caveat* must be stated. Kauffman's evolution of the biosphere by increasing diversity is, like the hypercycle of Eigen, a purely quantitative approach, i.e., the measure for diversity is just the number of different types of entities – molecules, or in the case of economy, goods, which Kauffman also mentions. In this sense this is still first order dynamics, with selection as a final arbiter between the different forms of diversity. I believe that Spencer also meant his definition in just this quantitative way. Third order dynamics, as proposed in this book, takes into account the possibility that certain systems, in particular cognitive and sociocultural ones, are diversified *structurally,* which means that they are differentiated with respect to general rules and geometry. To be sure, in systems with third order dynamics *quantitative* diversity also plays a part, but I think that quantitative diversity is, in this case, a result and not a cause: quantitative diversity in the sense of Kauffman emerges in systems capable of third order dynamics *because* of structural diversity or heterogeneity, respectively. In particular third order dynamical systems are, in an abstract sense, not directly dependent upon their environment: they develop their own criteria for evolutionary success and manipulate their environment accordingly. Only in (2000) Kauffman speculates about the possibility of "a self-tuning universe to pick the appropriate values of its constants, to tune its own laws" (257) and thus hints at the idea that I expressed with the concept of third order dynamics; Hawking (1988), by the way, already also hinted at the possibility of a universe that evolves together with its laws, and changes them by its own evolution too. It is up to physicists, of course, as Kauffman himself says, to decide upon the validity of these speculations, which he just sketches rather generally. In our case of sociocultural (and cognitive) evolution, however, there is no speculation necessary. History and research in cognitive development both give strong evidence of the fact that these evolutionary processes can and must be explained by the concept of third order dynamics.

Yet the fact that Kauffman as well as Eigen and others before him emphasise the importance of selforganising dynamics, which rely upon the selforganised emergence of diversity, though only in a quantitative way, are perhaps also indicators for a hidden third order dynamics in the prebiotic realm. Future research has to decide if these ideas mark, as

Kauffman hopes, perhaps the cornerstone of a new science of complexity.

Let us now turn back to our comparatively modest task of explaining sociocultural evolution. Apparently sociocultural evolution – and perhaps cognitive *phylogenesis* as well – in a certain sense repeated the universal scheme of the unfolding of the different types of dynamics. In the beginning early tribal societies were mainly regulated by the "biological heritage" of humankind and got along with the dominance of first order dynamics. This would explain why these societies changed only slowly: second order dynamics was used only in cases where it was absolutely necessary, and the trajectories generated by the SCA were rather quickly caught in the attractors of the respective cultures; in particular, the main mechanisms of role generating were only rudimentarily unfolded. The agrarian state empires evolved by higher degrees of second order dynamics and low degrees of third order dynamics as well, which explains their high levels of culture in all aspects; yet the degrees of heterogeneity were not sufficient, that third order dynamics could unfold its accelerating effects to transcend the cultural attractors. Only in the special case of the early European society did third order dynamics emerge completely as the – for the time being – last and highest form of dynamical complexity.

If these at present still rather speculative considerations are valid then the question if there are historical laws can be answered in a twofold sense. On the one hand sociocultural evolution is apparently regulated by the general principles of evolution, which have been just analysed. In this sense, but perhaps only in this sense, we may speak of universal "laws" which explain the general path of human history. On the other hand it cannot be denied that the concept of "historical law" is mostly used in another fashion, i.e., laws in the sense of the natural sciences, which explain the particular paths of history. The general evolutionary principles are obviously not of the same logical type as laws, if one understands laws as statements like " if conditions A, B,C, ... exist and if the causal relation(s) R connects A,B,C, ... with effects X,Y and Z, then X,Y and Z will occur". To answer the question about historical laws more precisely it is therefore necessary to examine a bit more thoroughly the relation between sociocultural evolution and history.

In the preceding chapters I have often mentioned the fact that the dynamics of complex systems is generated by their rules of interaction and that it is possible to classify these rules by the different parameters discussed, ordering parameters in the case of first order dynamics, meta parameters in the case of second order dynamics, and the evolutionary parameter in the case of third order dynamics. The knowledge about the values of the different parameters allows one to determine *in principle* the possible trajectories of the systems. Yet this is of course not enough to predict the *actual* trajectory that the system will follow in its development. To know this it is necessary to have sufficient information about the initial states of the system, about the influence of the environment with regard to possible changes of states by environmental disturbances, about environmental conditions with regard to necessary changes of the rules and about the influence of the environment in regard to particular cultural inventions. To borrow a term from physics: one must know not only the general logic of the system, expressed in the rules of interactions, the meta rules and the different parameters, but also the different boundary conditions that determine the actual course. In other words, the general logic of the system defines a space of possibilities for the system's development, the boundary conditions operate as constraints, which select the actual course.

In Chapter 3 I emphasised the fact that evolutionary processes are even more difficult to explain than these general remarks suggest. Boundary conditions or constraints, respectively, do not unequivocally select the actual paths of development, but the system usually has the choice between different solutions for the adaptive problems it must solve, the problems are mathematically underdetermined. Which solution the system chooses is mainly dependent upon the history of the system, which is also responsible for the values of the meta parameters. Random events, which are not explainable by either evolutionary principles or boundary conditions or the system's history must also be taken into regard. To be sure, when selecting a particular path of development, each system is subject to the general evolutionary principles and in this sense it is regulated by laws. However, the principles do not determine the selection processes themselves, and whether these selection processes are subject to concrete laws in the form of "A, ... by R causes X, ..." is quite another question, which I can answer only tentatively in this book (see below).

In the beginning of this essay I mentioned the fact that there is still no general consent in respect of the relation between the concepts of sociocultural evolution on the one hand and that of history on the other (cf. Habermas 1976). Of course, historians will certainly give definitions for these relations other than a mathematical systems theorist like myself. However, in a pragmatical fashion it is perhaps sufficient to define sociocultural evolution as the *general* process by which the human species unfolded its capabilities in the way discussed in this book; this process is regulated by the evolutionary principles. History on the other hand is the ensemble of concrete processes that were subject to evolutionary principles, particular boundary conditions and sometimes even random processes. Historical laws in this sense, if there are any, that regulate the historical processes, must accordingly be found in the interplay between these two or three determinants.

5.2 THE RELATIVE INEVITABILITY OF THE WESTERN WAY

At the end of this essay one more question can also be answered, i.e., the question if the emergence of modern societies with their particular characteristics like industrial capitalism, functional differentiation and the like, are an inevitable result of sociocultural processes. Several theorists of sociocultural evolution like, e.g. Sanderson (1995) and Turner (1997), apparently believe in such an inevitability, though they give no precise reasons for this belief.

Another approach to this problem has recently been given, e.g., by Huntington. In his famous essay "The Clash of Civilizations" (1996) he distinguishes between "modernization" and "Westernization" and claims that though the former is indeed inevitable since the rise of the Western civilisation the latter is definitely not, because the cultural traditions of non Western societies are so strong that they will force these societies into other cultural directions. "Modernization", in Huntington's terms, seems mainly to be the taking over of industrial capitalism and urbanisation; the political structures of Western societies like, e.g., parliamentary democracy and general cultural-political values like human rights and the strong emphasis laid upon individualism in Western societies, are strange to other "civilizations" and will probably not been taken over. Yet Huntington too argues only with plausibilities and gives no convincing proofs of his arguments.

By applying the evolutionary principles to this problem several more exact answers are possible. In a very general sense the emergence of modern societies was indeed unavoidable. This follows from the general principle of heterogeneity described above, which states that the emergence of the different kinds of dynamics had to occur with a rather high probability. In our case this means that to the degree sociocultural systems became more complex. i.e., more heterogeneous during the course of history, an inevitable process by itself, sooner or later a society literally had to emerge, with values of the evolutionary parameter sufficient for the unfolding of third order dynamics. It is certainly no accident that the early European societies happened to be just this case because of their origins in the socio-political form of military feudalism, with the resulting sociocultural heterogeneity on the one hand, their high degree of national heterogeneity on the other hand, and their status as "follow-up" cultures as a third factor. Given these starting conditions, the rest was indeed inevitable.

To presume such an unavoidable development is *not* to say that sociocultural evolution must have led with necessity to modern capitalism and bourgeois democracy. This would stipulate something like a goal of sociocultural evolution, which is simply not tenable. The results of the unfolding of third order dynamics could have been otherwise, e.g. the emergence of some kind of socialism without the inhibiting effects we know from the fate of the so-called socialistic states in Eastern Europe. Because complex systems always have to select between different options, the unfolding of third order dynamics in another part of the world, that is in societies with other cultural traditions, could have produced different results with regards to socio-economic structures. That is the difference between sociocultural evolution and concrete historical processes defined above: inevitable was the unfolding of third order dynamics sometime and somewhere; the particular results due to the fact that this happened in early Europe could have been otherwise, because the general logic does not determine the outcome unequivocally. In this sense the argument of Huntington seems convincing, although one has to take into account that once a society with third order dynamics has emerged, its undeniable success has strong influences on other societies that are not so far evolved.

Yet the problem of the unavoidability of the Western way is a bit more complicated than scholars like Huntington, with their distinction between modernisation and Westernisation, seem to believe. One of the distinguishing characteristics of Western culture was and is its claim for universal principles. To be sure, these principles cannot be found, e.g., in the Christian heritage of Western culture, because other religions claim with the same right equal universality. However, the cultural achievement that is most characteristic for European and Western culture, that is modern science, can rightly claim universality in contrast to all other competing forms of world views. Nobody seriously doubts that $E = mc^2$ expresses a universally valid result of human cognition, regardless of to which culture anybody belongs to. Nobody outside of the Christian-Jewish faiths on the other hand believes in the literal validity of the Genesis. Science as a product of Western culture is also a cognitive achievement that is valid independently of any particular culture.[57] At least in this respect Western culture rightly claims a universality that other cultures lack and which civilisations competing with the Western one have to acknowledge and take over.

Similar considerations have to be undertaken in regard to Western political-cultural values like human rights, in particular equality and freedom of the individual. There is strong evidence that these political achievements are not only due to specific European cultural traditions but that they are, in particular, necessary effects of functional differentiation, generated by an SCA with third order dynamics. Let us consider equality first:

An SCA, operating with third order dynamics, leads to the autonomy of different roles and the generation of new roles, which are also rather autonomous with respect to the old ones. Autonomy means in particular the disappearance of social hierarchies as a *structuring feature of the whole society* because sociocultural inhibition also means, among other aspects, political dominance of one role in regard to other roles. That does *not* mean the disappearance of hierarchies altogether; such a claim

---

[57] I omit the case of fundamentalistic sects because they do not belong to the mainstream of Western culture.

for Western societies would be quite absurd. It means the transfer of hierarchical structures into the different functional subsystems, which emerge as the result of third order dynamics. A manager has no authority outside his firm over other people and in particular not over individuals whose roles belong to other subsystems, like, e.g., a student at a university, although inside the firm there are quite established hierarchies, as everybody knows. If, in contrast to stratificatorily differentiated societies in modern societies, there are no *global* hierarchical relations, i.e., valid for the whole society, how are the relations between members of different subsystems determined?

The political answer to this question was given with a famous term of the French revolution: the general societal relations are defined by the concept of *citoyen,* that is the concept of the *general* social structure in terms of *formal equality* among all members of the society. Indeed, no other answer is logically possible in a society characterised by strong role autonomy: global hierarchies, i.e., hierarchies that are binding for the whole society, would reduce role autonomy, which would lessen in turn the efficiency of the role occupants, which would mean a regressing of the society. Therefore *formal* equality is an inevitable consequence of the effects that third order dynamics has generated, and not just a particular value of the European culture. With quite different concepts but a very similar logic, law theorists, inspired by Marx, have explained the emergence of the equality of all citizens in regard to law as an unavoidable consequence of the rise of industrial capitalism, that is, the necessary security of the capitalistic entrepreneurs against the old feudal powers.

A parallel argument can be given with regard to the value of individual freedom. Because freedom is an ambiguous concept I deal here only with the freedom to choose one's own professional career – a freedom that the peasants or craftsmen in medieval Europe lacked totally. Of course, freedom in this sense does not mean that everybody is free to take up any profession he likes. Each profession is regulated by rules of access and most of them demand long phases of professional training. However, each *citoyen* is free to decide if he/she wants to undertake a particular career and to orient his/her life to the goal of achieving it. Again the emergence of role autonomy demands as a logical necessity the absence of *global* rules, which decide about access to the particular roles. Only the occupants of specific rules can have the right to decide about rules of access, that is about the rules that regulate the reproduction of the role specific subsystems during the succession of generations. Global regulations, executed by some central authority, which are not defined by the role occupants would again lessen role autonomy and thus reduce the efficiency of the role occupants.

A classic example of this inevitable progress was the reformation of the medieval universities by the famous founding of the Berlin university by Humboldt and Schleiermacher, the model for the modern research university (Ben-David 1972): the access to university education should be dependent only on the individual abilities of the student. Criteria like social status or wealth of the parents should be of no importance. Of course, things were a bit more complicated, but with these new rules of access the development of the modern university system was determined.

I skip the according arguments for other dimensions of individual freedom like, e.g., the differentiation between the public and the private spheres in modern societies. They all boil down to the fact that to the degree that third order dynamics generates high levels of role autonomy, cultural-political consequences like the introduction of formal equality and individual freedom for the *citoyens,* that is to the members of these societies were indeed unavoidable. To be sure, no society *must* take over these consequences: each non Western society is free to stop at certain points in their own development and stick to some cultural traditions. Yet that would mean the reducing of third order dynamics, i.e., stopping their own evolutionary dynamics in certain aspects, and thus lessen their capability to compete with societies like the Western ones, which do not put cultural constraints on their development. Societies with reduced evolutionary dynamics would become or stay peripheral societies, to again borrow the concept of World Systems Theory. In this sense, societies with a non European cultural tradition are just not free to choose between modernisation and Westernisation: they either follow the European path of development until the introduction of the main sociocultural rules like formal equality and freedom, and cultural achievements like science or they stay behind and become a mere victim of the processes of globalisation which are a result of European third order dynamics.

It is finally time to return to the old antagonism between Enlightenment and Romanticism, with which I started this essay. Obviously both sides are right, and wrong together. The philosophers of the Enlightenment were right insofar as there are indeed general regularities in history, and European societies are indeed a measure for sociocultural evolution. However, they were wrong insofar as they took this idea too literally and too concretely, which was due to the times, in which they lived. "Regularities" and "measure" can only be understood in terms of the abstract evolutionary principles discussed above; it may not be understood that the European development is *literally* the way all societies have to go. Cases like Japan or the South Asian "Tiger states" already demonstrate that things will be not so simple, although the present difficulties of these societies seem to indicate that they are subjects to the inevitabilities just mentioned: there is no half-way to modernisation without a price, that is the price of reduced efficiency and reduced dynamics.

The partisans of Romanticism were right in the sense that each culture indeed goes its own way until the specific attractor is reached. However, they were wrong in their belief that cultures cannot be compared. Toynbee has already answered this question quite satisfactorily. Therefore in my opinion it is time to end the fruitless debates about progress, Eurocentrism, the incompatibility of cultures and the like. Each culture is subject to the general evolutionary principles and, additionally, to its environment. The historical fate of the different cultures is a result of these factors – no more, but also no less.

Several times I have mentioned the fact that after the unfolding of third order dynamics in Europe, with the resulting emergence of the modern societies of the Western kind, all other societies must follow this type of evolution or become or stay secondary, respectively. In *this* sense the Western societies are now indeed the measure for all other societies, and their fate will determine directly or indirectly the fate of all societies. Therefore I finish this essay with some considerations on the future of this dominant form of sociocultural systems.

5.3 SOME FINAL REFLECTIONS ON THE PREDICTABILITY OF MODERN SOCIETIES

It seems inescapable, after having reconstructed the courses of sociocultural evolution, to draw a picture about the future of contemporary, i.e. modern societies. Sanderson (1995) at the end of his eminent book sketches a very gloomy perspective on the future of mankind. This looks very bad, according to Sanderson's rather pessimistic opinion of human character as egoistic and driven only by the wish "to satisfy their own needs and wants" (loc. cit., 12), because the materialistic needs will drive modern societies with an inevitable force into ecological disaster.

To be sure, the ecological dangers are not to be neglected and whether mankind will be reasonable enough to avoid planet-wide catastrophes is at this time an open question. Yet the certainty with which Sanderson predicts this sombre future is a bit astonishing. He neither gives exact evolutionary mechanisms as a precise explanation of the past, nor is he able to demonstrate if and why evolutionary principles that lead us to the present will also be the unchanging forces that generate our future. In the scientific sense of the term the prediction of Sanderson is no prediction at all, but just an expression of a pessimistic world view and a negative opinion of mankind in particular.

The scientifically interesting question is, of course, not whether men are "good" or "bad", whatever that means. The question is whether predictions of complex systems are possible at all, and if so, under what conditions. Let us examine a bit more thoroughly therefore the concept of predictability.

According to the usual results of modern physics, systems are predictable if the rules that regulate the dynamics of the systems are "t-invariant", that is the rules or physical laws can be applied to explain the history of the system as well as to predict its future. The astronomical laws of Kepler and Newton are perhaps the most famous example for such t-invariant laws: they serve to compute planetary constellations thousands of years ago and they allow one to predict an eclipse of the sun a hundred years in the future. Theoretical physicists always look for t-invariant laws for different reasons (cf. Barrow loc. cit.), and as far as I know most theoretical physicists firmly believe that true universal laws will always be t-invariant.

It is well known that since thermodynamics things are not so easy, even in theoretical physics. The "arrow of time" cannot be neglected any more in some fundamental equations. However, the dynamics of thermodynamical systems can also be predicted though only by statistical methods. Therefore, even after thermodynamics and the fundamentally stochastic laws of quantum mechanics, theoretical physics did not have to abandon the dream of predictability. The same holds for the discovery of "chaotic" systems which allow predictions only within a space of possibilities (cf. Gell-Mann 1994). It seems that the classical condition of t-invariance is sufficient but not strictly necessary for predictability: if one abandons *deterministic* predictability, predictions are possible even under conditions of restricted t-invariance, though only with a certain "fuzziness", i.e., the admission of stochastic deviations.

Since Darwin the question has been raised again and again as to whether evolutionary theories also allow predictions. To be sure, the arrow of time is deeply integrated in all evolutionary theories and mechanisms and therefore evolutionary laws are never t-invariant in the strict sense. Not only do the importance of random processes like mutations forbid any classic t-invariance, but the problem lies even deeper. I mentioned several times in this essay that complex adaptive systems always have to choose between different options when they have to adjust their rules to certain environmental conditions. The problems they have to solve are mathematically underdetermined and therefore there are almost always different solutions for a particular problem that are equally favourable. This can be studied in detail, e.g., with mathematical models like the genetic algorithm. This fact causes in turn a certain impossibility to compute adaptive systems "backwards": given a certain structure, i.e. rules of interaction and some additional meta rules, and a certain state of the system at time t, then it is not possible to unambiguously determine the structure and state of the system at time t-1. The history of such systems can be understood unequivocally only by looking at the empirical facts; the computing backwards of such systems gives again only a space of possible structures and states.

This fundamental uncertainty about systems whose rules of interaction and meta rules are not t-invariant holds even for non adaptive and deterministic non-linear systems like cellular automata (CAs): if one knows their rules and states at time t, then it is possible to compute their future unequivocally by running computer simulations. However, it is generally not possible to unambiguously determine their history, i.e., their preceding states, although the rules of the CAs do not change at all (Wuensche and Lesser 1992), because different states in the past could have lead to the same state in the present, with the same rules. So we have the astonishing fact that there are deterministic systems that allow precise predictions but not unequivocal reconstructions of their past without "empirical" knowledge about it. Historical examinations of complex systems can never be wholly substituted by mathematical systems analysis but can "only" be complemented.

Based on empirical facts about the history of biological evolution it is obviously possible to model rather exactly the past course of "the origin of species" (Darwin). "In principle" it should be possible to model the future of biological evolution too, as is the case with the CAs just mentioned, although the fundamental principles of biological evolution are basically stochastic: the well known general principles of biological evolution allow at least the sketching of spaces of possible developments. In fact of course this task is quite impossible. How should one reason about the evolutionary future of a biological species if we do not know whether it will become extinct in the next hundred years? Not only that, but in particular the very fact that our species is permanently changing the evolutionary conditions, i.e., the ecological environments of nearly all other living species, forbids any evolutionary predictions that do not at least take into account our own interactions with our physical and biological environment. Therefore, although a *general* prognosis of biological evolution seems quite possible in a mathematical sense, a factual prognosis will be possible only by also considering sociocultural evolution. So what about the predictability of sociocultural systems and perhaps also cognitive ones?

In a very general sense it seems nowadays, in contrast to classic t-invariance, that on the one hand we have a fundamental asymmetry in regard to the relation of explaining the past and predicting the future: it is generally not possible to reconstruct the past by knowing only the rules and present states of complex systems. However, it is often possible to predict the future of these systems, though mostly only with a certain probability. Even these restricted possibilities of prognosis always have to assume that the *fundamental* laws of the systems remain constant. That assumption of course can be made in regard to systems with dynamics of only first order. It can be made also with respect to systems of second order dynamics, like biological ones, but only in respect of the constancy of the meta rules and the meta parameters. The prediction problem is mainly one of not knowing exactly the environmental boundary conditions that select between the possibilities the systems have. However, predictions are *principally* possible in a mathematical sense as long as the fundamental properties of such systems, like their meta parameters, i.e., their adaptive behaviour remain constant. It is always possible, for instance, to predict the probable evolutionary trajectory of a single species if one applies the mathematical model of the genetic algorithm. Given enough empirical knowledge about the particular genome and enough computing power, it can be shown when and with what results, i.e., phenotypes, the species will reach an evolutionary attractor – *ceteris paribus*.

Sociocultural systems on the other hand are representatives of third order dynamics and in these cases things become even more difficult. Third order dynamics means that not only rules of interaction, ordering parameters and meta parameters are open to change, but also the very conditions that regulate the evolutionary course of these systems. To be sure, most societies known from history were regulated by third order dynamics only to a rather small degree; therefore their evolutionary fate can be explained by applying only the principles of first and second order dynamics. Modern societies are another case because with regard to these systems nearly "anything goes", as Paul Feyerabend once remarked with respect to science.

The analysis of third order dynamics in the preceding subchapters could suggest a mistaken impression, i.e., that this type of dynamics, once unfolded, will go on forever and will be limited only by physical thresholds like the size of the brain in the case of cognitive ontogenesis or the material resources and ecological carrying capacity available to third order societies.[58] Yet we know from researches into cognitive ontogenesis that things are more difficult: even processes of third order dynamics can be slowed down or stopped under certain conditions. There is no reason why things should be different with sociocultural systems. Sociocultural processes can be slowed or stopped and even inverted. This can be explained by the basic mechanisms of the SCA:

One of the main assumptions was that the evolutionary dynamics of sociocultural systems is regulated by an interplay of inhibiting and reinforcing factors. The inhibiting factors in particular were defined as the cultural boundaries that on the one hand generate the paradigmatic definitions of problems and suited problem solving algorithms, and on the other define limits of the perception of problems. In regard to the *social* structure of a society the inhibiting factors also function as *integrating* factors, which give the society a certain unity and prevent the breaking up of the society into autonomous and isolated parts. Indeed, clusters of similar roles that have no or only weak *cultural* connections to clusters of other roles will have obtained this only by also weakening the *social* relations to different roles, or the according role clusters, respectively. The integrative forces of a society are not only, but to a very important degree, those of its culture, that is the strength of relations among different roles. It is well known in contemporary social theory that this is one of the main problems of modern societies (cf. Luhmann 1986). The very (third order) dynamics that enabled these societies to evolve in the way they did, by lessening the inhibiting factors between different roles, has long become a menace with regard to the necessary integration of society. Although the concept of the *citoyen* and the "universality" of client roles (Luhmann), i.e., the right to benefit from all subsystems like education, medicine, law or polity, are strong integrating factors, they are perhaps not enough.

Considering this feature of modern societies it seems quite possible that there may some day be a reduction of third order dynamics by again strengthening the inhibiting, i.e., integrating factors. After all, humans need assurances with regard to their social and cultural home; modern

---

[58] "Carrying capacity" describes the ecological measure of an environment in regard to ecosystems. The greater the carrying capacity of the environment, the larger the ecosystem can be, that is, the more environmental resources can be spent by the ecosystem.

societies tend to overstrain their members in this respect. Culture is finally not only a cognitive space but also a place where one belongs to and feels at home – "a basic human need no less natural than that for food or drink or security or procreation" (Berlin 1982,12).[59] The renaissance of traditional, in particular religious belief systems, ethnic traditions and regional identities like "Welshman" or "Breton", are indicators for such countermovements, although they seem rather unimportant at present compared to the large processes of "globalisation" with the exception perhaps of religious movements (cf. Huntington loc. cit.). If these observations are correct, then systems of third order dynamics are ambiguous not only with respect to their history but also to their future.

Therefore the task of constructing predicting models of modern societies seems quite hopeless, considering the number and different levels of parameters that are principally open to change. It is not impossible to construct mathematical models, which capture all these spaces of variability and define future trajectories of modern societies, classified in regard to their degrees of probability. The enlarged SCA of Subchapter 4.2. already gives some ideas what kind of models these must be. However, because predictions, as I mentioned already, have to make some *ceteris paribus* assumptions about the constancy of certain mechanisms, it seems rather arbitrary currently to select a particular constancy from the possible ones. Perhaps things will change in this respect and science *does* make progress after all; let us wait for and see.

The probably most famous and most fertile science fiction author of all time, the professor of biochemistry Isaac Asimov, has tried to sketch a science of future social processes with his well known concept of "psychohistory", described in his famous "Foundation" series. Asimov originally used the paradigm of statistical thermodynamics for this task, obviously assuming that the rules of interactions between people will not

---

[59] This famous definition of Berlin is no contradiction to the definition used in this essay: the knowledge that is valid in a specific society is always the knowledge that is needed to feel "at home in the universe", to quote Kauffman. In particular, the connections between the different parts of the knowledge determine whether the universe (and one's own society) is a whole complete place, and not merely an ensemble of isolated parts. Nobody could feel at home in such an ensemble (see above Chapter 2).

change in future times. Being a natural scientist this assumption seemed quite reasonable to him and to his successors, who carried on the writing of the Foundation series and who are natural scientists or also trained in the natural sciences.[60] Although these books are beautiful pieces of science fiction, they demonstrate quite clearly that the prediction of societies cannot be done by the established methods of scientific prognosis, a fact that also seemed to become clear to the different authors at the end. The assumption of constancy of rules of interaction is not valid in these fields of research; we saw that for even more cases of system parameters and system structures the constancy assumption is also not necessarily valid. Even more sophisticated methods than statistical mechanics like chaos theory, and other advanced theoretical tools of modern (natural) science, are not fit to do the job. The task of social science, as far as it concerns the future of societies, is obviously not that of prognosis in the classical sense of the term.[61]

I mentioned above that it is *logically and mathematically* quite possible to predict the courses of biological evolution but not factually because of numerous boundary conditions, not least the one our own interactions with biological nature. Yet the contemporary progresses of the biological sciences in the realms of molecular biology and genetic engineering suggest another possibility: we are factually able to understand and predict the future course of biological evolution *because we make it ourselves.* In a literal sense life on earth becomes more and more the subject of our own experiments, and in this way predictable as the effect of our own actions. Whether this will lead to favourable results for mankind and the other living species is a question that I cannot decide; the important point here is that the *observations* of biological evolutionary processes can and will be substituted by the *production* of them.

---

[60] This was done in the nineties by Greg Bear, Gregory Benford and David Brin.

[61] The famous objections by Popper and Merton against the possibility of social prognosis in the terms of "self-destroying and selff-fulfilling prophecies" are in my opinion not as serious as these great theorists seemed to believe. People are quite able to ignore predictions even if these are in the negative - for example ecological ones. Therefore the logical core of these arguments is of course still valid, but the factual importance of them can perhaps often be neglected.

In the 18th century the Italian philosopher Giambattista Vico remarked that we understand only those things that we can make. He wanted to argue with this famous consideration against the possibility of understanding nature because we do not make it, and for the program of a science of society because we obviously make society ourselves, by our social actions and interactions. It is a bit ironic that the history of science proved Vico wrong: in laboratory experiments we "make" nature in an artificial way and with mathematical theories we understand nature as the product of our experimental actions. In contrast, a real science of society was not possible for the same reason: we cannot make laboratory experiments with social processes and we did not have the mathematical concepts to understand society in a precise manner.

Theories and concepts like those presented in this essay, although they are still preliminary, are no tools for the prognosis of sociocultural futures, but they may be the basis for social planning. It is not the task of such social theories, equipped with elaborated mathematical tools, to predict a future that is not subject to classic forms of prediction. However, these theories can be the foundations of an understanding of society in an enlarged sense of Vico: by understanding mathematically the main mechanisms that drive societies on their particular courses of evolution, and by experimenting with these theories via the medium of elaborated computer programs, it will be possible to understand the consequences of our own actions for future states of societies. In other words, we will be able to construct sociologically valid *scenarios,* which tell us in a precise manner what may happen if we carry on the way we did in the immediate and the distant past. We can then decide if we like these scenarios of possible outcomes or not; in particular we will be able to understand what is to be done to avoid unfavourable outcomes or to guarantee those that we deem favourable. In this sense the dream of Vico may be fulfilled in that we understand society because we are able to make it in a *conscious* way.

In the preceding subchapters third order dynamics has been characterised as a special form of emancipation from the environment. Cognitive systems, like us, are obviously able to evolve according to this type of dynamics. In a certain sense this exhibits a kind of freedom: we are neither automata regulated by our genes, as reductive biological approaches seem to claim, nor pure subjects to environmental stimuli, as traditional behaviorism believed. We are more, i.e. capable of third order dynamics and able to emancipate ourselves from biological initial cognitive conditions as well as from environmental constraints. Our problem is what to do with these possibilities, going ecologically bankrupt as Sanderson and others believe, or ending in nuclear holocausts or trying to "muddle through" (Holland), in order to make things a little better in and for each generation.

The greatest philosopher of the Enlightenment, Immanuel Kant, characterised in a famous definition Enlightenment as "the emancipation of constraints not understood". Mathematical theories of sociocultural evolution do not *predict* a future, which consists only of possibilities, but make it possible to understand our past and how to shape our future on the basis of constraints perhaps understood at last.

REFERENCES

Alexander, J., Giesen, B., Münch, R. and Smelser, N.J. (eds.), 1987: *The Micro-Macro-Link*. Berkeley: University of California Press

Anderson, P., 1974: *Lineages of the absolutist state*. London: New Left Books

Andresen; H., 2002: *Interaktion, Sprache und Spiel. Zur Funktion des Rollenspiels für Sprachentwicklung im Vorschulalter*. Tübingen: Narr

Arendt, H., 1963: *On Revolution*. New York: The Viking Press

Axelrod, R., 1984: *The Evolution of Cooperation*. New York: Basic Books

Bagley, R.J. and Farmer, J.D., 1992: Spontaneous Emergence of a Metabolism. In: Langton et al. (eds.)

Bandura, A., 1986: *Social foundations of thought and action. A social cognitive theory*. Englewood Cliffs: Prentice-Hall

Barrow, J. D., 1991: *Theories for Everything. The Quest for Ultimate Explanation. Oxford*: Oxford University Press

Bartholomew, J.R., 1989: *The formation of science in Japan*. New Haven: Yale University Press

Bateson, G., 1970: *Mind and Nature. A Necessary Unity*. London: Chandler

Bateson, G., 1972: *Steps to an Ecology of Mind*. London: Chandler

Bell, E.T., 1937: *Men of Mathematics*. New York: Simon and Schuster

Ben-David, J., 1972: *The Scientist's Role in Society*. Englewood Cliff (NJ): Harper

Berger, P. and Luckmann, T., 1966: *The Social Construction of Reality*. New York: Doubleday

Berlin, I., 1982: *Against the Current*. London: Hogarth

Bernal, J.A., 1954: *Science in History*. London: Watts

Blute, M., 1979: Sociocultural Evolutionism. An Untried Theory. In: *Behavioral Science* **24**, 46 - 59

Boerlijst, M. and Hogeweg, P., 1992: Self-Structuring and Selection: Spiral Waves as a Substrate for Prebiotic Evolution. In: Langton et al. (eds.)

Böhme, G., van den Daele, W. and Krohn, W, 1977: *Experimentelle Philosophie*. Frankfurt (M): Suhrkamp

Boyd, R, and Richerson, P.J., 1985: *Culture and the evolutionary process*. Chicago: University of Chicago Press

Briggs, J. and Peat, D., 1993: *Turbulent Mirror*. New York: Harper and Row

Brown, D.E., 1991: *Human Universals*. Philadelphia: Temple University Press

Campbell, D.T., 1988: *Methodology and Epistemology for Social Science*. Chicago: University of Chicago Press

Carley, K., 1997: Organization and Constraint-Based Adaption. In: R.A. Eve, S. Horsfall and M.E. Lee (eds.): *Chaos, Complexity and Sociology. Myths, Models and Theories*. London: Sage

Cavalli-Sforza, L.L. and Feldman, M.W., 1981: *Cultural transmission and evolution: A quantitative approach*. Princeton NJ: Princeton University Press

Chase-Dunn, C., 1989: *Global Formation. Structures of the World-Economy*. London: Basil Blackwell

Chomsky, N., 1965: *Aspects of the Theory of Syntax*. Cambrige MA: MIT Press

Churchland, P. and Sejnowski, T., 1992: *The Computational Brain*. Cambridge MA: MIT Press

Cohen, M.D., Riolo, R.L. and Axelrod, R., 2000: The Role of Social Structure in the Maintenance of Cooperative Regimes. In: *Rationality and Society* **13**, 1: 5 - 32

Cosmides, L. and Tooby, J., 1987: From evolution to behavior. Evolutionary psychology as the missing link. In: J. Dupré (ed.): *The latest on the best. Essays on evolution and optimality*. Cambridge MA: The MIT Press

Dawkins, R., 1976: *The Selfish Gene*. Oxford: Oxford University Press

Dawkins, R., 1986: *The blind Watchmaker*. New York: Norton

Dennett, D.C., 1995: *Darwin's Dangerous Idea. Evolution and the Meanings of Life*. New York: Touchstone

Depew, D.J. and Weber, B.H., 1995: *Darwinism Evolving. Systems Dynamics and the Genealogy of Natural Selection*. Cambridge MA: The MIT Press

Doreian, P. and Stokman, F., 1997: The Dynamics and Evolution of Social Networks. In: P. Doreian and F. Stokman (eds.): *Evolution of social Networks. Amsterdam*: Gordon and Breach

Downs, A., 1967: *Inside Bureaucracy*. Boston: Little, Brown and Company

Dreyfuss, H.L. and Dreyfuss, S., 1987: *Künstliche Intelligenz*. Reinbek: Rohwohlt

Durham, W. H. and Weingart, P., 1997: Units of Culture. In: Weingart et al (eds.)

Durham, W.H., 1991: *Coevolution. Genes, culture and human diversity*. Stanford: Stanford University Press

Edelman, G.M., 1992: *Bright Air, Brilliant Fire - On the Matter of the Mind*. New york: Basic Books

Eder, K., 1976: *Die Entstehung staatlich organisierter Gesellschaften*. Frankfurt (M): Suhrkamp

Eder, K., 1991: *Geschichte als Lernprozess? Zur Pathogenese politischer Modernität in Deutschland*. Frankfurt (M): Surhkamp

Eigen, M. and Schuster, P., 1979: *The Hypercycle. A Principle of Natural Selforganization*. Berlin: Springer

Eisenstadt, S.N., 1998: Social Division of Labor, Construction of Centers and Institutional Dynamics. A Reassessment of the Structural-Evolutionary Perspective. In: G. Preyer (ed.): *Strukturelle Evolution und das Weltsystem*. Frankfurt (M): Suhrkamp

Evans-Pritchard, E.E., 1976: *Witchcraft, Oracle and Magic among the Azande*. Oxford: Oxford University Press

Falk, R. and Jablonka, E., 1997: Inheritance. Transmission and Development. In: Weingart et al. (eds.)

Farmer, J.D., 1990: A Rosetta Stone for Connectionism. In: S. Forrest (ed.): *Emergent Computation*. Physica D **42**, 1 - 31

Feyerabend, P., 1970: Consolations for the Specialist. In: Lakatos and Musgrave (eds.)

Fisher, R.A., 1930: *The General Theory of Natural Selection*. Oxford: Clarendon

Flohr, H., 1991: Brain Processes and Phenomenal Consciousness. In: *Theory and Psychology* **1 (2)**: 245-262

Freeman, L., 1989: Social Networks and the Structure Experiment. In: L. Freeman (ed.): *Research Methods in Social Network Analysis*. Fairfax: George Mason University Press

Geertz, C., 1973: *The interpretation of cultures*. New York: Basic Books

Gell-Mann, M., 1994: *The Quark and the Jaguar*. New York: Freeman

Giddens, A., 1984: *The Constitution of Society. Outline of the Theory of Structuration*. Cambridge: Polity Press

Goodall, J., 1986: *The Chimpanzees of Gombe. Patterns of Behavior*. Cambridge MA): Belknap Press of Harvard University Press

Gould, S.J., 1977: *Ontogeny and Phylogeny*. Cambridge MA: Harvard University Press

Gould, S.J., 1982: Darwinism and the expansion of evolutionary theory. In: *Science* **216**, 380 – 387

Götschl, J. (ed.), 2001: *Evolution and Progress in Democracies*. Dordrecht: Kluwer Academic Publishers

Gumerman, G.J. and Gell-Mann, M. (eds)., 1994: *Understanding Complexity in the Prehistorc Southwest*. Reading MA: Addison Wesley

Habermas, J., 1968: *Technik und Wissenschaft als "Ideologie"*. Frankfurt (M): Suhrkamp

Habermas, J., 1976: *Zur Rekonstruktion des Historischen Materialismus*. Frankfurt (M): Suhrkamp

Habermas, J., 1981: *Theorie des kommunikativen Handelns II*. Frankfurt (M): Suhrkamp

Hart, H., 1959: Social theory and social change. In: L. Gross (ed.): *Symposium on Sociological theory* (196 - 238). Evanston (Ill.): Row and Peterson

Hawking, S.W., 1988: *A Brief History of Time. From the Big Bang to Black Holes*. New York: Bantam Books.

Helbing, D., 1995: *Quantitative Sociodynamics. Stochastic Methods and Models of Social Interaction Processes*. Dordrecht: Kluwer Academic Publlihsers

Hofbauer, J. and Sigmund, K., 1984: *Evolutionstheorie und dynamische Systeme. Mathematische Aspekte der Selektion*. Hamburg: Paul Parey

Hofstadter, D.R., 1986: *Metamagical Themas*. Harmondsworth: Penguin

Holland, J., Holyoak, K.J., Nisbett, R.E. and Thagard, P., 1986: *Induction*. Cambridge MA: MIT Press

Holland, J.R., 1975: *Adaptation in Natural and Artificial Systems*. Ann Arbor: University of Michigan Press

Huntington, S.P., 1996: *The Clash of Civilizations*. New York: Simon and Schuster

Huxley, J.S., 1942: *Evolution, the Modern Synthesis*. London: Allen and Unwin

Jablonka, E., Lachmann, M. and Lamb, M.J., 1992: Evidence, mechanisms and models for the inheritance of required characters. In: *Journal of Theoretical Biology* **158**, 245 - 268

Jacobs, N., 1958: *The origin of modern capitalism and Eastern Asia*. Hong Kong: Hong Kong University Press

Kauffman, S., 1992: *The Origins of Order*. Oxford: Oxford University Press

Kauffman, S., 1995: *At Home in the Universe*. Oxford: Oxford University Press

Kauffman, S., 2000: *Investigations*. Oxford: Oxford University Press

Klüver, J. and Müller, W., 1972: Wissenschaftstheorie und Wissenschaftsgeschichte. Die Entdeckung der Benzolformel. In: *Zeitschrift für allgemeine Wissenschaftstheorie* **3**

Klüver, J. and Schmidt, J., 1999 a: Social Differentiation as the Unfolding of Dimensions of Social Systems. In: *Journal of Mathematical Sociology* **23 (4)**, 309 - 325

Klüver, J. and Schmidt, J., 1999 b: Control Parameters in Boolean Networks and Cellular Automata Revisited: From a logical and a sociological Point of View. In: *Complexity* **5**, No. **1**, 45 - 52

Klüver, J., 2000: *The Dynamics and Evolution of Social Systems. New Foundations of a Mathematical Sociology.* Dordrecht: Kluwer

Kohonen, T., 1987: *Self-Organization and Associative Memory.* Berlin-Heidelberg: Springer

Kosko, B. 1987: Adaptive Bidirectional Associative Memories. In: *Applied Optics* **26**, n. **23**, 4947 - 4960

Kosko, B., 1988: Bidirectional associative Memories. *IEEE Transactions of Systems. Man and Cybernetics.* Vol. SMC-**18**, 49 - 60

Kuhn, T.S., 1962: *The Structure of Scientific Revolutions.* Chicago: University of Chicago Press

Kuhn, T.S., 1970: Reflections on my Critics. In : Lakatos and Musgrave (eds.)

Lakatos, I. and Musgrave, A. (eds.), 1970: *Criticism and the Growth of Knowledge.* Cambridge: Cambridge University Press

Lakoff, G., 1987: *Women, Fire and Dangerous Things. What Categories reveal about the Mind.* Chicago and London: The University of Chicago Press

Langton, C. G., 1992: Life at the Edge of Chaos. In: Langton et al. (eds.)

Langton, C., G., Taylor, C., Farmer, J. D. and Rasmussen, S. (eds.), 1992: *Artificial Life II.* Reading MA: Addison Wesley

Lansing, S., Kremer, J.N. and Smuts, B.B., 1998: System-dependent Selection, Ecological Feedback and the Emergence of Functional Structures in Ecosystems. In: *J. theor. Biology* **192**, 377 - 391

Lepenies, W., 1976: *Das Ende der Naturgeschichte.* München: Oldenbourg

Lévy-Strauss, C., 1958: *Anthropologie Structurale.* Paris: Librairie Plon

Lewin, R., 1992: *Complexity. Life at the Edge of Chaos.* New York: Macmillan

Lewontin, R., 1970: The units of selection. In: *Annual Review of Ecology and Systematics* **1**, 1 - 18

Luhmann, N., 1984: *Soziale Systeme.* Frankfurt (M): Suhrkamp

Luhmann, N., 1986: *Ökologische Kommunikation*. Opladen: Leske and Buderich

Luhmann, N., 1996: *Die Gesellschaft der Gesellschaft*. Frankfurt (M): Suhrkamp

Mainzer, K., 1997: *Thinking in Complexity. The Complex Dynamics of Matter, Mind and Mankind*. Berlin: Springer

Maynard Smith, J., 1974: *Models in Ecology*. Cambridge: Cambridge University Press

Maynard Smith, J., 1982: *Evolution and the Theory of Games*. Cambridge: Cambridge University Press

Maynard Smith, J., 1996: Conclusions. In: W.G. Runciman, J. Maynard Smith and R.I.M. Dunbar (eds.): *Evolution of Social Behaviour Patterns in Primates and Man*. Proceedings of The British Academy 88. Oxford: Oxford University Press

Mead, G.H., 1934: *Mind, Self and Society*. Chicago: Chicago University Press

Michalewicz, Z., 1994: *Genetic Algorithms + Data Structures = Evolution Programs*. Berlin: Springer

Milgram, S., 1967: The small world problem. In: *Psychology Today* **1**, 61 -67

Needham, J., 1970: *Clercs and Craftsmen in China and the West*. Cambridge: Cambridge University Press

Needham, J., 1972: Human Law and the Laws of Nature. In: *The Grand Titration. Science and Society in East and West*. London: George Allen and Unwin

Nelson, B., 1969; Science and civilazation, "East" and "West". Joseph Needham and Max Weber. In: R.J. Seeger and R.S. Cohen (eds.): *Philosophical foundations of Science*. Boston Studies in the Philosophy of Science **11**, 445 - 493. Dordrecht: Reidel

Parisi, D., Ceconi, F. and Corini, A., 1995: Kin-directed altruism and attachment behaviour in an evolving population of neural networks. In: N. Gilbert and R. Conte (eds.): *Artificial Societies. The Computer Simulation of Social Life*. London: UCL Press

Parsons, T. and Platt, G., 1973: *The American University*. Cambridge MA: Harvard University Press

Parsons, T., 1968: *The Structure of social Action*. New York: Academic Press

Piaget, J., 1975: *Die Entwicklung des Erkennens*. Stuttgart: Klett

Pinker, S., 1994: *The Language Instinct*. New York: Morrow

Rasmussen, S., Knudsen, C. and Feldberg, R., 1992: Dynamics of Programmable Matter. In: Langton et al. (eds.)

Reynolds, R., 1994: Learning to cooperate using cultural algorithms. In: N. Gilbert and J.E. Doran (eds.): *Simulating Societies: The Computer Simulation of Social Phenomena*, pp. 223 – 244, London: UCL Press

Ritter, H. and Kohonen, T., 1989: Self-organizing semantic maps. In: *Biological Cybernetics* **61**, 241 - 254

Rosch, E., 1973: Natural Categories. In: *Cognitive Psychology* **4**, 328 - 350

Rosen, R., 1991: *Life Itself. A Comprehensive Inquiry into the Nature, Origin, and Fabrication of Life*. New York: Columbia University Press

Roth, G., 1996: *Das Gehirn und seine Wirklichkeit. Kognitive Neurobiologie und ihre philosophischen Konsequenzen*. Frankfurt (Main): Suhrkamp

Russell, B., 1922: *The Problem of China*. London: Miller

Sanderson, S.K., 1990: *Social evolutionism. A critical history*. Oxford: Basil Blackwell

Sanderson, S.K., 1995: *Social Transformations. A General Theory of Historical Development*. Oxford: Blackwell

Schein, E.H., 1985: *Organizational Culture and Leadership*. San Francisco: Jossey-Bass

Schelsky, H., 1962: *Einsamkeit und Freiheit*. Düsseldorf: Schwann

Schmid, M., 1998: Soziologische Evolutionstheorien. In: G. Preyer (ed.): *Strukturelle Evolution und das Weltsystem. Theorien, Sozialstruktur und evolutionäre Entwicklungen*. Frankfurt (M): Suhrkamp

Schwartzmann, H., 1978: *Transformations. The Anthropology of Children's Play*. New York: Plenum

Spengler, O., 1926/28: *The Decline of the West (Der Untergang des Abendlandes)*. New York: Alfred Knopf

Spengler, T., 1979: Die Entdeckung der chinesischen Wissenschafts- und Technikgeschichte. In: T. Spengler (Hrsg.): Joseph Needham: *Wissenschaftlicher Universalismus (= selected collection and translation of Needham's works)*. Frankfurt (M): Suhrkamp

Sperber, D., 1996: *Explaining Culture*. Cambridge, MA: MIT Press

Stichweh, R., Reyer, H.-U. and Uszkoreit, H., 1999: *Memorandum zu einem Institut für Evolutionswissenschaft*. Bad Homburg: Werner Reimers Konferenzen

Stoica. C., 2000: *Die Vernetzung sozialer Einheiten.*

   Hybride interaktive neuronale Netzwerke in den Kommunikations- und Sozialwissenschaften. Wiesbaden: DUV

Tarski, A., 1956: *Logic, Semantics, Metamathematics*. Oxford: Oxford University Press

Thomas, K., 1998: Das Ethnische und das Staatliche. In: G. Preyer (ed.): *Strukturelle Evolution und das Weltsystem*. Frankfurt (M): Suhrkamp

Thornhill, N.W., Tooby, J. and Cosmides, L., 1997: Introduction to Evolutionary Psychology. In: Weingart et al (eds.)

Tomasello, M., 1999: *The Cultural Origins of Human Cognition*. Cambridge MA: Harvard University Press

Toynbee, A., 1934 - 61: *A Study of History* (12 vols.) Oxford: Oxford University Press

Trigger, B.G., 1998: *Sociocultural Evolution. New Perspectives on the Past*. Oxford: Blackwell

Turner, J.H., 1997: *The Institutional Order*. Reading MA: Addison Wesley

Turner, J.H., Borgerhoff Mulder, M., Cosmides, L., Giesen, B., Hodgson, G., Maryanski, A., Shennan, S.J., Tooby, J. and Velichkowsky, B., 1997: Looking Back. Historical and Theoretical Context of Present Practice. In: Weingart et al (eds.)

Turner, V. W., 1969: *The Ritual Process. Structure and Anti-Structure*. London: Routledge and Kegan Paul

Ulanowicz, R.E., 1994: The propensities of evolving systems. In: Kahil, E.L. and Boulding, K.E. (eds.): *Social and natural Complexity*. Cambridge: Cambridge University Press

Vanberg, V.J., 1994: *Rules and Choice in Economics*. London: Routledge

Waddington, C.H., 1956: *Principles of Embryology*. New York: Macmillan

Waldrop, M.M., 1992: *Complexity. The Emerging Science at the Edge of Order and Chaos*. New York: Simon and Schuster

Wallerstein, I., 1974: *The Modern World System I*. New York: Academic Press

Weingart, P., Mitchell, S.D., Richerson, P. and Maasen, S. (eds.): *Human by Nature. Between Biology and the Social Sciences*. Madwah-London: Lawrence Erlbaum

Wilson, E.O., 1975: *Sociobiology. The New Synthesis*. Cambridge MA: Harvard University Press

Wuensche, A. and Lesser, M., 1992: *The global Dynamics of Cellular Automata. Attraction Fields of One-Dimensional Cellular Automata*. Reading MA: Addison Wesley

Zilsel, E., 1976: *Die sozialen Ursprünge neuzeitlicher Wissenschaft*. Frankfurt (M): Suhrkamp.

INDEX

THEORY AND DECISION LIBRARY

SERIES A: PHILOSOPHY AND METHODOLOGY OF
THE SOCIAL SCIENCES
Editors: W. Leinfellner (*Vienna*) and G. Eberlein (*Munich*)

KLUWER ACADEMIC PUBLISHERS – DORDRECHT / BOSTON / LONDON